CHANGING FAITH

# Changing Faith

*The Dynamics and Consequences of Americans'*
*Shifting Religious Identities*

Darren E. Sherkat

NEW YORK UNIVERSITY PRESS
*New York and London*

NEW YORK UNIVERSITY PRESS
New York and London
www.nyupress.org

References to Internet websites (URLs) were accurate at the time of writing.
Neither the author nor New York University Press is responsible for URLs
that may have expired or changed since the manuscript was prepared.

Library of Congress Cataloging-in-Publication Data
Sherkat, Darren E., 1965–
Changing faith : the dynamics and consequences of Americans' shifting
religious identities / Darren E. Sherkat.
pages  cm
Includes bibliographical references and index.
ISBN 978-0-8147-4126-9 (cl : alk. paper) — ISBN 978-0-8147-4127-6
(pb : alk. paper)
1. United States—Religion.  2. Identification (Religion)    I. Title.
BL2525.S535  2014
200.973—dc23          2013049748

New York University Press books are printed on acid-free paper,
and their binding materials are chosen for strength and durability.
We strive to use environmentally responsible suppliers and materials
to the greatest extent possible in publishing our books.

Manufactured in the United States of America

10  9  8  7  6  5  4  3  2  1

Also available as an ebook

# CONTENTS

## ACKNOWLEDGMENTS

This book is the culmination of over two decades of research which began as a seminar paper for Anthony Oberschall. Tony was a fervent believer in the power of demography for shaping social movements, and his persistent questions about the sources of right-wing movements in the United States led to my investigation of the trends and patterns in religious affiliation in the 1970s and 1980s. My collaborations with John Wilson helped to hone the concepts and theories guiding my research, and my collaborative work with Chris Ellison forged the basis for taking ethnicity seriously in the demography of religion.

This book would never have been written were it not for the encouragement and support of Jennifer Hammer at NYU Press. Jennifer repeatedly prodded me to consider turning my papers into a book and has been exceptionally supportive, efficient, and tolerant while I have trudged along constantly reanalyzing new data and rewriting the text. Andrew Katz did a wonderful job copyediting the manuscript and correcting my many errors.

I am also profoundly indebted to my research assistant, Derek Lehman, who diligently read each chapter, inserted citations and references, and taught me how to use Endnote. I appreciate the comments and support of my former undergraduate mentors, Burke Rochford, Jean Blocker, and Doug Eckberg, and my graduate mentors, Ken Land, Ed Tiryakian, Tom DiPrete, and Joel Smith. I have benefited from the advice and counsel of Penny Edgell, Lisa Keister, Alfred Darnell, Roger Finke, David Gay, Michael Humphries, Rodney Stark, David Bromley, Jay Demerath, Evelyn Lehrer, Larry Iannaccone, Walter Gove, Clark Roof, Jim Wright, Rob Benford, Reginald Bibby, Esther Wilder, and hosts of others. I also benefited from the insights of my former students Anthea Butler, Sally Smith Holt, Lubna Asif, Fawaz Alanezi, Robert

Wiley, Nadia Amin, Dean Eatman, Ben Moulton, Sarah Cunningham, Kylan de Vries, Amelia Ketzle, Kristie Lipford, Kristie Perry, S. J. Creek, Greg Maddox, and Melissa Powell Williams.

My family makes working an easy task, and I thank my spouse, Alison Watts, and my children, Jackson Watts, Owen Watts, and Ashley Sherkat Eldridge. Mostly, this effort is the product of my upbringing by my wonderful parents, Geraldine Frances Roberts Sherkat and Mehdi Sherkat. My understanding of American religion was forged in their own diverse experiences.

# Introduction

*Making Sense of American Religion*

Religious identifications play a profound role in how Americans relate to one another, influencing whom we marry, how we raise our children, our educational and occupational opportunities and choices, and our moral and political commitments. Yet, as a nation of immigrants, the way that religious identifications operate to structure social relations is also intimately connected to ethnicity, assimilation, and nativity. Religious identifications structure the social world differently for the ancestors of African slaves and the descendants of Anglo-Saxon slaveholders—even though both very often identify as Baptist, Methodist, or Pentecostal. Our diverse array of religious groups operate in an ethnically diverse society that is constantly shifting because of our consistently high rates of immigration. Religious change cannot be properly analyzed or explained without attention to how identifications are rooted in ethnic experiences and shaped by processes of assimilation and segmentation. This book examines how religious identifications have shifted over four decades (1972–2012), the sources of those dynamics, and the impact of religious identifications for religious beliefs, family relations, social status, and political commitments—with a focus on how ethnicity continues to structure all of these dynamics and an eye toward how coming generations will alter the religious landscape.

Starting with Alexis de Tocqueville's (1835/1840) *Democracy in America*, commentators on American religion have remarked on the fluidity of Americans' attachments to religious groups. While in most nations people cling to the religion of their family and clan, Americans, it is said, are relatively free to choose their religious commitments. The result of this freedom of association is considerable dynamism in American religion; religious denominations have risen and fallen in popularity and influence over the course of the nation's history. Yet Tocqueville was observing an America dominated by Anglo-Saxon Protestants— an America where ethnicity was less likely to constrain choices about religious commitments and where social class was the primary force driving Protestant denominationalism (Finke and Stark 1992; Niebuhr 1929). Most investigations ignore how much of this religious dynamism has been a function of immigration, fertility, and other demographic processes, rather than shifts in freely chosen religious commitments. What is also intriguing about the United States is that religion continues to be quite consequential in a variety of arenas of social life, unlike in other developed parts of Europe and Asia. Religious identifications are central to understanding the dynamics of American religion, and the cognitive nature of these identifications provides an important framework for understanding the changeable nature of religion in the United States. Identification is different from group membership, and while identifications are often made toward organized religious groups —identifying as Southern Baptist or Catholic, for example—often people's religious identifications are less directed—such as when people simply identify as "Protestant" or "Christian" or Hindu, without specifying a particular organized faith community. Identification with religion can also be rejected, and this book will examine the growing trend of rejecting religious identification.

Religious change is a confusing topic, because both religious denominations and the people who populate them are constantly shifting religious and organizational allegiances. Denominations which once offered poor worshipers otherworldly forms of religion to the tune of raucous ecstatic worship sometimes transform over time into staid traditions catering to affluent congregants with formulaic ritual and highly educated ministers (Finke and Stark 1992; Niebuhr 1929). The dynamics of transformation result in part from shifts in the social status of congregants over the course of generations. First-generation farmers and laborers may be comforted by an ascetic religion which denounces worldly gain, but later generations often find the old-time religion intellectually unappealing and socially constraining. When later generations become powerful within a religious group, they often mobilize to change the type of religion offered by the denomination (Finke and Stark 1992). The transformation of religious groups from ecstatic otherworldly sects to more worldly organizations has long been defined by sociologists as the sect-church transformation (B. Johnson 1963; Niebuhr 1929; Stark and Bainbridge 1985; Troeltsch 1931).

In the 19th century, the Methodist Church was an otherworldly sect, requiring members to adhere strictly to religious prescriptions and proscriptions and rejecting the importance of secular education and worldly involvements (Finke and Stark 1992). Indeed, Max Weber spoke of this character of Methodism in the early 20th century, describing "the soteriological orgies of the Methodist type" (Weber 1978, 486). Yet, even as Weber was commenting on the nature of Methodism— largely on the basis of his 1904 visit to North Carolina— Methodism was already in the process of transforming into a much more worldly religion. By the middle of the 20th century, Methodism was a mainstay of American mainline religion, professing a moderate take on salvation and offering services structured around formal sermons delivered by ministers educated in elite seminaries such as Northwestern, Duke, Vanderbilt, and Emory. Now, many Methodist congregations are driven by a more inclusive liberal theology, women are common in the pulpit, and some United Methodist congregations have conducted same-sex commitment ceremonies against the instructions of the United Methodist Church (Udis-Kessler 2008). Over the course of the 20th century, the Methodist sect transformed from a sectarian group to a moderate church with liberal leanings.

The alteration of the character and content of any religious group is likely to conflict with the tastes of many members, and some yearn for the old-time otherworldly faith. Defectors from these newly transformed churches may form their own more otherworldly sect through schism, and hence the cycle of transformation is termed the Sect-Church-Sect cycle (B. Johnson 1963; Montgomery 1996; Sherkat 2002; Stark and Bainbridge 1985, 1987). But the availability of diverse religious groups in the United States makes it more likely that disgruntled congregants will simply switch to a more compatible otherworldly denomination. The cycle of religious change may be completed through religious switching rather than through schism. Yet ethnicity provides an important barrier to religious switching, and ethnic boundaries have defined the contours of organizational diversity throughout the history of the United States. Moreover, religious switching often benefits more liberal religious denominations and not just otherworldly religious sects, as some scholars have claimed (e.g., Finke and Stark 1992; Iannaccone 1994). Freedom of religious choice works both ways; and in many generations, more worldly and universalistic liberal churches expand their ranks through religious switching (Newport 1979; Roof and McKinney 1987; Sherkat 2001b; Stark and Glock 1965).

American religion has been complicated by diverse waves of immigration and by a racial gulf forged in slavery. Many religious organizations made decisions either to resist or to assimilate to the dominant Anglo culture in the United States, and ethnically determined barriers to affiliation and identification with religious groups have shifted substantially over the past three centuries. From the nation's founding, American religion was divided across ethnic lines based on varied European ancestries, and African Americans were required to develop their faiths in segregated institutions, almost exclusively in the Baptist and Methodist traditions (Ellison and Sherkat 1990; Frazier 1964; Lincoln and Mamiya 1990; Sherkat 2001a, 2002). Indeed, the conflict over slavery divided white Presbyterian, Methodist, Disciples of Christ, and Baptist denominations along regional lines and left an indelible mark on the character of white southern Protestantism. African American religious institutions are quite different from white denominations hailing from the same nominal faith—the beliefs and social organization of white Baptists and Methodists are very different from their African American counterparts. American religion remains strongly divided by faith tradition and patterns of worship, and the political, personal, and social consequences of religion vary by race (Emerson and Smith 2000).

Catholicism in the United States has historically unified diverse ethnicities by tolerating linguistic diversity—creating a varied set of ethnic Catholic churches (Finke and Stark 1992). During the 20th century, European Americans assimilated rapidly into an Anglo-American culture, and religious institutions and religious switching played a crucial role in the process (Hamilton and Form 2003; Roof and McKinney 1987; Stark and Glock 1965). Over time, ethnic Lutheran and Reformed denominations made deliberate attempts at assimilation, and mergers created Presbyterian and Lutheran denominations that deemphasized

European ethnicities. In 1965, the United States lifted amendments to the Immigration and Nationality Act, opening immigration to people from eastern Europe, Asia, and Africa who previously were prevented from becoming American citizens. These "new immigrants" differ substantially from previous waves. Most immigrants now originate from non-European countries, and substantial proportions hail from nations that are predominantly non-Christian (Alanezi and Sherkat 2008; Ebaugh 2003; Ebaugh and Chafetz 2000; Jasso et al. 2004). Like African Americans, these new immigrants are unlikely to assimilate fully into Anglo-American religion; instead they are forging their own religious institutions both within established Catholic and Protestant churches and in other faith traditions.

Religious collective identities—cognitive conceptions of how distinctive forms of religion bind a group together—have become part of the national discourse as diverse traditions have sought to find common ground for transposing their faiths into the political realm (Sherkat 2006). In the 1970s and early 1980s, American Christians were split between those who identified as being "born again"—a collective identity based on a shared theology of Christian salvation—and people for whom such an identity was irrelevant or unimportant. As a "born again" identity faded in salience among its identifiers—having been spoiled by various televangelist scandals in the 1980s—the identity of "evangelical" filled the role as a unifying identity for conservative Protestants. "Evangelical" is an identity based on an orientation toward worldly engagement—borrowed from the more sociological term designating groups that proselytize. The issue of identities versus identifications with specific religious organizations is an important one. A focus on transient identities is not an effective sociological strategy for monitoring social change or examining how religion influences other realms of social life. While some religious commentators have argued that identities are a useful marker or are preferred because they are the desired self-identifications of religious devotees, the ephemeral and contested nature of identities makes them impossible to track over time.

The focus of this book is on changes in religious identification and their consequences since the early 1970s. For this period, there are excellent data for tracking religious identifications, shifts in these commitments, religious beliefs, and participation in religious organizations.

The General Social Survey (GSS) was first conducted by the National Opinion Research Center (NORC) in 1972 and has been conducted regularly ever since. This allows the presentation of comprehensive data on American religion from 1972–2012, using comparable measures over time. The United States has not examined religion in the U.S. Census since 1956, and the Census of Religious Bodies never did allow an examination of the religious propensities of individuals or the consequences of religion for people and groups (Finke and Stark 1992). While there are other survey research sources available over time, all of them have inconsistent measures of religious identification, lacking the detail and diversity present in the GSS. Other data sources, such as Gallup and Pew, fail to obtain scientifically justifiable response rates for making inferences about the religious propensities of the American population, while the GSS has consistently maintained response rates over 70% of the people targeted for interview. Indeed, recent works using the Baylor Survey and the Pew Religious Landscape Survey (which only managed to interview under a quarter of targeted respondents) make exaggerated claims about the religious beliefs and commitments of Americans and underrepresent the proportion who reject religious identification and overestimate rates of religious commitment (Stark 2008).

## Defining Religious Commitments

Religions are social groups that produce and maintain explanations about the meaning and purpose of life, and many humans value explanations about such important matters (Stark and Bainbridge 1985, 1987; Stark and Finke 2000). These explanations go beyond the natural world, invoking some supernatural leap of faith. Many people find religious explanations comforting and rewarding. These explanations are distinctively religious because of their appeal to a supernatural realm. Without a supernatural element, explanations of the purpose of life are secular philosophies. Most religions also promise additional benefits for believers as part of their explanations for the meaning and purpose of life, with some benefits only enjoyed after death. Rodney Stark and William Sims Bainbridge (1985, 1987) deemed these promises "supernatural compensators," and they include promises of postmortem benefits to the faithful (such as heaven or nirvana), as well as punishments for infidels (such as damnation to eternal torture or rebirth as a lowly life form). Explanations may be directly rewarding, but they are not the same as heaven and hell—rewards and punishments which only accrue in an afterlife. Rich sets of exclusive supernatural compensators drive many extreme influences of religion on social behavior, while explanatory rewards about the meaning and purpose of life motivate different types of religiously inspired behavior. Many religious groups, particularly sectarian Protestant groups espousing "prosperity gospel," also make promises of rewards in this life and claim that devotees of the exclusive faith will be rewarded in this life, as well as in the next.

## Religious Traditions

Tradition is the highest order conceptual component of sociological taxonomies of religion. Religious traditions are rooted in a common set of beliefs about the supernatural and how the supernatural interacts with the natural world. Most religions codify these beliefs in sacred texts, which are interpreted by communities of believers. The most common major faith traditions in the United States are Christianity, Judaism, Mormonism, Buddhism, Islam, Unitarianism, and Hinduism (in order of their current prevalence). Table I.1 shows the distribution of religious affiliation for all respondents in the 2002–2012 General Social Survey (GSS). The United States remains overwhelmingly a Christian nation,

*Table I.1. Percentage of Adherents to Religious Traditions in the United States: 2002–2012 General Social Surveys*

| Religious tradition | 2002–2012 GSS |
| --- | --- |
| Christian | 78.0% |
| None | 16.2% |
| Jewish | 1.8% |
| Mormon | 1.3% |
| Buddhist | .6% |
| Muslim | .5% |
| Unitarian | .3% |
| Hindu | .3% |
| Other Eastern | .2% |
| Native American | .1% |
| Number of cases | 16,042 |

and table 1.1 shows that the main competitor to Christianity is nonidentification. About 78% of Americans profess some form of Christianity,
while over 16% have no religious identification. Jews remain the next-
largest religious tradition at just under 2%. Mormons are the third-
largest tradition with 1.3%, while Buddhists garner 0.6% of adherents.
Islam, Unitarian Universalism, and Hinduism each accounted for less
than 0.5% of religious identifications in 2002–2010 GSS data.

Religious commentators and activists may be quick to argue, for
example, that Mormonism is a Christian faith—a direct claim by the
Church of Latter-Day Saints which is contested by those who belong to
some other Christian groups. However, for sociologists, the identification of a religious tradition requires a strict adherence to the content of
religious explanations produced in that tradition. The Book of Mormon
is a very substantial and novel addition to the Christian tradition and
one that constitutes a shift in the nature of supernatural explanations.
New sacred texts define a new tradition, just as Christianity and Islam
added to the Abrahamic tradition of Judaism to forge new traditions;
the Book of Mormon is seen by sociologists to spell out a new faith.

All religious groups begin as cults—new religious movements offering a distinct set of explanations about supernatural rewards and compensators (Stark and Bainbridge 1985, 1987). Most new religions start
with a considerable repertoire of preexisting cultural capital. That is, the
vast majority of new cults meld together explanations from one or more
prior traditions, and cults which present exceptionally novel supernatural rewards and compensators tend not to be very successful and
usually die out after one generation of adherents (Stark and Bainbridge
1985). In the 19th century, the United States saw the cult of Mormonism
rise from Christianity, and at the same time in Persia, the cult of Baha'i
borrowed elements from several traditions to forge a new syncretism.
Unitarians (many of whom originated in Christian Congregationalism
in the United States) rejected the divinity of Jesus, which requires their
reclassification as a cult movement. Now after more than two centuries, Unitarian Universalism constitutes a unique religious tradition.
After more than a century of survival, it does not make much sociological sense to continue to refer to newer traditions as cults. Yet neither
should we consider them a part of the older tradition. Instead, these
groups constitute new religious traditions.

## Religious Denominations

Religious denominations are sets of organizational units within a common tradition. They are organizations which coordinate collective activities across several congregations. Congregations are an elemental form of religious organization, bringing individuals together, usually with a religious leader (a priest or priestess), for routine collective action. Denominations always maintain a degree of diversity in the way individual congregations or leaders interpret the religious explanations of the religious tradition (only new traditions and cults are able to maintain homogeneity). Formal organizational ties are what define denominations. In the United States, it is easy to identify separate organizational connections associated with denominations in Christianity, Judaism (Harrison and Lazerwitz 1982), Mormonism, Islam, Hinduism, and Buddhism. Because most religious traditions are rare in the United States, it is impossible to systematically analyze denominationalism in Hinduism, Buddhism, Judaism, Mormonism, or Islam in the United States in a quantitative study such as this one. However, Christian denominations can be examined in a fair degree of detail in the GSS.

Christian denominationalism in the United States follows historical patterns of immigration and organization building. Some religious denominations were planted as part of mission efforts of national and international churches, such as the Roman Catholic Church, various Orthodox bodies (most of which have now merged into a unified Orthodox Church of America), several national Lutheran churches (particularly German, Norwegian, Swedish, and Danish, which have subsequently merged and also split), and the Anglican Communion (which is the Episcopal Church in the United States, though some conservative congregations now associate with other national Anglican bodies). While these international Christian denominations have a firm and longstanding organizational infrastructure, it is important to remember that most religious denominations in the United States have a brief and fractured history. There are more than twenty-three hundred religious groups operating in the United States, and the vast majority of these are diminutive Christian denominations encapsulating a limited number of congregations (Melton 2003). Most American Christian denominations have been forged out of alliances among a

fairly small number of ministers in specific locales. Small denominations often develop ties with like-minded congregations and similar
denominations to form a larger denomination. American religious history is filled with examples of denominations coming together in small
meetings, falling apart over theological, organizational, or political
issues, and then coming together with other Christian groups at a later
point in history.

The ebb and flow of organizational connections often cross seem-
ingly distinct "denominational" boundaries. An excellent example is the
union of Presbyterians and Baptists who forged the Christian Church
in the 19th century. Within fifty years, the union split (and not along
former denominational lines) to form the more liberal Disciples of
Christ (Christian Church) and the more conservative Churches of
Christ. Within a tradition, there is often an impulse to confront diversity through reconciliation of beliefs and the formation of a coalition
of denominations to share resources, though differences of theological
interpretation always persist. In the Christian parlance, these coalitions
of similar religious organizations are called "ecumenical organizations,"
and they have played a strong role in the unification of denominations
with similar religious views. Contrary to the claims of some scholars
(e.g., Finke and Stark 1992), ecumenical organizations are common for
both liberal and conservative groups, and ecumenical movements often
give rise to denominational mergers.

The General Social Survey identifies 205 separate "Protestant" denominations. On close inspection of the technical appendix of this survey, this "Protestant" total includes several new religious movements,
including Mormonism (which is denominated by the Latter-Day Saints
and the Reorganized Latter-Day Saints, which broke from the LDS in
1872 and renamed itself the Community of Christ in 2001), Mind Science, New Age, Swedenborgianism, and New Age Spirituality. These
data do not capture the full diversity of religious organizational ties
to Protestantism even for the respondents of the GSS. Many people
would not necessarily be able to specify the exact Baptist, Presbyterian,
Lutheran, or other denomination with which they identify, even if they
are active members of a congregation tied to a specific denomination.
There are several separate Presbyterian denominations in the United

States (Presbyterian Church of America, Presbyterian Church USA, Cumberland Presbyterian Church, Reformed Presbyterian Church, Evangelical Presbyterian Church, Bible Presbyterian Church); each has an independent organizational foundation, and they profess somewhat different beliefs about Christianity. But the denominational distinctions are lost on most lay members, particularly if they are not very active in their congregation, and research cannot focus on identifications with specific denominations because respondents often cannot make those distinctions. Indeed, the largest Presbyterian denomination (Presbyterian Church USA) did not form until 1983, when southern and northern branches came together after separating over the slavery issue in the 19th century. The Presbyterian Church of America (the second-largest body) was formed in 1973, after splitting from the Presbyterian Church in the United States (the southern church). In 1982, the Presbyterian Church of America forged a coalition with the Reformed Presbyterian Church, Evangelical Synod, which was itself formed by a merger in 1965 between the Evangelical Presbyterian Church and the Reformed Presbyterian Church in North America, General Synod. Given all the organizational mergers and schisms in Presbyterianism, few Presbyterians who grew up before 1965 are currently in the same denomination in which they were raised—even if they are lifelong members of the same congregation.

Table 1.2 shows the distributions of the largest Protestant denominations in the General Social Survey code book: respondents were asked to name their specific Protestant denominational identification, and these were given a code (found in the first column of the table) to enable researchers to group denominations into meaningful classifications. The majority of self-proclaimed Presbyterians (51%), Lutherans (56%), and Baptists (53%) cannot identify their specific denomination, and 46% of Methodists are unsure about their precise denominational affiliation. In some denominations, particularly in Baptist bodies, it is hard to delineate the denominational tie of a particular church. For a congregation to become "Southern Baptist" or "National Baptist," it only needs to be accepted by and affiliate with a national or local Baptist alliance and to pay the association fee. Some Baptist congregations are members of several associations. This is especially common for large African

American congregations, which may be simultaneously members of
the Progressive National Baptist Convention, the National Baptist Convention, and even the Southern Baptist Convention—a predominantly
white denomination which has attracted fellowship from some African
American Baptist congregations. Baptist churches often retain names
and signage proclaiming "Free Will Baptist" or "Missionary Baptist"
when in fact the congregation is allied with the National Baptist Convention USA or the Southern Baptist Convention. Many Southern and
National Baptist churches have "disfellowshipped" from those conven-

*Table 1.2. Denominational Identifications for
Some Major Protestant Denominations in
the General Social Surveys*

| Code | Frequency |
| --- | --- |
| 10 AM BAPTIST ASSO | 543 |
| 11 AM BAPT CH IN USA | 239 |
| 12 NAT BAPT CONV OF AM | 163 |
| 13 NAT BAPT CONV USA | 113 |
| 14 SOUTHERN BAPTIST | 3,075 |
| 15 OTHER BAPTISTS | 731 |
| 18 BAPTIST-DK WHICH | 5,465 |
| 20 AFR METH EPISCOPAL | 168 |
| 21 AFR METH EP ZION | 70 |
| 22 UNITED METHODIST | 2,329 |
| 23 OTHER METHODIST | 129 |
| 28 METHODIST-DK WHICH | 2,261 |
| 30 AM LUTHERAN | 515 |
| 31 LUTH CH IN AMERICA | 176 |
| 32 LUTHERAN-MO SYNOD | 568 |
| 33 WI EVAN LUTH SYNOD | 118 |
| 34 OTHER LUTHERAN | 137 |
| 35 EVANGELICAL LUTH | 216 |
| 38 LUTHERAN-DK WHICH | 1,578 |
| 40 PRESBYTERIAN C IN US | 312 |
| 41 UNITED PRES CH IN US | 394 |
| 42 OTHER PRESBYTERIAN | 145 |
| 43 PRESBYTERIAN, MERGED | 138 |
| 48 PRESBYTERIAN-DK WH | 1,028 |
| 50 EPISCOPAL | 1,181 |
| 60 OTHER-SPECIFY | 6,511 |
| 70 NO DENOMINATION | 2,335 |
| 98 DK | 34 |
| Protestant total / total N | 30,672 / 51,020 |

tions over theological, financial, or political issues. Yet a regular member of a congregation may be unaware of the change in denominational ties, which may be known only to deacons, board members, or members who regularly attend congregational business meetings.

A growing number of Americans report that their religious affiliation is "nondenominational," or they simply identify as Protestants or Christians with no particular denomination. It is unclear what these identifications mean. Many congregations claim to be "nondenominational" when in fact they belong to an alliance of congregations which share religious materials, mission resources, ministerial training, and religious authority—which is a denomination by sociological definition. The Vineyard denomination is a great example of a coordinated set of self-proclaimed "nondenominational" churches. Despite their protestations, they are not actually nondenominational congregations; they are Vineyard, which is a fairly new denomination. Denominations may be a new alliance with little formal organization, or they may have a long-standing and well-developed set of ties. Often, individual congregants are simply not aware of their congregation's formal ties, and churches may further mask this membership by taking names from geographic locations or biblical places or events. Recently, many Southern Baptist Convention (SBC) churches have taken on generic names—in my town, First Baptist Church of Carbondale became "The View"—and there is almost no indication of their connection to the SBC in any of their promotional materials or signage. Of course, some "nondenominational" respondents attend truly independent churches, while others are only nominally Christian and do not regularly attend church anywhere. In the latter case, what respondents seem to mean is that they are not Catholic, but they consider themselves to be Christian and, by default, Protestant.

People who respond that they have no religious identification are also a diverse and growing group. Many are uninterested in religion (such as atheists or agnostics), while others are unwedded to a particular religion (having diverse religious tastes). Some people who report no religious identification prefer Christianity, Judaism, or some other faith tradition but lack an attachment to a specific congregation or religious organization.

*Identities and Attachment*

Social and personal identities structure much of what people do, and identities are central to much social scientific theorizing about religion, ethnicity, and sexuality. Social groups often need a collective identity —what Harrison White and Charles Tilly have referred to as "catness" (Tilly 1978; White 2008), implying that everyone who is a part of that group thinks of themselves as part of a social category. And people who are linked to groups often take this social connection to be part of their personal identities, placing these identities on par with more individuated identities such as parent or spouse. Common variants include ethnic, occupational, sexual, and regional identities. Journalistic and activist appeals to identities tend not to acknowledge their multiplex and changing character, and even most sociological treatments have only a passing connection to the well-developed sociological literature on identities and their dynamics (cf. Thoits 2003). Identities are contested and changeable, and that is readily apparent in contemporary American religion (Dillon 1999). It is common for insiders and outsiders to contest what identities mean. The resulting conflicts demobilize efforts to forge coalitions and often result in the development of separate or new collective identities (Gamson 1995, 1997; Jelen 1991; Whittier 1995). In the past fifty years, Americans of African heritage have identified as Colored, Negro, Afro-American, Black, and now African American. Similar identity conflicts are evident in sexuality groups (Gamson 1996) and among feminists (Whittier 1995). While identities provide an important area of study in their own right, transient identities do not provide a clear basis for analyzing social change. The lack of a connection between identities and sociological concepts commonly used to study religion also makes their application unwieldy and fraught with error. Appeals to a "subcultural identity" (cf. C. Smith 2000) do not adequately delineate the elements of these subcultures, how they can be separated from specific sets of religious beliefs, or how identity groups are populated and reproduced.

In the sociology of American religious history, identities have been used strategically to create coalitions of diverse religious actors. "Protestant" as an identity does not mean very much in the contemporary context. But "Protestant" does have a clear historical referent: Protestant denominations are Christian denominations which split from the Roman Catholic Church. Notably, many other Christian denominations did not branch from Roman Catholicism, such as Orthodox and Coptic denominations. Protestantism also came to be a collective and individual identity amplified to encompass diverse groups coming from varied national and theological Protestant traditions (Calvinist, Baptist, Lutheran, Anglican, and Methodist). In the West, the amplification of Protestant identity was crucial for forging political coalitions against Catholics, which in the United States eventually resulted in the prohibition of alcohol and ensuring that public school curricula were distinctively Protestant and exclusively English (Bowles and Gintis 1976; Finke and Stark 1992). Yet even in that crusade, "Protestant" as an identity was not the same as its historical meaning, since one of the largest Protestant denominations in the United States was abjectly opposed to Prohibition and culturally distinct from the Anglo-dominated politicized Protestantism—the Lutherans. The historical meaning of Protestantism as a set of movements breaking from Catholicism was displaced by a distinctively American collective identity meant to include only English-speaking Protestants, who were often further delineated as "White, Anglo-Saxon, Protestants" (Roof and McKinney 1987). Notably, by the mid-20th century in the United States, the target of "Catholic" as an oppositional identity has become less salient, and "Protestant" identity had faded in meaning and importance.

By the early 20th century, the fragmentation within and among Protestant denominations led to an interdenominational movement identified as "fundamentalism." In a historical context, fundamentalism originated among Presbyterians at Princeton Seminary who wanted to steer their denomination toward what they considered to be the key biblical principles (Marsden 1980). But across other denominations, "fundamentalism" was embraced as a collective identity. Churches and denominations proudly added it to their names, and religious conservatives openly referred to themselves as fundamentalists—collective identities became relevant for individuals.

Fundamentalist identities declined in salience after the negative publicity received by conservative Christians as a result of the Scopes trial and other religious controversies of early 20th-century Christianity (Berkman, Pacheco, and Plutzer 2008). Yet the term "fundamentalist" is also a sociological concept. It denotes adherence to textual inerrancy or traditional strictures. These dual conceptions of fundamentalism can be confusing, since many groups and individuals that adhere to a fundamentalist religious perspective do not claim to be "fundamentalists" in terms of their collective or self-identifications. Indeed, some fundamentalist groups and individuals are offended if they are referred to as fundamentalists. In the 1970s, conservative Christians adopted a new identity to try to forge a coalition across diverse denominations, taking up the "born again" theological belief as central to collective identity. "Born again" became a collective and individual identity, placarded on bumper stickers and trumpeted from mainstream magazines and newspapers. President Jimmy Carter proudly proclaimed that he was "born again" according to his faith (Carter was a lifelong Southern Baptist until he renounced the denomination over the issue of patriarchy in the 1990s). The problem with a theological position as an identity is that not all denominations hold the same theological orientations. Being "born again" denotes adult salvation experiences common to the freewill side of the Baptist tradition, which rejected the theological belief in predestination. Adult salvation experiences are not at all required for many other Baptists and other kinds of Christians such as those from the Calvinist and Reformed traditions, Primitive Baptists, perfectionist Methodists, and a host of other denominations.

When "born again" Christianity lost favor as a collective identity, "evangelical" became the focal collective identity for conservative Christians of the Protestant tradition. The adoption of "evangelical" as a new identity has produced a lot of confusion about American religion. "Evangelical" is a proper, though Christian-focused, term denoting a religious group with an orientation toward proselytization. "Evangelical" is included in the names of many denominations, including the most liberal branch of the Lutherans (the Evangelical Lutheran Church of America; ELCA). The Evangelical Lutherans are only "evangelical" in the sense that they wanted to combine distinct national Lutheran bodies. Evangelical Lutherans do not proselytize; hence, they are not "evangelical" in the sociological sense of that concept. Notably, most ELCA members would not identify themselves as "evangelical" as the term is currently used by conservative Christians as a politicized religious identity. Many other nonevangelical (nonproselytizing) groups embrace the collective identity of "evangelical." Members of conservative Presbyterian and Reformed groups have adopted this moniker in solidarity with the new coalition of conservative Christians, yet Christians from the Calvinist-inspired Reformed and Presbyterian traditions adhere to principles of predestination which make proselytization futile. Contemporary evangelical identities have little correspondence with the sociological concept of evangelicalism. Moreover, the waning success of political movements forged by "evangelical" Christians will likely cause that identity to lose salience and eventually be replaced with another identifier. Focusing on variable identities is pointless if the goal is to assess enduring shifts across diverse groups and wider expanses of history, and whatever the value of analyzing identities, we lack high-quality data on these types of Christian identities over time.

This book examines how identifications with religious traditions and denominations vary over generations and across ethnic groups. Religious traditions and denominations will be separated in as much detail as possible in the GSS data. By retaining as much distinction as possible in religious identifications, their unique dynamics and ethnic roots will be apparent—and the intersection of religious and ethnic identification will be evidenced in the different ways that these identifications influence family life, social status, and political commitments.

## Status, Sect, and Church

Beginning with Max Weber (1978) and refined by his student Ernst Troeltsch (1931), sociologists have used the concepts of "sect" and "church" to make sense of diversity within religious traditions. Early specification of the sect-church typology focused on how social stratification leads to diverse theodicies—beliefs which explain the earthly fates of the faithful and the infidel. The religion of the privileged classes tends to focus on worldly rewards as evidence of the grace of the gods. In contrast, the lower classes tend to desire a form of religion that amplifies otherworldly rewards and discounts earthly gain. The wealthy want a religion which makes them comfortable with their positions and legitimates the earthly social structure. The poor prefer a religion which provides them with dignity and gives a promise that their earthly suffering will be rewarded in the afterlife (Weber 1978).

As Protestantism began to differentiate organizationally, the relationships between social status and religious affiliation became clearer. Some denominations cater to wealthy elites, while others serve the downtrodden masses. In the United States, the status ordering among denominations was linked to ethnic migration patterns and political and economic domination (Babchuk and Whitt 1990; Demerath 1965; Stark and Glock 1965). Religious groups serving early Anglo immigrants —the Episcopalian, Presbyterian, and Congregationalist groups—were high-status "churches." Later mission efforts which operated primarily among the poor were conducted by otherworldly sects, principally of Methodist and Baptist organizational and theological heritage (Finke and Stark 1992).

In the early 20th century, sociologists began to expand the criteria associated with the concepts of "sect" and "church." Most classifications of sect and church follow the basic arguments of Troeltsch (1931). By this formulation, "sects" are seen not only to produce otherworldly religious explanations as their product but also to have little formal authority or hierarchy in their organizations. This sectarian form of religion contrasts with "churches," which were deemed hierarchical and formal in their organization. Sects were supposed to have limited official dogma and to rely on the prophetic interpretations of largely uneducated ministers, while churches had an established theological repertoire purveyed by highly trained priests. Sects focused on otherworldly goods, while churches stuck to earthly considerations. Sects are seen as a radical protest against the existing social order, while churches are conservative and accepting of secular society. Sects are small, churches are big. Sects are exclusive, while churches are inclusive and universal.

The criteria used by early sociologists to typologize sects and churches resulted in an unmanageable set of distinctions which no actual religious groups can instantiate (B. Johnson 1963). In the real world, there are many churches which are small and exclude most of the population from full membership, while many sects are very large and welcome the masses. Sects often have hierarchies and dogma, while churches are commonly congregational in organization and eschew dogma. Many sects focus heavily on worldly gain and promote a conservative orientation to the social order, while many churches preach against worldly acquisitiveness and militate for changing social structures. There are simply too many criteria to eventually come to a binary classification of religious groups or to meaningfully array them on a continuum.

Benton Johnson (1963) made a major conceptual breakthrough by jettisoning the many varied criteria used to classify sect and church and attending to a single characteristic which could be used to forge a continuum from sect to church: tension with broader society. Since Johnson's pathbreaking article, most sociologists have accepted this scheme: sects are religious groups in a high state of tension with dominant society, while churches are religious groups accepting of the social order. Rodney Stark and Roger Finke (2000) and Laurence Iannaccone (1988, 1994) point to the importance of religious strictures for generating tension with broader society, arguing that these edicts place sects in tension with dominant society—which presumably condones and makes normative the flouting of religiously inspired virtue. As Iannaccone puts it, high-tension sects require that "pleasures are sacrificed, opportunities forgone, and social stigma is risked or even invited. The problem is epitomized by the burnt offering, a religious rite designed specifically to destroy valuable resources" (1994, 1182).

Despite the allure of a simple continuum based on tension with secular values, Johnson's scheme fails to provide an adequate and accurate description of the conditions experienced by various religious groups. Are Southern Baptists sectarian? What about the Assembly of God? If yes, then how are they at tension with broader society? What is broader society? Both of these groups are rightly considered to be different from more liberal religious groups and nonreligious people and institutions. Yet both also embrace worldly gain and are profoundly supportive of the existing social order, and there is very little that could possibly put them at odds with American society. While Baptists, Pentecostals, and other "high tension" groups do require that members make substantial monetary contributions to their organizations, these funds are not burnt; instead they are used to create collective value for members. Just as memberships to sports clubs are used to buy new equipment and hire trainers, tithes to sectarian groups are used to pay leaders and provide state-of-the-art facilities for the production of collective religious services and to provide other nonreligious commodities—such as children's day care, gymnasiums, bus services, and activities for the elderly and infirmed (Sherkat 1997). There is some evidence that sacrifices and stigmas have impacted the life chances of sectarians (Darnell and Sherkat 1997; Keister 2008, 2011; Sherkat 2012; Sherkat and Darnell 1999); however, sectarian disadvantage is rooted in life-course factors and the status-attainment process and not in the overt ideologies of wealth and income attainment fostered by these groups. There have been two Southern Baptist presidents of the United States, and the Assembly of God (a fundamentalist Pentecostal denomination) claims the affiliation of several high-ranking elected officials, a recent attorney general in John Ashcroft and former vice presidential candidate Sarah Palin. Members of these and other sectarian denominations have successfully integrated into many powerful institutional arenas in the United States (Lindsay 2007).

What about religious prescriptions and proscriptions? What are these sacrifices which elicit stigma that prevent the attainment of secular value? Most American sects ban the use of alcohol, which may create some social awkwardness. Yet many people do not drink for reasons of taste and health, and it does not create "tension" with society. The same can be said for drinking coffee for Mormons. Many people do not drink coffee. It may be a personal sacrifice, or it may not, depending on one's preferences. For people who grow up not drinking coffee, it is very likely that they would find the drink noxious, and the same can be said for alcohol—most preferences are adaptive to prior consumption (Elster 1979; Sherkat 1997; Sherkat and Wilson 1995). Do sexual strictures elicit tension with society? Sexual behaviors are private and largely undetectable by others, particularly by people who are not close friends or family members. For most social interactions, one's sexual behaviors are irrelevant. While some commentators point to the hypersexuality of some elements of popular culture (Regnerus 2009; C. Smith 2000), vivid sexuality and promiscuity portrayed in some popular cultural media are hardly to be taken as a prescription for normal social behavior. Data from the 2012 GSS show that over 23% of Americans were celibate in the last year, and another 62% were monogamous. The abstinence-until-marriage approach favored by sectarian Christians and conservative Catholics has dominated American public policy toward sexuality since 1980. Extramarital sex is proscribed by all major religious groups in the United States, and it is strongly condemned in "broader society." Adultery is cause for termination from the U.S. military and from a variety of other employers. Indeed, twenty-six states retain criminal statutes prohibiting adultery. Proscriptions against homosexuality are only sacrificial strictures for people who desire homosexual relations. And homosexuality is viewed negatively in many quarters of American society, both religious and secular (Sherkat et al. 2011). Not engaging in homosexual behavior does not invite stigma or increase one's risk for social sanctions. It is hard to see how "traditional" sexual values place a group at tension with American society—except when these groups politicize their values and attempt to control nonmembers' behaviors.

The sect-church scheme breaks down in the other direction as well. In the contemporary United States, it is the liberal Protestants and Unitarians who seem to be at tension with "broader society." Liberal groups have consistently opposed popular wars, supported racial integration, militated for unpopular rights for women and immigrants, and fought capital punishment (which is enormously popular in the United States). During Barack Obama's first presidential campaign, his relationship with Rev. Jeremiah Wright was strongly criticized, forcing Obama to denounce his former minister. While Rev. Wright is more flamboyant than most, his denomination is the mainline liberal United Church of Christ, and his message of opposing oppression abroad and helping the poor at home fits squarely within the UCC's mainstream—though it provokes heated tension within "broader society." Tension with society cannot be an arbiter because it is inconsistent over time. Depending on the whim of majorities and the will to sanction, any group can come into tension with the social order, and any group can come to control the social order. What we need is a way to distinguish similar types of religious groups on the basis of their own endogenous characteristics.

## Conceptualizing Religious Differences

Religious groups have many distinctive organizational and theological features which can be classified using sociological concepts. They have different patterns of control over resources, varied participatory structures, and differences in how they view membership. Religious groups also vary in core beliefs about supernatural rewards and compensators for adherents, in how they adhere to a textual tradition, in their understandings of the supernatural and natural world, in their views of the scope of supernatural power, and in their views on supernatural rewards and compensators for people outside their own faith. Throughout, this book will employ these concepts when discussing patterns of religious change and influence.

Organizational structures can have a profound influence on the trajectory of denominations since they allocate the power to control religious production. Organizations with substantial hierarchies and well-developed bureaucracies will function differently from organizations characterized by democratic leadership and minimal hierarchies influencing the use of resources. In Christian parlance, these forms are called "episcopal" and "congregational," not to be confused with the denominations sharing those names. It is useful to jettison these Christianized concepts in favor of the more general organizational concepts of "hierarchical" versus "horizontal" control.

Another concept of religious organization also uses the term "congregational," here referring to participatory structures—do people congregate regularly for routine collective action, or is the religion primarily meditative or devotional? The congregational style of worship is ubiquitous in the Abrahamic traditions. Christians, Jews, and Muslims are expected to regularly participate in collective services. But the congregational form of participation is not as common in Hinduism, Buddhism, Jain, and other traditions, in which prayer and devotion are expected and not tied to particular collective services. Interestingly, in the United States, many traditionally devotional religious groups adopt a congregational style in response to their experiences in the United States (Yang and Ebaugh 2001).

Religious groups have different structural responses to membership, with some groups vigorously seeking to recruit strangers, while others make it difficult or impossible for an outsider to join. In Christian parlance, as noted earlier, religious groups that proselytize are called "evangelical." Given the problems with the common usages of this concept, it seems best to think of religious groups as relatively *open* to membership or *closed* to outsiders. Extremely open groups will proselytize vigorously, such as the Jehovah's Witnesses, Mormons, and Hare Krishnas. Closed groups only grant membership based on birth, such as many Orthodox Jewish denominations, the Amish, and Mennonites.

Most people are socialized into a particular religious group, and they remain in that group. But what if people switch? How easy is it, or how hard? The Hare Krishna provides a nice contrast between their hyper-proselytization and their stringent requirements for actual membership. Many recruits to the Hare Krishna (known as ISKON, the International Society for Krishna Consciousness) believe in the main precepts and goals of the movement (cognitively, they have changed what they want in religion to this variant of sectarian Hindu), yet they are not accepted as "real" members until after a lengthy initiation and demonstration of their knowledge of and fealty toward the movement (Rochford 1985, 2007). Mormons also have stages of membership linked to proselytiza-tion efforts, since an outsider may be immediately turned off by talk about golden plates or magic underwear (Stark and Bainbridge 1985). In contrast, many denominations have no real accounting of member-ship or requirements for who joins. People pass freely from one reli-gious group to another. Indeed, denominations and congregations have a hard time keeping up with these transfers, and clearing the rolls is an ongoing problem of religious accounting (Hoge and Roozen 1979). At the individual level, which is this book's primary concern, identifi-cation is the subjective domain of the respondent. If someone claims to be affiliated with a denomination, then he or she is. If people do not attend a congregation or formally join, then they are not counted among members from the view of the denomination, but individuals may identify with a group without holding a formal membership. Most religious change happens across readily traveled paths—switching to relatively closed groups such as the Amish, Mennonites, or Judaism does not occur often enough to have an impact on religious change.

"Fundamentalism" is an important sociological concept that refers to the degree to which a group adheres to edicts presented in the sacred texts of its tradition. Fundamentalism as a concept is similar to the old concept of "orthodoxy," which is unwieldy because of its conflation with the Orthodox denominations in Christianity—and because the oppo-site of orthodox, unorthodox, has negative connotations. Of course, how a denomination interprets its sacred tradition will vary consider-ably over time, and denominations and traditions will also have less organized fundamentalist movements. A strong measure of funda-mentalism is belief about the inerrancy of sacred texts and/or about the degree to which sacred texts should be taken literally. Viewed this way, about a third of Americans are fundamentalists who believe that the Bible is the absolute word of god and that it should be taken literally word for word. Yet very few Christians in the United States adhere to dietary prescriptions and proscriptions which are articulated quite clearly in their sacred texts. Indeed, "fundamentalists" from all religious traditions pick and choose among the many prescriptions and proscriptions and supernatural explanations identified in the sacred texts of their faiths. The GSS finds Catholics, Jews, and liberal Protestants among adherents counted as fundamentalists. Fundamentalism taps something very important and is inclusive of diverse groups, yet it is also inherently polysemic—taking on multiple meanings depending on the perspectives of those who are making an interpretation (Sewell 1992; Sherkat 1998).

Another concept for distinguishing among religious groups is their views about the relative exclusivity of religious benefits. Can other religions lead to heaven? "Exclusivism" is the view that only the faithful members of a particular group will enjoy religious rewards and compensators, while all others will be subjected to eternal punishment. At the other end of the pole is "universalism," the view that all religions and all individuals enjoy supernaturally derived rewards and compensators. More than any other concept, this one best separates religious groups with regard to how they influence members' religious orientations and trajectories of religious identification. The definition of "liberalism" or "conservatism" lies not in tangible connections to scriptural orthodoxy writ large but instead to specific beliefs about the types of religious compensators awaiting people who hold other religious faiths (or none at all). Do only the faithful of a particular tradition go to heaven? And are there negative supernatural compensators for nonbelievers? Unfortunately, no high-quality studies have assessed this component of religious belief.

Christian religious groups have varying perspectives on eschatology, beliefs about future events. For many groups, particularly those with fundamentalist orientations toward scriptural authority, there is a pervasive belief that Abrahamic scriptures predict an end or serious shift in the nature of the human occupation of Earth. Many Christians interpret the Book of Revelations as prophesying a great battle between good and evil, before or after which there will be a return of the god Jesus to Earth to establish a theocratic planet. In general, religious groups that believe in an end of normal human life are termed "millenarian," which refers to the Christian belief in a thousand-year reign of Jesus on Earth. These types of understandings are pervasive across a variety of religious traditions. In Christianity, not all groups adhere to these prophetic interpretations, and there is considerable variation in how prophesies are interpreted among those who do hold millenarian orientations. Some believe that Jesus's return to Earth will precede theocratic rule (premillennialism), while others believe that humans must create a godly society for a thousand years before Jesus will return (postmillennialism). Many premillennialists believe that true Christians will enjoy an exclusive benefit of being "raptured" into heaven before the great battle between good and evil.

Religious groups vary in their style of collective worship. For some groups, worship is formula driven, with a specified liturgy and a sermon delivered by a well-trained professional clergy member. In other religious groups, services are more free-form, theatrical, and enabling of extemporaneous lay participation in the service. These latter types of religious groups are often called "charismatic." Charismatic worship styles can be found in a variety of religious denominations, even among Catholics (Neitz 1987). However, this style is more often practiced in sectarian denominations. Charismatic worship is often associated with Pentecostalism, which is a very specific religious belief associated with several Christian denominations, particularly the Assembly of God, Pentecostal Holiness, and the Church of God in Christ. Pentecostals believe that the Holy Spirit (a manifestation of a triune god in Christian beliefs) enters the bodies of the faithful and causes them to speak in other languages (a phenomenon known as "glossolalia"). Notably, glossolalia is viewed quite negatively by groups which do not believe in it, particularly other sectarians—for whom it is considered evidence of demon possession.

## Classifying Denominations: A Practical Guide

Denominations are important socializing agents, providing distinct institutional foundations for instilling religious belief and structuring religious practices. The organizational diversity of American religious denominations exceeds the variation in religious understandings and practical forms. Because of this, it is possible to cluster together sets of denominations with common religious orientations. Still, some traditions have theological, ritual, or ethnic foundations which require separate inspection. Since this book's goal is to examine the shifting religious commitments of individuals, it needs to be noted that there are also practical limits on available data for less prevalent religious commitments.

Most classification schemes for religious groups in the United States separate denominations based on "liberalism" or "fundamentalism" (T. Smith 1990). At the "liberal" end are the old "mainline" Protestant groups—Episcopalians, United Church of Christ, and Presbyterians. "Moderate" Protestant groups typically include the Methodists, Disciples of Christ, Lutheran, and Reformed groups. Conservative or "fundamentalist" groups include a wide range of denominations, such as Southern Baptists, Assembly of God, Churches of Christ, Nazarenes, and a large number of smaller sectarian groups.

The tripartite classification scheme proposed by Tom Smith (1990) is useful for some purposes; however, it also masks considerable diversity within the three categories. Recent attempts to expand the classification system to seven categories (Steensland et al. 2000) are also fraught with problems. Specifically, this scheme fails to separate Lutherans, Baptists, and Episcopalians as unique denominations and lumps together all African American Protestants, ignoring their considerable diversity and history of segregated denominationalism (Sherkat 2001a, 2002). This scheme also lumps together distinctive liberal and moderate Protestant traditions and places many moderate Protestant groups into the misnamed "evangelical" category.

Denominations and traditions should be broken down as finely as the data allow. But the small numbers in non-Christian traditions and data barriers do not enable detailed examinations of these groups or investigations of denominationalism in Hinduism, Judaism, Mormonism, Buddhism, or Islam. This book outlines a thirteen-category classification system based on tradition, denominational similarity, and ethnicity similar to that used by James Kluegel (1980) and Wade Clark Roof and William McKinney (1987). The categorization delineates (1) liberal Protestants, (2) Episcopalians, (3) moderate Protestants, (4) Lutherans,

(5) Baptists, (6) sectarian Protestants, (7) Mormons, (8) other Protestants, (9) Catholics, (10) Jews, (11) Unitarians, (12) people who identify with other religions, and (13) people with no religious identification. First, it classifies several mainline Protestant groups into a "liberal Protestant" category. Members and leaders of these denominations almost uniformly reject fundamentalism, exclusivism, and eschatological prophesy, embracing instead a contextualized view of scriptures, a universal orientation toward supernatural compensators, and a realistic conception of the trajectory of human prospects. Liberal Protestants also reject the notion of negative supernatural compensators; beliefs in a literal hell or devil or in end-times visions are rare in liberal Protestant denominations—even among more conservative groups such as the Presbyterian Church of America, fundamentalism and a literal hell and devil are relatively rare understandings of the proper nature of the supernatural. Liberal Protestant denominations include Presbyterians, United Church of Christ, and Congregationalists (an old term for the United Church of Christ which many respondents and churches retain). This scheme separates Episcopalians from other liberal denominations because of their distinctive ethnic and liturgical features. Episcopalians are closer to Catholics in their ritual practice, and their Anglican heritage remains influential and distinctive.

In the "moderate Protestant" category are Methodists, Reformed groups, American and Northern Baptists, and Disciples of Christ. Moderate groups have a more reverential view of the sacred texts of Christianity, and they tend to believe that positive supernatural compensators will only be enjoyed by fellow Christians. Members of moderate Protestant groups are also more likely to believe in hell and the devil, embracing negative supernatural compensators for those who are not of their mold. Some moderate Protestants also embrace eschatological prophesy and tend to be more postmillennialist if they buy into these beliefs. Some treatments put Methodists in the liberal camp (e.g., Stark and Glock 1965; Steensland et al. 2000), but doing so is not appropriate when dealing with national samples and individual-level data. While elite Methodist seminaries such as those at Northwestern, Duke, and Emory are quite liberal, this is not at all true of most ministers or the laity—particularly in the South, where there are large concentrations of Methodists. This scheme excludes Lutherans from the moderate group and analyzes them separately, including the more conservative Wisconsin and Missouri synods, because Lutherans are, first and foremost, an ethnic church for northern European immigrants, and 56% of Lutherans do not identify with a specific denomination in their responses to the GSS. Most Lutheran churches gave services in languages other than English until World War I, when anti-German and anti-immigrant sentiment forced a switch to English (Finke and Stark 1992). Lutherans are also highly ritualized in their worship style. While Martin Luther rejected key elements of Catholic theology, the sect he spawned retained much of the ritual tradition of the Catholic Church.

Baptists are a large and quite distinctive sectarian group in the United States. With the exception of the liberalized Northern and American Baptists, most Baptist denominations and independent Baptist congregations are fundamentalist in their beliefs about sacred texts, they adhere to an exclusivist view of supernatural rewards and compensators, and most entertain beliefs about eschatological prophesy. Southern Baptist minister Rick Warren, who presents himself as a moderate-to-liberal Southern Baptist, responded to a Jewish questioner at the Aspen Institute that he believes that Jews will not be allowed in heaven (Riley 2008). Another Southern Baptist minister, the late Jerry Falwell, famously preached that "God almighty does not hear the prayer of a Jew" (Hyer 1980). Most white Baptists are in churches affiliated with the Southern Baptist Convention, but an increasing number of Baptist congregations are independent of a specific fellowship—they retain a denominational identification while lacking formal organizational ties to any specific Baptist convention. There are several unique features of Baptists, including an evangelical orientation toward outsiders, a strong horizontal and lay-led organizational structure, and a rejection of Pentecostalism. "Baptist," perhaps more than any other Protestant denominational identification, is a collective and personal identity, similar to "Catholic" (Dillon 1999). The horizontal organizational structure of Baptist groups creates both prospects and problems for white and African American Baptist groups.

Beyond the Baptists is a diverse array of sectarian denominations. Common to these sectarian denominations are fundamentalist orientations toward scriptural authority, exclusivist beliefs about supernatural compensators, and usually a strong focus on eschatological prophesy.

Many of these denominations are open or evangelical in their orientation toward outsiders, but some of them are insular and keep away from people who do not share their faith. Many are Pentecostal and charismatic, such as the Assembly of God and the Church of God in Christ, yet quite a few others, such as the Churches of Christ, have reserved worship styles and reject Pentecostalism. Some, such as the Churches of Christ, have horizontal organizational structures, but others are ruled over by a singular leader, and lay members have little say in congregational or denominational decisions.

Catholics are a large and important category, and much of this book will focus on the dynamics of affiliation among Catholics. The cumulative GSS will often allow the profitable examination of identification as Mormon, Unitarian, Jewish, nondenominational Christian, other religion, and no affiliation as separate categories.

The dynamics of religious commitments among African Americans are quite different from those found in other American ethnic groups, and the structure of the African American religious marketplace is defined by the experiences of slavery. During slavery and after emancipation, the Methodists and Baptists garnered the commitments of the vast majority of slaves and former slaves. African American Catholics come from unique experiences in places where Catholic slaveholding was prevalent (particularly in Louisiana). Catholicism is associated with higher status attainment among African Americans (Frazier 1964; Glenn 1964; Hunt and Hunt 1975), and immigrants of African and Afro-Caribbean origin are also more likely to be Catholic.

African American Methodism operates in several separate denominations: African Methodist Episcopal, African Methodist Episcopal-Zion, and Colored Methodist Episcopal, as well as in largely segregated United Methodist congregations. Methodism garners the commitments of a large fraction of the African American population, and these denominations have a uniquely hierarchical organizational structure. The strong hierarchy of the Methodist tradition made it more effective for mounting large-scale organizational projects (Lincoln and Mamiya 1990), and it has traditionally served the African American middle class (Sherkat 2001a, 2002).

The next chapter provides an overview of how religious affiliations changed from 1972 until 2012. First, it will show changes in religious identification across four decades of the General Social Survey. Second, it will show how these shifts are revealed by generational changes in religious origin and affiliation. Finally, it will investigate how race and immigrant status influence these distributions over time. This book provides the most comprehensive and systematic quantitative portrait of religious change in the United States, and it will demonstrate what those changes mean for American society in the realm of family life, social status, and political commitments.

# 1

## Religious Identification in America

Religious identification is a personal cognitive attachment to a religious group or tradition and may also reveal an actual or potential tie to religious organizations. Cognitive commitments to religious groups are important for structuring marital ties, for establishing childrearing patterns, and for providing lifelong socialization on how religion might impact the family, social life, status attainment, and political engagements. A connection to a religious group, even if it is only a cognitive identification, provides a source of institutional support for beliefs and behaviors. Identifications are usually a product of prior religious participation, and they are strongly associated with religious participation in the groups with which people identify. Most people who participate in religious groups also donate tangible resources to them, both financial and voluntary. GSS data show that 72% of respondents who report a religious identification have given money to a religious congregation in the past year, and 82% of people with some religious identification attended a religious service in the past year. Cognitive identifications with religious groups are strongly linked to the mobilization of resources by religious organizations.

Because of the connection of shifts in religious identification to religious mobilization, they provide an important image of religious change. Changes in the proportion of Americans holding particular religious identifications are a function of several factors, including differential fertility across religious groups, cohort replacement through the dying off of older identifiers, immigration, and people switching their religious identifications. These changes occur both over time and across generations. Fertility, of course, will only reveal itself as a key factor structuring religious identification in subsequent generations. And fertility effects will be strongly influenced by religious intermarriage and religious switching. Immigration is a constant feature of the

United States' demography, and over time immigrants have come in successive waves of immigration from varied religious and ethnic backgrounds. Religious switching can vary over time and also across generations (Roof and McKinney 1987; Sherkat 2001b) but is most often a single occurrence in the early life course (Roof 1989; Sherkat 1991). This chapter examines trends in religious identification and how these vary across generations and ethnic groups.

Over the past forty years, the ethnic composition of the United States has changed considerably through both fertility differentials and immigration. Ethnicity and immigration play a strong role in determining religious identifications, and changes in immigration policy after 1965 have changed the ethnic composition of different generations of Americans (Ebaugh 2003). Figures 1.1 and 1.2 show the ethnic and immigrant composition of the GSS samples by decade. Notably, data from the 1970s come only from 1977 and 1978 (the GSS was not conducted in 1979), when the question about immigration was added to the study. In the late 1970s, 69% of GSS respondents were native-born whites with both parents also born in the U.S. This total does not decline very much over time, but it does dip to 65% in the 2000s. The decrease in the proportion of nonimmigrant whites is offset by an increase in the proportion of African American and "other race" respondents. In the late 1970s, just over 10% of GSS respondents were nonimmigrant blacks, and only a tiny fraction (0.1%) of GSS respondents were nonimmigrants from other racial backgrounds. By the 2000s, the proportions of nonimmigrant African Americans inched up to almost 13%, while 2.2% of GSS respondents had two U.S.-born parents and claimed a race other than white or black.

The shifting ethnic composition of the U.S. becomes even more pronounced when immigrants are examined. The proportion of Americans who have at least one parent born outside the United States has been fairly constant at about 20% of GSS respondents since the late 1970s; however, the race and ethnicity of immigrants has shifted considerably. Figure 1.2 shows that in the late 1970s, almost 19% of GSS respondents were white first- or second-generation immigrants, while in the 2000 surveys, just over 12% of respondents were white first- or second-generation immigrants. In the late 1970s, black and other race immigrants *together* only accounted for 1.4% of GSS respondents. Since

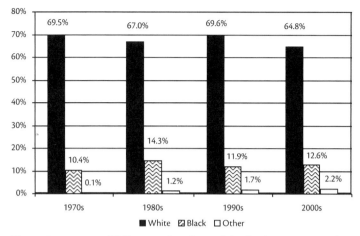

Fig. 1.1. Percentages of GSS respondents beyond the third generation in the U.S. by racial category and decade

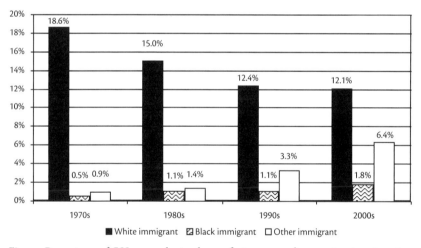

Fig. 1.2. Percentages of GSS respondents who are first- or second-generation immigrants by race and decade (1977–2012 GSS)

2000, the GSS samples have been 1.8% first- or second-generation black immigrant, and 6.4% first- or second-generation immigrants from other races. In the 1970s, GSS respondents were overwhelmingly white—69% native born and 19% white immigrants—88% of respondents were white. In more contemporary data since 2000, whites make up about 77% of respondents—12% of these being white immigrants. Nonwhites have gone from accounting for only 12% of the sample in the 1970s to making up 23% of GSS respondents. And in the 1970s, nonwhites were overwhelmingly native-born blacks—87% of nonwhite respondents. In the post-2000 surveys, only 55% of nonwhites were native-born blacks.

Most treatments of American religion either ignore race and ethnicity or segment the experiences of African Americans and immigrants in a way that sidelines their importance. That strategy is a useful shortcut for dealing with the overwhelming diversity within American religion, particularly given the rapid assimilation of ethnic Europeans into Anglo-American culture and religion. But ignoring ethnic and racial diversity is not a viable strategy for understanding the future of religion in a changing nation. The assimilation of European ethnics into a homogenized set of Anglo-Christian denominations was a very unusual sociological occurrence (Hamilton and Form 2003), and that homogenization is not quite complete (as will be shown in analyses comparing western and eastern European Americans); and the American experiences of the new immigrant groups which have arrived since 1965 will likely proceed in a quite different fashion (Ebaugh 2003).

## The Demography of Religious Change

Normal demographic processes are the engine of much social change, and shifting religious commitments are no different. Every year, new Americans are born, die, or immigrate to the U.S. Migration out of the U.S. has not been a strong demographic influence on the structure of the U.S. population, though that could change in the future. If new generations and immigrants differ substantially from older generations, then eventually the character of the nation will appear more like the younger generations. Over time, older generations die off and are replaced by younger generations, what sociologists refer to as cohort replacement. Cohort replacement is what drives many of the dynamics of religious commitments. Figure 1.3 charts the median birth year of respondents to the GSS in the four decades examined. In the 1970s, the median GSS respondent was born in 1932. That means that half of the GSS respondents in the 1970s were born prior to 1933. In the surveys conducted since 2000, the median GSS respondent was born in 1960— meaning that half of the respondents were born in 1960 or later.

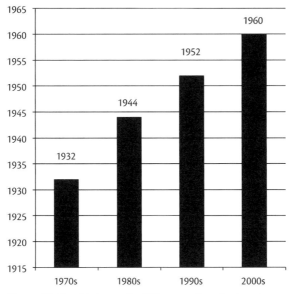

Fig. 1.3. Median birth year for GSS respondents by decade

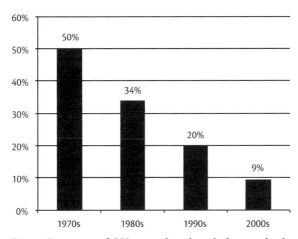

Fig. 1.4. Percentage of GSS respondents born before 1933 by decade

Figure 1.4 provides a dramatic sketch of generational replacement in the GSS by examining the proportion of respondents born before 1933, which is the median for the first decade of data collection. While 50% of respondents in the 1970s were born before 1933, that figure plunges to 9% for the respondents since 2000. The older generations are dying off, and younger cohorts are more important for understanding the nature and trajectory of social life.

## Trends in Religious Identification

In the past two decades, two competing grand theories have been the focus of explanation for trends in religious affiliation: supply-side rational-actor theories and the secularization thesis. According to the supply-side perspective, religious denominations are producing a product, and the quality of that product will drive consumer behavior. Proponents of the supply-side "strict church" thesis (Iannaccone 1994) argue that mainline Protestant religious groups are in decline because they fail to offer strong religious products. From this view, liberal religion is mushy and undemanding, offering few (or no) exclusive supernatural rewards and compensators. Supply-side theorists argue that liberal religious denominations are challenged in the provision of basic religious services, since the contributions of committed religious activists are watered down by the presence of shirkers who are not tolerated by exclusivist sectarian groups. In contrast, sectarian religious groups offer clear and exclusive supernatural compensators—promises of heaven only for their faithful. And because sectarian groups exclude the less faithful, their religious activities are also more effective and efficient (Iannaccone 1994). In direct contrast, secularization theories argue that as the United States becomes more secular, religious attachments will become less important. Hence, secularization proponents expect to find that nonaffiliation is increasing, that religious switching is more common, and that more fundamentalist and exclusivist religious groups will decline or only increase through fertility differentials (Greeley and Hout 2006; Hout, Greeley, and Wilde 2001).

Grand theoretical accounts generally fall short of providing useful explanations for complex sociological processes, in large part because they tend to ignore competing explanations and the diverse set of social forces that impact sociological factors. Table 1.1 presents the distribution of the thirteen religious classifications across the four decades of the GSS. Notably, there is ample support for and divergence from the expectations of both supply-side theories and secularization theories of religious change. First, in line with the expectations of supply-side

*Table 1.1. Trends in Religious Identification: GSS 1972–2012*

| Identification | 1970s | 1980s | 1990s | 2000s |
|---|---|---|---|---|
| Liberal Protestant | 6.4% | 5.7% | 5.2% | 3.7% |
| Episcopalian | 2.7% | 2.5% | 2.4% | 1.9% |
| Moderate Protestant | 13.0% | 13.1% | 12.7% | 9.8% |
| Lutheran | 8.4% | 6.8% | 7.0% | 4.4% |
| Baptist | 21.3% | 20.3% | 17.6% | 15.5% |
| Sectarian Protestant | 7.6% | 9.0% | 8.0% | 8.8% |
| Mormon | .8% | 1.9% | 1.2% | 1.2% |
| Other Protestant | 3.2% | 3.9% | 4.6% | 9.7% |
| Catholic | 25.8% | 25.3% | 25.1% | 24.1% |
| Jewish | 2.4% | 2.0% | 2.1% | 1.9% |
| Unitarian | .2% | .2% | .3% | .3% |
| Other religion | 1.3% | 1.9% | 3.3% | 2.8% |
| None | 6.9% | 7.4% | 10.7% | 16.0% |
| Number of cases | 8,751 | 13,751 | 12,783 | 18,731 |

theorists, liberal Protestant groups hold a declining share of Americans' religious commitments. In the 1970s, over 6% of respondents identified with a liberal Protestant group, and nearly 3% aligned with the Episcopal Church. In the surveys conducted in the 2000s, liberal Protestant bodies hold the identifications of under 4% of respondents, and Episcopalians garnered 2%. The number of moderate Protestants also fell from 13% of respondents to under 10%, while the proportion of Lutherans plunged from over 8% to over 4%.

While supply-side theorists have argued that the decline of "mainline" Protestant groups is evidence of the superiority of sectarian religious denominations, the data do not support this side of their argument. Sectarian religious groups are not gaining market share. Baptist bodies have decreased their share from over 21% of Americans to fewer than 16%—close to the *combined* losses of liberal Protestants, Episcopalians, and moderate Protestants. Other sectarian groups grew modestly from 8% to over 9% between the 1970s and the 1980s but fell back below 9% in the 1990s and held steady in the early 2000s. So while the less exclusivist liberal and moderate religious groups do seem to be experiencing the decline suggested by supply-side theories, their losses are not resulting in gains for the strictly exclusivist Baptist and sectarian denominations.

Looking at other religious groups, table 1.1 shows that the proportion of Catholics in the GSS is remarkably stable over the four decades.

Catholicism garnered the identifications of about 25% of Americans in the 1970s, and it held the commitments of 24% in the surveys conducted since 2000. Despite an alarming shortage of priests (Schoenherr, Young, and Cheng 1993) and conflict over birth control, abortion, women's rights, Vatican II, and a host of pedophilia scandals, Catholicism garners the identifications of the largest plurality of Americans.

Between the 1970s and the 2000s, an increasing proportion of Americans listed their religious identification as "other Protestant." In the 1970s, just over 3% reported this as an identification, yet in the surveys in the 2000s, almost 10% were Christians with no particular denomination. Both of our grand narratives of religious change could claim victory on this point. Supply-side partisans claim that nondenominational groups are sectarian in their orientation, and hence the growth of this group fits the expectations of strict-church theories. Secularization theorists argue that these "other Protestants" are simply people who do not care enough about religion to identify with any group (Kosmin and Keysar 2006). Later, we will examine the beliefs and religious commitment of these other Protestants to see which of these theses, if either, is more correct.

Mormons, Unitarians, and Jews hold fairly stable across the four decades of the study. There is a notable upward tick in the percentage of Mormons in the 1980s, but this is almost certainly a function of shifts in sampling units of the GSS (sampling units in the GSS are geographic areas from which respondents are randomly selected, and these units change). Because Mormons (and Jews) are regionally concentrated, a shift in regional sampling units could have a considerable impact on their reported proportions.

In line with the expectations of secularization theorists, the proportion of Americans who have no religious identification has increased dramatically since the 1970s. While about 7% of GSS respondents in the 1970s had no religious identification, this proportion more than doubled to nearly 16% in the surveys conducted since 2000. In the surveys conducted since 2000, about the same proportion of Americans were found to have no religious identification as identify with Baptist groups.

The proportion of Americans who identify with other religious traditions has also increased. In the 1970s, only 1.5% of respondents identified with traditions other than Christianity, Mormonism, and Judaism.

Yet in the surveys conducted since 2000, 3.1% of respondents identified as Muslim, Hindu, Buddhist, Sikh, Unitarian, or other traditions. Notably, that makes these traditions taken together more popular identifications than Episcopalian, Jewish, or Mormon. Non-Christian religion is no longer an esoteric sideline.

## Generations and Religious Change

Trends over time are largely a function of generational differences and cohort replacement. The religious character of the United States thirty years from now will be built on the religious identifications of the latest cohorts of Americans, and the members of the World War II generation whose commitments have characterized American religion will all be dead. Yet we cannot be too focused on the absolute differences between cohorts. Religious ties often follow common patterns of aging and development. People often leave religion or switch religious affiliations early in the life course and then return later in life (Wilson and Sherkat 1994), and in cross-sectional data such as the GSS, generations are being compared at quite different points in the life course. Indeed, people born before 1933 were never interviewed at an age less than thirty-nine, and even the youngest among them was at least seventy-nine years old at the time of the 2012 survey. In contrast, GSS respondents who were born in 1960 and later—who constituted 50% of respondents in surveys since 2000—have only been observed at a maximum of age fifty-two, and many were interviewed at ages as young as eighteen. Caution is warranted when making inferences about long-term changes based on generational differences, because age and life-course statuses intersect with generations in repeated cross-sectional data.

The distributions of religious identifications across generations echo the findings in the trend data and present an even more substantial suggestion of change. Table 1.2 shows that the declines in the percentage of Americans who identify with liberal and moderate Protestant groups are even steeper than was apparent in the trend data. Taken together, liberal and moderate Protestant denominations, the Episcopal Church, and Lutheran groups held the commitments of nearly 38% of respondents born prior to 1925, but this figure drops more than 7% in the 1925–1943 cohort. Indeed, among the youngest cohort born since 1971,

*Table 1.2. Religious Identification by Generation: GSS 1972–2012*

| Identification | Pre-1925 cohort | 1925–1943 cohort | 1944–1955 cohort | 1956–1970 cohort | 1971–1994 cohort |
|---|---|---|---|---|---|
| Liberal Protestant | 8.2% | 6.5% | 4.8% | 3.4% | 2.2% |
| Episcopalian | 3.2% | 2.9% | 2.2% | 1.7% | 1.0% |
| Moderate Protestant | 17.9% | 14.4% | 11.5% | 9.8% | 6.5% |
| Lutheran | 8.9% | 7.2% | 6.1% | 5.1% | 3.1% |
| Baptist | 19.1% | 19.7% | 17.6% | 17.4% | 14.8% |
| Sectarian Protestant | 8.8% | 8.8% | 9.1% | 8.9% | 7.9% |
| Mormon | .9% | 1.2% | 1.3% | 1.5% | 1.2% |
| Other Protestant | 3.5% | 4.5% | 5.9% | 7.2% | 9.9% |
| Catholic | 22.1% | 24.5% | 24.8% | 26.3% | 24.8% |
| Jewish | 2.8% | 2.3% | 2.2% | 1.4% | 1.3% |
| Unitarian | .3% | .4% | .3% | .2% | .1% |
| Other religion | .9% | 1.5% | 2.9% | 3.3% | 4.1% |
| None | 3.6% | 6.1% | 11.5% | 13.9% | 23.1% |
| Number of cases | 9,691 | 12,892 | 13,505 | 13,938 | 6,354 |

only 13% claim an affiliation in any of these traditional "mainline" liberal or moderate denominations.

While supply-side theorists may be emboldened by the shrinking shares of the more universalistic liberal and moderate denominations, the supply-side expectation that liberal losses lead to gains among exclusivist sectarian groups is inaccurate. As was true in the trend data, Baptists and sectarians also have a declining share of religious identifications in younger cohorts. Baptist groups held the identifications of about 20% of the cohorts born before 1943, but this figure trails off to fewer than 15% of those born after 1970. Other sectarian groups hold steadier, garnering the identification of about 9% of respondents across all the generations born prior to 1970; however, this figure dips to under 8% for respondents born after 1970. If we ignore the rest of the religious marketplace, the supply-side narrative appears to hold true—sectarian groups do garner the commitments of a larger share of Protestants. But Protestantism is shrinking, and sectarian commitments are as well— from 28% of respondents in the pre-1925 cohort to fewer than 23% in the post-1970 generation.

While traditional denominations within Protestantism are in decline, Catholicism's share of religious identifications is increasing across generations. In the oldest cohort, 22% of respondents identified as Catholic, while in the youngest cohort this increases to about 25%. Indeed, in the

1956–1970 cohorts, over 26% of respondents claimed a Catholic identification. Another growing identification is "other Protestant," which increases from 3.5% of identifications in the oldest cohort to almost 10% in the youngest generation.

Table 1.2 also shows that Jewish identification is declining across cohorts. Nearly 3% of respondents born prior to 1924 claimed a Jewish identity, while only 1.3% of the youngest generation identified themselves as Jewish. As in the trend data, other non-Christian groups are on the rise. If we combine Unitarians and the other traditions, just over 1% of respondents in the pre-1925 cohort were from other non-Christian religions, while over 4% of the cohort born after 1970 identify with a faith other than Christianity or Judaism.

In line with the expectations of secularization theories, the largest gains in identification across cohorts accrue to nonidentification. Fewer than 4% of respondents in the oldest generation had no religious identification, but this figure increases across cohorts to over 23% in the youngest cohort. Still, it should be remembered that all the respondents in the younger generations were interviewed very early in the life course. As they age, many in these younger generations will affiliate with religious groups and will shift their identifications. The next chapter will explore these trends in a different fashion by focusing on the impact of religious switching in these totals.

## Religion and Ancestry

The United States has always been a nation of immigrants. The indigenous population of North America was not as large as in most parts of the world, and they suffered tremendously from disease, war, and genocide over the course of the first three centuries of European contact (Thornton 1987). Migration to the United States was always highly selective, and religious influences on migration are evident throughout U.S. history. The Anglican Church of Great Britain did not hold the sentiments of the majority of migrants to the U.S., and the Revolutionary War further marginalized the Episcopal Church. Indeed, British immigrants were more likely to be Calvinists from the Puritan and Presbyterian traditions or Methodist sectarians fleeing the oppressive monopoly of the Church of England, and they were much more likely to be nonreligious (Finke and Stark 1992). Religious minorities are significantly more likely to migrate than are members of majority traditions in any nation (Alanezi and Sherkat 2008; Form 2000; Hamilton and Form 2003), and so the United States found itself populated by a diverse set of immigrants, many of whom held an unpopular faith in their nation of origin—or they were nonreligious people fleeing the strictures of theocracies.

Not all immigrants have been welcome in the United States, and potential immigrants from many nations had reason to fear for their safety and livelihood. It would have been unthinkable for a person of African ancestry to move to the United States for much of its history, and immigrants from China and Japan experienced considerable hostility in the late 19th century. Indeed, hostility toward Asian immigrants was a key motivation for a series of Asian exclusion laws in the 19th and early 20th centuries; and these remained largely in effect until the passage of the Immigration and Nationality Act Amendments of 1965. Now, new Americans from different parts of the world are having an impact on the structure of American religious identifications.

The GSS asks respondents about their national ancestry; but not all nations are included in the lists, and some nonnational classifications are also in the mix ("Africa," "Middle East," "Latin America"). Nevertheless, this indicator of nationality can be used to sort out differences in origins across broad groups of Americans. And, notably, it also taps whether the primary nationality embraced by respondents is Native American, a category unexplored in most research (Garroutte et al. 2009). Table 1.3 presents the religious identifications of GSS respondents from six national-origin groups: (1) western European, (2) eastern European, (3) African, (4) Latin American, (5) Native American, and (6) Asian.

While we tend to think of white Americans as homogeneous, their ethnic heritage still plays a part in structuring their religious identifications. Most GSS respondents hail from western Europe, and people from this part of the world are much more likely to be liberal Protestants, Episcopalians, Lutherans, and moderate Protestants. In contrast, eastern Europeans are much more likely to be Catholic, with nearly 49% of respondents identifying as Catholic, compared to 26% among western Europeans. Particularly striking is the difference in the proportion

*Table 1.3. Religious Identification by Ethnicity: GSS 1977–2012*

| Identification | Western European | Eastern European | African American | Latin American | Native American | Asian |
|---|---|---|---|---|---|---|
| Liberal Protestant | 7.1% | 2.3% | 1.0% | .5% | 2.7% | 3.5% |
| Episcopalian | 3.1% | 1.2% | 1.3% | .3% | .9% | .4% |
| Moderate Protestant | 12.9% | 3.5% | 18.5% | 1.5% | 10.0% | 3.8% |
| Lutheran | 9.5% | 4.5% | .6% | .7% | 2.2% | 1.5% |
| Baptist | 12.6% | 2.2% | 43.6% | 3.4% | 30.5% | 4.0% |
| Sectarian Protestant | 7.2% | 2.6% | 12.8% | 9.4% | 17.3% | 4.5% |
| Mormon | 1.7% | .2% | .2% | .8% | 1.3% | .5% |
| Other Protestant | 6.2% | 3.4% | 4.7% | 4.5% | 8.3% | 4.3% |
| Catholic | 26.3% | 48.2% | 6.9% | 68.4% | 10.7% | 26.5% |
| Jewish | .7% | 17.8% | .2% | .3% | .1% | 1.3% |
| Unitarian | .4% | .2% | .1% | .1% | .1% | .1% |
| Other religion | 1.7% | 3.3% | 2.3% | 1.0% | 3.7% | 28.1% |
| None | 10.6% | 10.4% | 7.9% | 9.1% | 12.2% | 21.5% |
| Number of cases | 28,968 | 3,225 | 7,789 | 2,836 | 1,607 | 1,038 |
| % first- or second-generation immigrant | 14.7% | 39.4% | 8.8% | 74.1% | 3.0% | 90.1% |

of Jews and other non-Christians among whites from varied European backgrounds. Among Americans from eastern European origins, nearly 18% identify as Jewish, compared to less than 1% of western Europeans. In total, over 21% of Americans from eastern European origins adhere to a non-Christian faith, compared to under 3% of western Europeans.

Sectarian Christian groups are more popular among whites from western European backgrounds, with about 20% identifying as Baptist or with another sectarian denomination. In contrast, under 5% of Americans from eastern European backgrounds are Baptists or other sectarians. And it is not the case that eastern Europeans are irreligious; in fact, nearly identical proportions of eastern and western Europeans hold no religious identification (about 10% in the 1977–2012 cumulative GSS).

African Americans have very distinctive patterns of religious identification. Very few African Americans identify with liberal Protestant groups or with Lutheran bodies. Liberal Protestant denominations, the Episcopal Church, and Lutherans combined account for less than 3% of African American religious identifications—close to the total of combined non-Christian religious identifications (mostly Muslim).

The African American "mainline" denominations are the Baptist and Methodist groups, which have held the commitments of most African

Americans since before emancipation (Ellison and Sherkat 1990; Glenn 1964; Lincoln and Mamiya 1990; Sherkat 2002). There is considerably less religious diversity among African Americans—with over 62% of identifications falling in two denominational camps, Baptist and moderate Protestant. Almost 19% of African Americans identify with moderate Protestant groups, with most of these adhering to Methodist denominations. About 44% of African Americans identify as Baptists. Other sectarian groups hold the identifications of nearly 13% of African Americans—a substantially higher proportion than among whites of any ancestry.

There are relatively few African American Catholics, just 7% of African American respondents. Catholicism made inroads into African American communities in a few locales (particularly in Louisiana, in Maryland, and in the Mississippi River corridor), but it did not enjoy the predicted surge that was expected when African Americans were granted civil rights (Frazier 1964; Glenn 1964; Hunt and Hunt 2001). The vast majority of African Americans hold some religious identification. A lower proportion of African Americans have no religious identification than is found in any other ancestry group.

Latin Americans remain overwhelmingly Catholic, with 69% of Latin American respondents identifying with Catholicism. Still, Protestant inroads are apparent, and almost 13% of Latin Americans identify with Baptist or other sectarian Protestant groups—which foreshadows the success of these groups in conversion among Latin Americans.

No previous quantitative study has examined the religious commitments of a random sample of people who claim Native American as their central ancestry. The GSS finds 1,607 respondents who claim indigenous ancestry as their primary origin, and their religious identifications are unique. First, Native Americans are heavily Baptist and sectarian. Nearly 31% of those who claim indigenous origins identify their religion as Baptist, and 17% claim an identity with another sectarian group. An additional 10% are moderate Protestants. Only 11% of Native Americans claim a Catholic identity, and nearly 4% identify with other non-Christian religions (most of these claim indigenous religions such as Hopi or Navajo). Caution is warranted when interpreting these estimates, since the GSS sampling frame does not include Native American reservations. A minority and declining proportion of Native Americans live on reservations, though they may be quite distinct. It is likely that far higher percentages of indigenous people on reservations practice Native American faiths.

Asian Americans are an increasing segment of the American population and are quite diverse in national origin, including a sizeable "old stock" population of mostly Chinese and Japanese immigrants who weathered a century or more of ethnic hostility and a larger and diverse set of immigrants who have come since the late 20th century. Asians are far less likely to be Christians compared with other Americans, and over 28% hold a non-Christian faith. Asians are also much more likely to have no religious identification, with almost 22% claiming no religious identification. Less than half of Asian American GSS respondents identify as Christian. And this figure may be lower in the actual population since the GSS is biased against non-English speakers and may miss large pockets of Asians with limited English proficiency. Most Asian Christians are Catholic, and about 27% of Asian respondents identify as Catholic. Beyond that, Asian Christians distribute themselves almost evenly across other religious identifications—about 9% in Baptist and sectarian groups (combined) and around 9% in less exclusivist liberal and moderate denominations.

## Religion and Ancestry among Immigrants

About 20% of GSS respondents were born in another country or have at least one parent who was born elsewhere. These first- and second-generation immigrants have had less time to assimilate into the religious marketplace in the United States, and immigrants are increasingly coming from nations and backgrounds where the type of assimilation which took place among earlier European immigrants is unlikely to occur (Ebaugh 2003; Ebaugh and Chafetz 2000). Of course, for Asians and Latin Americans, ancestry is closely linked to immigrant status. Table 1.3 shows that over 90% of respondents who claimed an Asian ancestry were first- or second-generation immigrants, while 74% of respondents from Latin America were first- or second-generation immigrants. Western Europeans and African Americans have lower proportions of immigrants, but 39% of eastern Europeans are first- or second-generation immigrants. Respondents who report Native American ancestry were

*Table 1.4. Religious Identification by Ethnicity among First- and Second-Generation Immigrants*

| Identification | Western European | Eastern European | Latin American | Asian | African American |
|---|---|---|---|---|---|
| Liberal Protestant | 6.1% | 1.8% | .6% | 3.0% | 2.8% |
| Episcopalian | 3.8% | .6% | .4% | .5% | 5.7% |
| Moderate Protestant | 6.6% | 3.0% | .8% | 3.8% | 10.0% |
| Lutheran | 11.4% | 3.5% | .6% | 1.3% | .7% |
| Baptist | 3.7% | 1.0% | 2.9% | 3.8% | 17.6% |
| Sectarian Protestant | 4.2% | 2.1% | 9.8% | 3.7% | 15.5% |
| Mormon | .9% | .3% | .9% | 5% | .2% |
| Other Protestant | 5.4% | 3.2% | 4.0% | 3.4% | 8.1% |
| Catholic | 41.1% | 48.5% | 69.9% | 26.5% | 22.2% |
| Jewish | 1.9% | 22.9% | .4% | 1.3% | .5% |
| Unitarian | .4% | .5% | — | — | .3% |
| Other religion | 2.9% | 4.2% | .7% | 30.4% | 6.4% |
| None | 11.7% | 8.4% | 8.8% | 22.0% | 10.2% |
| Number of cases | 3,517 | 1,024 | 1,797 | 865 | 581 |

unlikely to be born outside the United States, and only 3% were first- or second-generation immigrants.

Looking at the first- and second-generation immigrants provides an interesting contrast with some of the findings based on ancestry, particularly for the Europeans. Table 1.4 shows that western European immigrants are much more likely to be Catholic, when compared to Americans from western Europe from prior waves of immigration: over 41%, compared to 26%. Immigrants from western Europe are also much less likely to claim identifications with Baptist groups or other sects— less than 8% claim a Baptist or other sectarian identity, compared to 20% among older-stock western Europeans. Predictably, fairly high proportions (11%) of immigrants from western Europe identify with Lutheran groups.

Because higher proportions of eastern Europeans are immigrants, their religious identifications look more like those of other Americans who claim eastern European ancestry. Among immigrants from eastern Europe, Jewish and other non-Christian identifications are even more popular, with 23% embracing Judaism and almost 5% adopting another non-Christian faith.

Latin American immigrants also look quite similar to other Americans of Latin American ancestry, with almost 72% embracing Catholicism. Latin American immigrants also have similar concentrations in other religious identity categories, including the proportion who identify as sectarians. This suggests that conversion to Protestantism is not simply something that takes place in the U.S. but is being brought with immigrants to the United States, as scholarship on Latin American Protestantism might suggest (Stoll 1990). Since over 90% of Asian Americans are first- or second-generation immigrants, the distribution of their religious identifications mirrors that found in table 1.3 for ancestry groups.

African and Caribbean immigrants are different from other African Americans, since the vast majority of people who claim African ancestry have lived in the United States for many generations. Immigrants with African and Caribbean origins are much more likely to identify as liberal Protestants when compared to other African Americans, and the proportion of Episcopalians among African immigrants is higher than in any other ancestry group. Nearly 6% of African or Caribbean immigrants are Episcopalian, which is even higher than among western European immigrants. Sectarian groups are popular among African immigrants, with almost 18% identifying with Baptists and over 15% with other sects. However, the Baptist totals are much lower than is found among African Americans in general. Immigrants of African origins are substantially more likely to be Catholic when compared to other African Americans—22% compared to 7%. And African and Caribbean immigrants often identify with other non-Christian groups. More than 6% of African immigrants have a non-Christian faith, and about half of these non-Christians are Muslim.

## The Structuring of Religious Change

Americans' religious identifications are changing, but simple explanations for those shifts do not identify the many factors that influence these changes. Linear theories such as those postulated by supply-side and secularization partisans do not help to explain the shifting structure of religious identifications in the United States. Contrary to the proclamations of supply-side theorists and conservative Christian activists, conservative Christian religious groups are not increasing their share of religious identifications in the United States. Indeed, identification with Baptist and other sectarian denominations is on the decline over time and across generations, and their losses mirror those found among mainline Protestant groups. Secularization theorists have more support in empirical reality, since the big winner in the shifting alignment of religious identifications is nonidentification with religion. Yet the grand, linear, evolutionary perspective put forward in classical and contemporary secularization theories is just as far-fetched as the supply-side stories yearning for a sectarian Christian America. Religious identification is not going away, and the vast majority of Americans hold religious identifications.

Grand theory is trumped by careful analyses of normal demographic processes. Religious identifications are shifting because of changes in the composition of the American population. The largest and most important shift in the population structure is the composition of immigrant groups—which constitute about one-fifth of the American population. Second, and related to this, younger generations have different religious alignments. Part of this is a function of the age structure of different ancestry groups, which is a function of both migration and fertility. Younger people are much more likely to migrate, and immigrant groups are largely composed of later generations. New immigrants and African Americans also have higher fertility rates, which makes them an increasingly important component of the structuring of religious identifications. As older cohorts are dying off, we are predictably seeing a decline in identifications with groups associated with old-stock Anglo populations (such as liberal and moderate Protestant bodies) and with western European immigrant groups (such as the Lutherans). Interestingly, Episcopalians are somewhat of an exception, owing largely to an influx of identifiers from Africa and the Caribbean. Catholicism is also buoyed by immigration; yet, given the influx of immigrants from heavily Catholic countries, their totals seem low.

This chapter has shown that religious identifications in the United States have changed over time and across generations and that ethnicity plays a strong role in those religious commitments. The United States is becoming less Protestant and less Christian in part because the immigrant groups populating the nation have changed and because younger generations are more likely to reject religious identification. Americans' religious identifications are not changing in a way that conforms to the expectations of supply-side rational-choice theories—conservative churches are not growing. Nor are Americans rapidly abandoning religious identification, as secularization theorists predict. Instead, the distribution of religious identifications appears to be more of a function of ethnic ties, waves of immigration, and generational replacement.

Many questions remain about how the structure of identifications has shifted and particularly how religious switching plays a role. This chapter has purposely avoided the issue of people changing their religious identifications over the life course. The empirical findings presented here chart only the distribution of current religious identifications, but the GSS also allows an investigation of the religious identification of respondents when they were growing up—at age sixteen. The next chapter will explore how voluntary shifts in religious identifications influence the dynamics of religious affiliation over time, across generations, and across varied ethnic groups. The flip side of religious switching is stability, which may be seen as a voluntary choice or a product of combination of religious socialization and social sanctions. People leave or stay in particular religious groups for a variety of reasons; and the religious benefits touted by supply-side theorists are only one part of the decision-making process. Chapter 2 will also investigate the predictors of religious switching using advanced multivariate statistical techniques to show how people tend to shift their religious identifications and how social status, ethnicity, gender, geographic mobility, and family factors influence changes in religious identification.

2

Religious Switching and Religious Change

Americans sometimes change their religious identifications over the course of their lives, and they are more likely to shift identifications than are people in other predominantly Christian nations (Breen and Hayes 1996; Hayes and McAllister 1995). Close to 40% of Americans shift their religious identification at least once during their lives (Roof 1989; Sherkat 1991). In most nations, religious identifications are bound by family and clan ties; yet Americans' religious attachments are less fixed. The result of this freedom of association is considerable dynamism in American religion, and these patterns of religious change have substantial consequence in a variety of arenas of social life. While many scholars and commentators like to amplify the voluntary aspect of religious commitments, it is important to remember that religious choices, like all choices, are made in social settings—where individual preferences and desires often succumb to social pressures which mete out rewards for some choices and punishments for others (Sen 1973; Sherkat 1997, 1998; Sherkat and Wilson 1995). Social constraints on religious choices are considerable, particularly for people embedded in ethnic communities where opportunities for social rewards are low outside their ethnic group and in rural and regional areas where social ties are consolidated across a variety of social realms—such as occupation, neighborhood, kinship, political associations, and religious congregations (Alanezi and Sherkat 2008; Ellison and Sherkat 1995b; Sherkat and Ellison 1999).

In the sociological literature, there have been two primary modes of explaining religious change, one focusing on the functioning of religious organizations and the second concentrating on broad cultural shifts. As we have seen, since the early 1990s, supply-side rational-actor models of religious change have been all the rage among sociologists and economists of religion, with theorists arguing that organizational factors are primarily responsible for the contours of affiliation and levels of religiosity in a given setting (e.g., Finke and Stark 1992; Iannaccone 1994). From this perspective, denominations which lose members are thought to have less effective religious production, while those gaining members from switching are deemed to produce more enticing religious products. However, this view of religious "production" often confuses the effective use of organizational resources to promote mobilization with the production of convincing explanations about the nature of the supernatural and how humans might obtain supernatural rewards or compensators. Indeed, supply-side partisans often slip into arguments which seem to claim that certain types of religious beliefs are more valuable than others (e.g., Iannaccone 1994), and it is unclear how that is consistent with a theory which is supposed to be based on collective production processes rather than the intrinsic quality of the product. If one set of beliefs is more preferred in a population, a demand-side theory best explains why some religious denominations do better than others.

Before the 1990s, the dominant perspectives on religious change focused on broad cultural shifts created by structural strains between existing religious value systems and institutions and economic and social shifts, arguing that people move to denominations which are more relevant given their cultural desires (Bellah 1976; Glock, Bellah, and Alfred 1976; Wuthnow 1976). Many religious commentators argued that cultural trajectories are linear and tend toward secularization. The dominant expectation for secularization theorists is that people will gradually move out of otherworldly religious groups, into more secular mainstream denominations, and eventually out of religion entirely (Berger 1967; Newport 1979; Stark and Glock 1965). For others, cultural movements vary across generations, and countercultural themes in the baby-boom generation were deemed to undermine commitments to organized religion (Bellah 1976; Wuthnow 1976, 1988). Linear theories of social change tend not to square with reality, and simple theories of secularization are rejected by most sociologists, including prominent former proponents such as Rodney Stark and Peter Berger. Other theories of cultural shifts are often overstated and underspecified. The "countercultural" generations of the baby boom were hardly uniform, and cultural critics tended to focus on a minority of baby boomers who sought to create an alternative culture—ignoring the vast majority who followed in the footsteps of their parents (Klatch 1999; Sherkat 1998; Sherkat and Blocker 1997; Sherkat and Wilson 1995).

Both supply-side rational-choice and cultural theories of religious change ignore the more mundane demographic factors which influence changes in commitments to religious groups and other voluntary organizations. Both perspectives view American society as uniform, and theorists from these traditions ignore the central importance of ethnic and racial cleavages, which provide a pivotal influence on American religion. This chapter discusses various explanations for trends and patterns of religious switching and the predictors of religious switching and apostasy. Using data from the 1973–2012 General Social Survey, it examines trends in religious switching and patterns of mobility across religious groups, including rates of apostasy—the rejection of religious identification. It focuses on how these trends and patterns vary across generations and across ethnic groups. Finally, it examines how ethnicity, gender, social status, and geographic mobility influence religious switching, apostasy, and which changes in identification are most and least likely, as well as what predicts individuals making improbable shifts in identification—such as when an Episcopalian comes to identify as a sectarian Protestant.

## Winners and Losers?

As noted, supply-side theorists of religious change argue that successful religious groups produce superior religious products and that groups which fail to produce valuable religious goods lose out in the religious economy (Finke and Stark 1992; Iannaccone 1994). Religious switching plays a key role in this process, since people are deemed to choose freely among a set of competitive "firms" operating in a local religious market. Supply-side theorists claim that religious production is enhanced by the "religious human capital" available in the congregation (Iannaccone 1990) and that "strict" sectarian churches have more adequate human-capital stocks because they exclude shirkers (Iannaccone 1994).

Supply-side theorists make bold claims about the success of sectarian religion, and their theories suggest that these groups should increase their shares in the religious marketplace because of religious switching (Iannaccone 1994). If these theories are on the mark, loyalty to religious groups should also be higher among sectarians. Few sectarians should want to leave religious groups producing such wonderful religious goods, and members of these groups should be steeped in religious human capital, which enables them to generate copious religious value (Iannaccone 1990). If supply-side theories are on target, there should be a clear pattern of religious switching from liberal Protestant denominations and nonreligion into conservative Protestant sects. We may also expect that Episcopalians might repatriate to the Catholic Church more often that Catholics defect to Anglicanism. Religious switching out of Catholicism may also be expected to increase in the generations following the Vatican II reforms, which reduced strictness. But other patterns of switching should be relatively trendless. Notably, supply-side theorists view preferences for religious goods as stable and ubiquitous, and they do not foresee an increase in apostasy—the rejection of religious identification. Supply-side theorists expect that apostasy will be highest among members of religious groups with low rates of religious participation (and therefore low levels of human capital)—such as liberal Protestant groups—or in religious groups that imbue capital which is hard to apply in other settings (such as for Jews, other non-Christians, or Catholics).

## Secularization in America?

One of the oldest theories in the sociological canon contends that religion will decline as a human social institution and that people will become less religious over time and across generations. Various statements of this secularization thesis have been made by both classical and contemporary scholars, from Auguste Comte and Max Weber to Peter Berger and Mark Chaves. The debate over secularization has become contentious, confusing, and counterproductive. We will not wade into the nuances of those discussions (see instead Bruce 2011; Chaves 1994; Hadden 1987; Lechner 1991; Stark 1999). Still, a practical variant of secularization theory can be applied to the analysis of religious change, and this produces testable expectations about religious switching. Simply put, if the United States is becoming more secular, then we should see higher rates of apostasy across generations, and we should see movement from more otherworldly sectarian religious groups into more worldly liberal groups. We should also see diminished rates of retention —which equates to higher rates of switching—across generations.

Many earlier theorists and researchers linked secularization to educational attainment. As secular learning replaces religious myths, it was argued, people would switch from otherworldly sects into more worldly mainline denominations and eventually become apostates (Newport 1979; Roof and McKinney 1987). This "up and out" theory of religious careers dominated most research on religious switching in the late 20th century. This chapter later develops how this perspective can be linked to status seeking and to theories of homophily in voluntary organizations (both of which differ from a linear secularization view).

## Countercultures and Religious Change

The social and political upheavals of the 1950s and 1960s led to much speculation about the potential for religious realignment. Echoing strain theories from studies of social movements and criminology, many religious commentators contended that an increasingly global environment, political turmoil, and other disruptions fueled a crisis of legitimacy for American religious institutions (Bellah 1976; Roof and Greer 1993; Wuthnow 1976). These social and religious crises are claimed to have had an enormous impact on baby boomers, creating a distinct generation with beliefs and attachments counter to those of previous generations. Indeed, the implied attractiveness of countercultural orientations to "bellwether" groups—especially young, educated baby boomers—led many observers to proclaim the 1960s counterculture as the driving force behind two pivotal "trends" that are claimed to be altering the religious character of the United States: (1) a distaste for biblical religion and (2) declining religious participation (Bellah 1976; Glock, Bellah, and Alfred 1976; Roof and Greer 1993; Wuthnow 1976).

Macrocultural theorists predicted that these social upheavals would swell the ranks of new religious movements and spur apostasy from traditional Christian denominations. However, macrocultural theories have also been used to try to explain the "growth" of conservative sects. Steven Tipton (1982) argued that the normlessness and individualism of the 1960s led many people to embrace traditional Christianity. Similarly, Christian Smith (2003) has argued that rapid social change has caused sectarian Christians to establish a counterculture enmeshed in communities imbued with a distinctive "subcultural identity."

Overall, these cultural theories point to a key split in religious identification across generations—beginning with the generations which reached maturity in the 1950s and 1960s. Beyond that, these theorists see macrosocial strains as producing everything from growing apostasy to burgeoning non-Christian movements to growth in sectarian Protestantism. They also predict a breakdown in the established patterns of attachments and a decline in the importance of institutional denominational identifications (Wuthnow 1993), replaced instead with broader Christian identities such as "born again" and "evangelical" (Hunter 1991; C. Smith 2003).

## Learning Religious Identifications

Grand narratives constructed by social theorists rarely do justice to the complexities of social life. Each of the three major perspectives used to explain religious change have a common simplicity. From the supply side, the simple answer is that conservative groups are better at production. For secularization theorists, religion is doomed to failure. For cultural theorists, all manner of change can be explained by reference to an amorphous "cultural consciousness" and equally ephemeral "structural strains." The sources of religious identification are a product of socialization, and religious firms are only one source of these identifications. Preferences for particular identifications are learned, and they shift over the life course in response to a variety of influences. Many factors motivating shifts in identification are unrelated to religion but are instead produced by other "selective incentives" (McCarthy and Zald 1977)—religious rewards and compensators emanating from explanations about the supernatural are not the only reason people make religious choices about identification and participation, and they may be only peripheral to people's religious decision making (Sherkat 1998, 2004; Sherkat and Wilson 1995).

In general, people learn religious identifications in childhood through socialization from a variety of agents. The family is the most important source for learning religious explanations and for providing identification with a particular religious group or tradition. Notably, there is no choice in this process. Children are taught what to value by parents, grandparents, siblings, and other trusted relations. Typically, alternative religious explanations are not even discussed by socialization agents, and they are caricatured and vilified when they are presented. Alternative religious explanations are thereby removed from the feasible set of religious products considered in religious decision making (Elster 1979; Kuran 1993, 1995). Children are taught to prefer a particular brand of religion, and with that usually comes identification with some organizational group. Preferences for those explanations are typically adaptive, meaning that they get stronger with repetition (Elster 1979; Sherkat 1998; Sherkat and Wilson 1995). Just as many people enjoy a particular brand of soft drink or breakfast food, familiar explanations about the supernatural are comfortable and generally preferred to novel ideas or typifications.

Exposure to alternative religious beliefs and identifications tends not to occur until later in childhood, usually through networks of friends and acquaintances in school. However, religious innovation can also come from within the family. Siblings, aunts and uncles, or other relations may introduce new ideas, which could lead to shifts in religious identification (Rochford 1985). This is one reason why exclusivist sectarian Christians and fundamentalists of all religious traditions are often oppositional to public education and seek to segregate their children from secular and alternative religious information. The presence of religious diversity means that their children will be exposed to, and perhaps even become friends with, children who hold quite different religious commitments.

Conversion from one religious group to another is almost uniformly accomplished through social ties (Rochford 1985; Stark and Bainbridge 1980). Indeed, in a classic study of conversion to the Unification Church (the "Moonies"), John Lofland and Rodney Stark concluded that "final conversion was coming to accept the opinions of one's friends" (1965, 871). People often identify as members of religious groups, even when they do not share the beliefs espoused by official doctrine—and this is even common for members of new religious movements (cults) which require high levels of participation and sacrifice from members (Lofland and Stark 1965; Rochford 1985). Preferences for religious explanations do not always drive choices about identification and commitment. Instead, people come to identify with religious groups and to hold preferences for particular religious understandings in response to social pressures.

## Social Influences on Religious Choices

Social networks not only convey learning about new religious understandings; they also influence the rewards and punishments associated with religious identities and activities. Social rewards derived from religious commitments are quite different from religious rewards and compensators (Sherkat 1997, 1998; Sherkat and Wilson 1995). Religious groups enable people to meet friends, business contacts, political connections, and intimate partners. They provide a setting where children can play and meet playmates. Religious groups coordinate activities for everything from sports to music to camping to motorcycle riding to hunting. Such activities are valuable in their own right, and people pay money to join secular clubs providing similar social connections. When individuals are enmeshed in social networks common to their own faith, there is considerable social pressure not to switch. The consolidation of social ties across family, work, and neighborhood often leads to "quasi-ethnic" feelings of religious identification (Harrison and Lazerwitz 1982; Sandomirsky and Wilson 1990; Sherkat 1991; Sherkat and Wilson 1995). In contrast, when a person's religious identity is different from those held by most of his or her friends, co-workers, and associates, there may be considerable pressure to switch.

Geographic mobility uproots individuals from preexisting social ties and places them in new environments where switching is more likely (Sherkat 1991; Sherkat and Wilson 1995). This is especially true when individuals move into or out of areas of the country dominated by particular types of religion, such as the Baptist belt in the South or the Catholic upper Midwest and Northeast (Ellison and Sherkat 1995a; Sherkat and Cunningham 1998). In contrast, immigrants from other nations often congregate in ethnic communities, which may increase the costs of leaving the faith (Alanezi and Sherkat 2008). But religion also influences migration decisions (Myers 2000), and immigrants may choose to come to the United States because they are, for example, Christian and living in less Christian environs (Alanezi and Sherkat 2008; Sherkat 2010a)

Intimate partners can have a profound effect on religious choices, and religious intermarriage is among the strongest predictors of switching religious identification (Sandomirsky and Wilson 1990; Sherkat 1991). Spousal conflict over religious issues can generate costs for maintaining a distinct identification, and spouses may switch out of sympathy for the religious commitments of their partner (Sherkat 1998; Sherkat and Wilson 1995). Religious groups that have low rates of intermarriage also have the lowest rates of religious switching (Sherkat 1991, 2010c).

In the 1960s and 1970s, research on religious mobility was dominated by status theories which posited that individuals would seek religious affiliations granting them high status in society. Following Rodney Stark and Charles Glock's (1965) theoretical and empirical work, researchers expected that high-status liberal denominations, such as the Presbyterians and Episcopalians, would have strong membership retention and would gain members from less prestigious groups. In contrast, low-status conservative sects, such as the Baptists, Churches of Christ, and various Pentecostal groups were expected to lose members and decline (Alston 1971; Kluegel 1980; Lauer 1975; Newport 1979). Some theorists view status seeking as an offshoot of secularization; however, others focus on choices being driven by social rewards—rather than by declining valuations of otherworldly religion. The focus on social influences is paramount in demand-side rational-actor theories applied to religious switching (Sherkat and Ellison 1999; Sherkat 1998; Sherkat and Wilson 1995) as well as to economic theories of conformity and conspicuous consumption (Akerlof 1997; Akerlof and Kranton 2000, 2010; Bagwell and Bernheim 1996; Bernheim 1994; Sen 1973, 1993). Consumption choices for members of high-status groups are made to bolster "invidious comparisons" vis-à-vis lower-status groups, while people of lower status engage in "pecuniary emulation" by mirroring the consumption patterns of higher-status groups (Bagwell and Bernheim 1996; Bernheim 1994; Veblen 2005). Status influences on religious choices may vary across periods and cohorts, just as fashion and other articles of conspicuous consumption go in and out of vogue or become salient status markers only for particular generations. Indeed, Roof and McKinney (1987) argue that status seeking was a common impetus for religious mobility in the conformist cohorts that reached adulthood in the World War II period and formed families in the postwar era.

Social connections are most valuable when they provide access to people who hold similar social status. Homophily drives patterns of affiliation and commitment in voluntary organizations because people value connections within social strata (McPherson, Smith-Lovin, and Cook 2001). People like to be with people who are similar to themselves with regard to education, income, ethnicity, and age. Individuals who differ from their peers in voluntary organizations are much more likely to disaffiliate (Popielarz and McPherson 1995; Sherkat and Wilson 1995). Age is especially important for structuring affiliation and commitment—people like to join groups populated by age-group peers and tend to defect from groups that are populated by people older or younger (McPherson and Rotolo 1996; Popielarz and McPherson 1995).

## Loyalty and Attractiveness: Religious Switching across Religious Groups

Since 1973, the General Social Survey (GSS) has asked respondents about their current religious identification and their religious identification when they "were growing up, say at about age 16." Religious switching is most common early in the life course and peaks at about age twenty-five (Roof 1989; Sherkat 1991). Most religious switchers (67%) report only making one switch, while 25% made two shifts, just over 6% report three shifts in identification, and less than 2% of GSS respondents report switching their identification four or more times. Detailed questions on multiple religious switching are only available in the 1988 data, so the focus here will be on overall switching from age sixteen to the time of the interview. This focus certainly masks multiple shifts which might occur over the life course and may especially ignore temporary apostates who leave religion early in the life course only to return to identification later (Wilson and Sherkat 1994).

Switching is defined here as a person's having a different identification at the time of the interview from the one expressed at the age of sixteen, with identifications grouped into thirteen categories: (1) liberal Protestant, (2) Episcopalian, (3) moderate Protestant, (4) Lutheran, (5) Baptist, (6) sectarian Protestant, (7) Mormon, (8) other Protestant, (9) Catholic, (10) Jewish, (11) Unitarian, (12) other religion, and (13) no religious identification. Switching across denominations is possible within

*Table 2.1. Religious Loyalty and Religious Switching*

| Identification | % loyal | % of current identifiers who switched | % of change from switching | % of respondents who currently identify (number of identifiers) |
|---|---|---|---|---|
| Liberal Protestant | 54.8% | 39.5% | −9.4% | 5.1% (2,715) |
| Episcopalian | 60.4% | 40.9% | 2.4% | 2.3% (1,230) |
| Moderate Protestant | 61.3% | 25.9% | −17.3% | 12.3% (6,530) |
| Lutheran | 68.2% | 26.6% | −7.0% | 6.2% (3,315) |
| Baptist | 70.2% | 19.5% | −12.8% | 18.0% (9,545) |
| Sectarian Protestant | 61.3% | 48.5% | 19.1% | 8.8% (4,679) |
| Mormon | 71.1% | 34.9% | 9.2% | 1.2% (662) |
| Other Protestant | 57.0% | 67.8% | 76.6% | 5.9% (3,123) |
| Catholic | 76.7% | 9.7% | −15.0% | 24.6% (13,096) |
| Jewish | 84.2% | 11.4% | −5.0% | 2.0% (1,069) |
| Unitarian | 43.7% | 78.6% | 104.2% | .3% (145) |
| Other religion | 63.5% | 56.7% | 46.6% | 2.5% (1,324) |
| None | 53.5% | 74.6% | 110.8% | 10.7% (5,709) |
| Total | 67.8% | 32.2% | | (53,142) |

several of the categories (e.g., sectarian Protestant, liberal Protestant, moderate Protestant); however, those moves would be across quite similar groups, and sample-size issues and limits on respondent knowledge prevent a more fine-grained approach. Overall, table 2.1 shows that 68% of GSS respondents report the same religious identification at the time of interview as they had at age sixteen, reflecting a switching rate of 32% across these broad categories of identification.

Loyalty differences across religious groups are of critical importance for evaluating theories of religious change. The highest rates of loyalty are among Jews, Catholics, Mormons, Baptists, and Lutherans. As chapter 1 demonstrated, loyalty to the faith does not necessarily translate into intergenerational stability in religious identifications, since both fertility and immigration also play a role, along with the ability to attract identifiers through religious switching. Notably, other than the "quasi-ethnic" and regionally concentrated Baptists, sectarian Protestants have relatively low rates of loyalty—in contrast to the expectations of supply-side theorists and "subcultural identity" advocates (Emerson and Smith 2000; Smith and Emerson 1998). Sectarians are about as loyal as Episcopalians and moderate Protestants. Liberal Protestants, other Christians, and Unitarians have relatively low rates of loyalty.

In addition to maintaining the loyalty of current identifiers, religious groups must attract people who have other identifications in order to make gains through religious switching. Table 2.1 presents the percentage of current identifiers who are switchers from another faith. Unitarians top the list, with about 79% of Unitarians having converted from some other group. Nonidentifiers are also quite likely to have grown up in some tradition, and 75% of nonidentifiers are apostates—people who rejected a former religious identification. Respondents who identify as Protestant with no specific denomination are also likely to have switched from a more institutionalized identity. As supply-side theorists would expect, a large proportion of sectarians originated in some other religious group, just under 49%. Yet very few Baptists switched into that identity. Indeed, with fewer than 20% of their members coming from switching, Baptists are even less attractive of new members than are Lutherans, a largely ethnic denomination which does not proselytize. Liberal Protestant groups and Episcopalians attract 40% of their current membership, reflecting fairly substantial appeal for switchers—as status theories suggest.

Catholic and Jewish identifications hold loyalty, but they are not attractive for switchers. For Catholics, under 10% switched into the faith, while switchers constitute about 11% of Jews. In contrast, other non-Christian traditions have attracted switchers, and 57% of those who hold other non-Christian identifications are switchers.

Table 2.1 also shows the big "winners" and "losers" in the shifting allegiances of religious identifiers. The big losers include moderate Protestants, who lost 17% of their original base of identifiers; Catholicism, which shrank by 15%; and Baptists, who saw a 13% reduction in their totals. The big "winners" are nonidentification and Unitarians—in

line with the expectations of secularization theories, these two identifications more than doubled because of switching. The "other Protestant" identification increased by almost 77%, and other non-Christian
groups boosted their ranks by 47% because of shifts in identifications.
Sectarian groups did grow by 19%, and liberal Protestants shrank by
9% because of switching, in accordance with supply-side expectations.
However, Episcopalians increased because of switching, while Baptists
shrank, which does not fit the simple supply-side narrative.

Generational differences in loyalty are hard to assess, since members of different cohorts are interviewed at different points in the life
course and have had greater or lesser opportunity to switch. Recall that
the introductory chapter showed that the average age of interview for
members of the pre-1925 generation is sixty-nine, and for the 1925–
1943 cohorts, the average is fifty-four. The youngest age of interview for
members of the 1925–1943 generation is thirty, which is well beyond
the median switching age (Roof 1989; Sherkat 1991). In contrast, the
remaining generations were interviewed at an average age of less than
forty, and the post-1971 generation was interviewed at age twenty-six,
on average. Because of the cohort differences in the age of interview, all
things being equal, the rates of loyalty are actually lower in the younger
generations. For example, if the rate of loyalty is 65% in the pre-1925
cohort and in the post-1971 generation, loyalty is stronger in the older
cohort since they have had more time to switch (though return switching can complicate this dynamic). However, within generations, it is
possible to compare rates of loyalty (see table 2.2).

Rates of loyalty vary across generations for religious groups, and loyalty is declining for some groups while increasing in others. Jews and
Catholics post the highest loyalty rates across all the cohorts, though
loyalty is declining for Catholics and Jews across cohorts. Mormons
also have high rates of loyalty in generations born prior to 1971, but in
the youngest cohorts, loyalty drops to 61% and ranks Mormons among
the least loyal groups in the youngest generation. Baptists and Lutherans are also consistently among the most loyal across cohorts.

Nonidentification is the least "loyal" grouping for respondents born
prior to 1956; most people who had no religious identification at age
sixteen picked up a religious identity prior to their GSS interview. However, in the younger generations born after 1956, nonidentifiers appear

*Table 2.2. Religious Loyalty by Generation: GSS 1973–2012*

| Origin identification | Pre-1925 cohort | 1925–1943 cohort | 1944–1955 cohort | 1956–1970 cohort | 1971–1994 cohort |
|---|---|---|---|---|---|
| Liberal Protestant | 61.8% | 51.3% | 50.2% | 56.2% | 61.3% |
| Episcopalian | 65.5% | 60.2% | 58.1% | 58.8% | 60.5% |
| Moderate Protestant | 60.7% | 60.0% | 61.3% | 63.9% | 60.3% |
| Lutheran | 72.9% | 69.5% | 65.7% | 66.5% | 62.8% |
| Baptist | 73.3% | 69.5% | 68.5% | 71.2% | 68.5% |
| Sectarian Protestant | 57.9% | 55.6% | 64.1% | 66.0% | 62.9% |
| Mormon | 75.8% | 74.2% | 72.4% | 71.2% | 61.2% |
| Other Protestant | 48.8% | 47.6% | 58.3% | 62.8% | 60.2% |
| Catholic | 87.3% | 82.2% | 73.1% | 74.4% | 69.9% |
| Jewish | 91.6% | 85.59% | 81.1% | 77.4% | 81.4% |
| Unitarian | 60.0% | 41.2% | 50.0% | 39.1% | 25.0% |
| Other religion | 48.1% | 61.9% | 65.6% | 63.3% | 69.2% |
| None | 33.0% | 29.6% | 46.7% | 59.6% | 71.5% |
| Total | 70.3% | 66.9% | 66.1% | 68.6% | 67.1% |
| Number of cases | 8,899 | 12,032 | 12,780 | 13,340 | 5,894 |

substantially more stable. Indeed, nonidentification is one of the most solid identities in the cohorts born after 1971—exceeding the loyalty found among Catholics of this generation. Unitarians also have low rates of loyalty, but there are too few of them to discern across generations. Among people born before 1944, sectarian Protestants have low rates of loyalty, fewer than 56% for those born between 1925 and 1943. Yet loyalty increased among sectarians who were born between 1944 and 1955 and remains fairly high in the two younger generations.

Liberal Protestant groups experienced a decrease in loyalty among identifiers born after 1925 and before 1956—dropping from 62% in the eldest cohorts to 50%. Yet loyalty appears to be on the rise in later generations. Religious identifications are more stable across generations for Episcopalians. Retention of Episcopal identification declined slightly from 66% to 60% in the two oldest generations, and loyalty is steady between 58% and 60% in the three younger cohorts. Moderate Protestants also have fairly stable retention across generations.

Younger generations are also increasingly loyal to non-Christian faiths other than Judaism. While these traditions retained fewer than half of their identifiers born prior to 1925, loyalty jumps to 69% in the youngest generation. Increased rates of immigration from non-Christian nations after the lifting of the Immigration and Nationality

Act in 1965 certainly play a role in this increase in loyalty. In the old-est generations, because of these immigration laws, most of the people raised outside Christianity and Judaism were immigrants married to U.S. citizens—who were almost uniformly Christian. Now, there are multigenerational families of non-Christians, and they are better able to continue to practice and identify with their religious tradition (Alanezi and Sherkat 2008; Ebaugh 2003; Sherkat 2010a).

Retention is one factor which influences the distribution of religious identifications over time, but another key issue is the relative attractive-ness of religious identifications. The overall gains and losses from reli-gious switching presented in table 2.1 vary considerably across genera-tions. Future trends in religious identification will be driven strongly by switching gains and losses in the younger generations. Table 2.3 presents the impact of religious switching on identifications across generations.

GSS respondents born before 1944 often switched to liberal Protes-tant and Episcopalian identifications. In the oldest cohorts, both Epis-copalian and liberal Protestant identifications increased because of switching, and Episcopalian identifications continued to grow from switching in the 1925–1943 cohort. This pattern of switching-induced growth in identifications for high-status, liberal Protestant denomi-nations fits the expectations of status theories of religious switching (Newport 1979; Sherkat 2001b; Stark and Glock 1965). However, liberal Protestant gains from switching turn into declines in the cohorts born after 1925, and Episcopal advantages also turn to losses in the cohorts born after 1956. Liberal Protestant groups lost hold of identifiers in the baby-boom cohorts and did not attract enough new identifiers to keep pace with their losses.

Losses from religious switching were heavy across generations for moderate Protestant groups and also for Baptists. While the former finding seems to fit the supply-side expectation that liberal groups will lose identifiers to more conservative denominations, the latter find-ing contradicts this expectation. Indeed, while losses from switching are fairly constant for moderates, losses from switching appear to be increasing for Baptists, in tandem with their decreasing rates of reten-tion found in table 2.2.

While Baptists are among the losers, other sectarian groups post

*Table 2.3. Gains and Losses from Switching by Generation: GSS 1973–2012*

| Origin identification | Pre-1925 cohort | 1925–1943 cohort | 1944–1955 cohort | 1956–1970 cohort | 1971–1994 cohort |
|---|---|---|---|---|---|
| Liberal Protestant | 8.0% | −3.0% | −22.0% | −19.0% | −15.0% |
| Episcopalian | 25.0% | 13.0% | −3.0% | −18.0% | −17.0% |
| Moderate Protestant | −18.0% | −15.0% | −20.0% | −16.0% | −21.0% |
| Lutheran | 1.0% | −1.0% | −10.0% | −12.0% | −23.0% |
| Baptist | −8.0% | −10.0% | −17.0% | −14.0% | −16.0% |
| Sectarian Protestant | 22.0% | 13.0% | 31.0% | 20.0% | 2.0% |
| Mormon | 29.0% | 25.0% | 21.0% | 2.0% | −28.0% |
| Other Protestant | 48.0% | 76.0% | 117.0% | 105.0% | 31.0% |
| Catholic | −1.0% | −6.0% | −19.0% | −20.0% | −25.0% |
| Jewish | −4.0% | −5.0% | −4.0% | −8.0% | −6.0% |
| Unitarian | 320.0% | 182.0% | 86.0% | 17.0% | 100.0% |
| Other religion | 1.0% | 33.0% | 90.0% | 46.0% | 32.0% |
| None | 57.0% | 69.0% | 193.0% | 103.0% | 102.0% |
| Number of cases | 8,899 | 12,032 | 12,780 | 13,340 | 5,894 |

gains from switching, and sectarian gains are particularly high in the 1944–1955 baby-boom generation. However, sectarians seem to be losing their attractiveness in the youngest generation—where gains are minimal at 2%. A similar pattern is found for Mormons. While Mormons gained considerably from switching in the cohorts born prior to 1956, switching increases declined to only 2% in the 1956–1970 generation—and Mormons lose 28% of their original identifiers because of switching in the 1971–1994 cohorts. Defection from the Mormons and their relative unattractiveness in the younger generations certainly contradicts the rosy picture of Mormon growth touted by supply-side theorists (Stark and Neilson 2005), though it matches findings from other studies of LDS trajectories (Lawson and Cragun 2012; Phillips and Cragun 2013).

The "other Protestant" classification shows heavy growth from switching in all generations but is a particularly attractive identity for cohorts born between 1944 and 1970. In the baby-boom generations, identifying as a Protestant with no particular denomination increased more than 100% because of switching from other identifications. Other non-Christian identities also made gains across generations from switching. With the exception of minimal growth in the oldest cohorts born before 1925, identification with non-Christian groups increased from switching, and these identifications nearly doubled from switching among the 1944–1955 baby boomers—increasing by 90% over their original totals.

Catholicism and Judaism lose identifiers at a higher rate than they attract converts, and both identities see losses from switching. Catholicism lost minimal totals from switching in the pre-1925 cohorts and only had modest losses in the 1925–1943 generation. However, religious switching reduced the proportion of Catholic identities in the post-1944 cohorts; rates of loss average nearly 20% for respondents born after 1944, and one-quarter of Catholic identifiers are lost from switching among those born after 1970. Decreases in Jewish identification are less substantial and are only 4% in the large 1944–1955 baby-boom generation. Because of the small number of original identifiers, Unitarian gains cannot be discerned across cohorts—though Unitarians are a clear winner in switching exchanges with other identities.

Relinquishing religious identification is a popular choice for religious switchers, and nonidentification increases substantially because of switching across all generations. Increasing rates of nonidentification are strongest in the 1944–1955 baby-boom generation—in which switching increased the original base of nonidentifiers by 193%. Nonidentification continues to double from its origin totals among respondents born after 1955. Overall, this pattern of growth from switching seems to follow generational dynamics, rather than a simple linear theory of growth and decline of conservative or liberal groups.

## Ethnicity, Loyalty, and Switching

Ethnicity plays a substantial role in the structure and velocity of religious mobility. Studies of religious switching have largely ignored the ethnic component, with rare exceptions focusing on the distinctive patterns and trends in religious mobility found among African Americans (Ellison and Sherkat 1990; Sherkat 2002). Table 2.4 shows rates of loyalty for a number of ethnicities. Rates of religious loyalty are lowest among Native American respondents, with 61% retaining their original identification. Latin Americans have the highest rates of retention, with 77% keeping their original faith. Western Europeans also have more fluid religious identifications than most other ethnicities, with

*Table 2.4. Loyalty of Religious Identification by Ethnicity: GSS 1973–2012*

| Origin identification | Native American | Western European | Eastern European | Asian | African American | Latin American |
|---|---|---|---|---|---|---|
| Liberal Protestant | 62.0% | 55.3% | 50.0% | 63.3% | 52.2% | 33.3% |
| Episcopalian | 47.8% | 61.6% | 58.3% | 42.9% | 57.5% | 44.4% |
| Moderate Protestant | 54.3% | 58.4% | 48.5% | 92.6% | 73.8% | 64.5% |
| Lutheran | 46.9% | 70.1% | 70.4% | 41.7% | 56.8% | 62.5% |
| Baptist | 67.2% | 63.9% | 51.4% | 45.2% | 77.0% | 55.1% |
| Sectarian Protestant | 63.1% | 56.2% | 65.1% | 87.0% | 75.0% | 69.3% |
| Mormon | 45.5% | 74.5% | 42.9% | 33.3% | 87.5% | 58.3% |
| Other Protestant | 54.4% | 56.2% | 61.5% | 63.2% | 60.7% | 57.4% |
| Catholic | 64.3% | 77.5% | 80.5% | 81.3% | 66.0% | 79.8% |
| Jewish | — | 73.1% | 88.4% | 76.9% | 90.0% | 33.3% |
| Unitarian | 71.4% | 42.6% | 50.0% | 100.0% | — | — |
| Other religion | 47.4% | 56.2% | 59.3% | 68.8% | 57.1% | 25.0% |
| None | 62.0% | 49.2% | 50.0% | 71.5% | 66.7% | 63.5% |
| Total | 61.2% | 65.7% | 76.3% | 72.6% | 73.5% | 76.6% |
| Number of cases | 1,537 | 27,272 | 3,039 | 988 | 7,267 | 2,614 |

about 34% leaving their identification of origin, compared to 24% for eastern Europeans—who are almost as loyal as Latin Americans. African Americans also have relatively stable religious identifications, with almost 74% retaining their original identification.

Differences in loyalties across ethnicities are often a function of the structure of religious identifications in the different ethnic categories. For example, high rates of retention among eastern Europeans is partly a function of the fact that large proportions are Catholic and Jewish—and Catholics and Jews tend to be more stable than Protestants. Interestingly, ethnicity serves to help boost the stability of religious identification in ways that suggest social influences on religious choices. For example, only about 20% of Latin American and eastern European Catholics switch to another religious identification; however, the corresponding figure for Native Americans is 36%, and 34% of African American Catholics leave the faith. Latin Americans' and eastern Europeans' ethnic communities consolidate ethnicity and Catholic identification, and because of this, there is social pressure to remain Catholic. In contrast, neither Native Americans nor African Americans have ethnicities bound to Catholic identification, and therefore leaving the faith is easier. Indeed, similar ethnicity-specific retention patterns are linked to high loyalty for African American Baptists, eastern and western European Lutherans, eastern European Jews, and Asians from non-Christian faiths.

Conversely, loyalty tends to be low for members of ethnic groups that are a minority in their religious identification. Non-European Mormons, African American Catholics, Latin American liberal Protestants, and Asian Lutherans and Baptists are substantially less loyal than are respondents of other ethnicities who were raised in these religions. Notably, some patterns do not support this finding, and there is relatively high loyalty among Asian sectarian, moderate, and liberal Protestants and for Latin American sectarian and moderate Protestants. Much of this may be explained by successful missions and bilingual services produced in these religious groups for Korean-, Chinese-, Vietnamese-, and Spanish-speaking constituencies. Indeed, religious ties often help with the immigration process, and this may further boost loyalty (Alanezi and Sherkat 2008; Sherkat 2010a).

How does ethnicity influence gains and losses from switching religious identification? And, in the same vein, which denominations are more attractive for the various ethnic groups? Table 2.5 explores the gains and losses from religious switching across ethnic groups. Religious switching results in differential fortunes for identifications across ethnicities. Episcopalians actually gain identifiers from switching among western and eastern Europeans, while they post losses from other ethnicities. Liberal Protestants also gain from switching among eastern Europeans and Asians. Both of these findings suggest that status-based switching plays some role and that ethnicity influences the boundaries of inclusion and exclusion in high-status denominations. Eastern Europeans and Asians may find it relatively easy to gain acceptance in high-status mainline Protestant groups, while African Americans and Latin Americans may not be afforded these status benefits. Moderate Protestants lose members from switching among western Europeans, African Americans, and Native Americans; however, they gain from switching among eastern Europeans, Asians, and Latin Americans.

Interestingly, Catholic identification declines because of shifts in identifications at about the same rate across all ethnic groups. In contrast, Baptists gain members from switching among Asians and Latin Americans; however, switching results in fewer Baptist identifiers in all other ethnicities. Sectarian Protestants chart increases from switching

*Table 2.5. Percentage Gained or Lost through Switching by Ethnicity: GSS 1973–2012*

| Origin identification | Native American | Western European | Eastern European | Asian | African American | Latin American |
|---|---|---|---|---|---|---|
| Liberal Protestant | −12.0% | −9.0% | 1.0% | 10.0% | −18.0% | −13.0% |
| Episcopalian | −35.0% | 7.0% | 50.0% | −43.0% | −22.0% | −11.0% |
| Moderate Protestant | −25.0% | −18.0% | 7.0% | 44.0% | −14.0% | 32.0% |
| Lutheran | 0% | −9.0% | 20.0% | 33.0% | 2.0% | 125.0% |
| Baptist | −13.0% | −14.0% | −7.0% | 26.0% | −15.0% | 14.0% |
| Sectarian Protestant | 4.0% | 8.0% | 79.0% | 91.0% | 57.0% | 76.0% |
| Mormon | −5.0% | 7.0% | 14.0% | 33.0% | 75.0% | 92.0% |
| Other Protestant | 84.0% | 74.0% | 55.0% | 111.0% | 93.0% | 149.0% |
| Catholic | −16.0% | −13.0% | −15.0% | −11.0% | −18.0% | −18.0% |
| Jewish | 0% | 7.0% | −8.0% | 0% | 80.0% | 167.0% |
| Unitarian | −96.0% | 94.0% | 250.0% | 0% | 400.0% | −100.0% |
| Other religion | −52.0% | 180.0% | 14.0% | −26.0% | 117.0% | 142.0% |
| None | −9.0% | 1,290% | 140.0% | 46.0% | 117.0% | 224.0% |
| Number of cases | 1,537 | 27,272 | 3,039 | 988 | 7,267 | 2,614 |

across all ethnicities, and their increases are marked among eastern Europeans, Asians, African Americans, and Latin Americans. The size of sectarian gains for these ethnicities is partly a function of the fact that relatively few Asians, Latin Americans, or eastern Europeans were raised in Protestant sects. Notably, while nonidentification posts sizeable gains from religious switching across all ethnic groups, growth among Asians and Native Americans is substantially lower than for other ethnicities (all of which show at least a doubling of the proportion of nonidentifiers).

## Leaving the Faith: Apostasy across Cohorts

"Apostasy" is a strong word and often evokes protest among researchers and theorists who like to argue that nonidentification does not indicate a rejection of religious belief. That may be so, to some extent, but not entirely, as will be shown in the next chapter. That there are "believers" who do not "belong" does not change the fact that respondents to the GSS (and similar surveys) are asked directly, "Are you Protestant, Catholic, Jewish, Other, or None"—and they choose "None." Obviously, if you are raised without a religious identification, you cannot have rejected religion. However, for people who report growing up with a

*Table 2.6. Apostasy by Origin Religious Identification and Generation: GSS 1973–2012*

| Origin identification | Pre-1925 cohort | 1925–1943 cohort | 1944–1955 cohort | 1956–1970 cohort | 1971–1994 cohort |
|---|---|---|---|---|---|
| Liberal Protestant | 2.5% | 6.6% | 12.9% | 14.5% | 21.9% |
| Episcopalian | 4.7% | 9.7% | 14.2% | 14.1% | 21.1% |
| Moderate Protestant | 2.6% | 4.7% | 8.2% | 9.8% | 17.5% |
| Lutheran | 1.6% | 5.6% | 10.7% | 9.5% | 17.8% |
| Baptist | 2.0% | 3.2% | 7.4% | 7.9% | 13.1% |
| Sectarian Protestant | 3.4% | 3.9% | 6.8% | 10.8% | 13.0% |
| Mormon | 4.8% | 5.8% | 9.7% | 17.6% | 27.1% |
| Other Protestant | 8.1% | 8.5% | 14.3% | 14.5% | 19.0% |
| Catholic | 3.0% | 5.9% | 11.3% | 10.0% | 17.0% |
| Jewish | 4.8% | 7.8% | 13.3% | 11.5% | 15.1% |
| Unitarian | 5.9% | 31.8% | 21.7% | 25.0% | — |
| Other religion | 11.7% | 9.4% | 15.1% | 18.5% | 22.5% |
| Total | 2.8% | 5.0% | 9.6% | 9.7% | 14.8% |
| Number of cases | 8,899 | 12,032 | 12,780 | 13,340 | 5,894 |

religious identity yet now embrace none, apostasy is not too strong a concept. They have rejected their former identity in favor of no religious identification.

As was demonstrated in chapter 1, nonidentification has become a popular option over the past forty years. Some of this growth is a function of a higher proportion of people being raised with no religious identity and retaining no identity throughout the life course—as table 2.2 showed regarding increased loyalty among nonidentifiers. However, much of the growth in nonidentification is a result of religious switching, and apostasy is widespread. But who leaves the faith? Table 2.6 presents rates of apostasy across cohorts and religious identities. Of course, many in the younger generations will take up a religious identity later in the life course (Wilson and Sherkat 1994). Apostasy is low in the pre-1925 cohort, with fewer than 3% rejecting their former religious identity; however, rates of apostasy increase in each cohort, topping out at nearly 15% in the 1971–1994 generation. In the baby-boom generation born between 1944 and 1955, apostasy stands at nearly 10%, which is just under that found in the 1956–1970 cohort.

Moderate Protestants, sectarian Protestants, and Baptists have relatively low rates of apostasy, though both groups also have increasing rates across generations, and sectarians exceed the average for people born between 1956–1970. Liberal Protestants and Episcopalians have somewhat higher rates of apostasy than average. Apostasy is consistently higher than average among Jews, Mormons, other non-Christians, and Catholics across all cohorts. This fits with expectations that in religious groups with quasi-ethnic social ties, religious switching will more often take the form of apostasy (Sandomirsky and Wilson 1990; Sherkat and Wilson 1995).

## Apostasy and Ethnicity

The dynamics of renouncing religious identification are also structured by ethnic ties. For some ethnic groups, shedding religious identifications may pose little risk, particularly when opportunities for status and social interaction abound. However, members of other ethnic groups may be constrained by overlapping social ties which make religious identification and participation less voluntary (Ellison and Sherkat 1995a; Sherkat and Ellison 1991; Sherkat and Wilson 1995).

Table 2.7 explores how religious identities and ethnicity structure rates of apostasy. Overall, rates of apostasy are highest for Asians, with nearly 11% rejecting a former identification. Over 8% of western and eastern Europeans and Native Americans reject identification. Rates are

*Table 2.7. Apostasy by Origin Religious Identification and Ethnicity: GSS 1973–2012*

| Origin identification | Native American | Western European | Eastern European | Asian | African American | Latin American |
|---|---|---|---|---|---|---|
| Liberal Protestant | 14.0% | 9.2% | 18.1% | 10.0% | 11.1% | — |
| Episcopalian | 13.0% | 11.5% | 20.8% | 14.3% | 10.0% | 11.1% |
| Moderate Protestant | 11.1% | 7.3% | 11.9% | 3.7% | 3.8% | — |
| Lutheran | 12.5% | 7.0% | 7.0% | 25.0% | 11.4% | 12.5% |
| Baptist | 7.3% | 6.7% | 16.7% | 12.9% | 5.0% | 14.1% |
| Sectarian Protestant | 6.7% | 6.6% | 9.3% | — | 6.3% | 13.6% |
| Mormon | 13.6% | 11.4% | 14.3% | 66.7% | — | 25.0% |
| Other Protestant | 11.8% | 13.8% | 12.3% | 26.3% | 11.0% | 21.3% |
| Catholic | 11.6% | 9.9% | 7.8% | 5.3% | 8.4% | 6.5% |
| Jewish | 50.0% | 14.4% | 7.6% | 7.7% | 10.0% | 33.3% |
| Unitarian | — | 20.4% | — | — | 100.0% | — |
| Other religion | 7.1% | 12.4% | 14.0% | 18.8% | 15.6% | 33.3% |
| Total | 8.5% | 8.3% | 8.4% | 10.8% | 5.4% | 7.4% |
| Number of cases | 1,537 | 27,272 | 3,039 | 988 | 7,267 | 2,614 |

lower for Latin Americans, and the lowest rates of apostasy are found among African Americans, which conforms to the semi-involuntary-institution thesis regarding African American religious commitments (Ellison and Sherkat 1990, 1995b, 1999; Sherkat 2002; Sherkat and Cunningham 1998; Sherkat and Ellison 1991). Apostasy is low among members of the majority religion of particular ethnicities. For example, Latin American and eastern European Catholics are less likely to become apostates than are Catholics from other ethnic groups. African Americans originally identifying with the "black mainline" Baptist and Methodist groups have lower rates of apostasy than do Baptists or moderate Protestants from other ethnicities, and "black mainliners" reject identification at lower rates than do African Americans from other denominational backgrounds. Among western Europeans, moderate Protestants, Lutherans, Baptists, and sectarians have lower rates of apostasy than do Catholics, while the relationship is reversed among eastern Europeans and Latin Americans. And eastern European Jews are less likely to renounce religious identification than are Jews from other ethnic origins.

Overall, patterns of apostasy seem to follow the expectations of theories which suggest that people maintain religious identities in large part because of social pressures to conform. These pressures are generally weaker for individuals from dominant ethnicities and for people from younger generations.

## The Social Sources of Switching and Apostasy

Sociologists explain changes in religious identification using a variety of status and demographic factors. People switch religious identities in response to life-course factors such as marriage, childrearing, geographic mobility, and changes in their educational attainment and income (Sherkat 1991; Sherkat and Wilson 1995). Religious switching and apostasy are also linked to gender differences in religiosity, with men more likely to become apostates and less loyal to their religious identity of origin (Iannaccone 1990; Sherkat 1991; Sherkat and Ellison 1991; Sherkat and Wilson 1995). The study of religious switching is complicated by the multiplicity of possible origins and destinations. To make sense of the social sources of religious switching, this chapter approaches the analyses in three different ways. First, it examines the act of switching to another identity. This is a global approach which gives primacy to the impact of simple demographic factors such as gender and geographic mobility—but also reveals how other status distinctions foster or hold back religious change. Second, it examines the predictors of renouncing religious affiliation—a directional measure of switching to one very important category. Third, because of the complexity of switching across the varied identities, it scales these relationships using log-multiplicative association models and creates empirical measures of switching distances by ethnicity and cohort (Goodman and Clogg 1992; Goodman and Hout 1998; Powers and Xie 2008; Sherkat 2001b, 2004).

Cohort and ethnic differences in switching and apostasy do not occur in a vacuum, and life course, geographic location, and status influences intersect with cohort and ethnic patterns to foster religious change. To take into account these competing influences, this chapter focuses on multivariate statistical models predicting the odds of switching religious identification and apostasy versus retaining one's original religious identity. Table 2.8 presents the effects of generations and ethnicities on the odds of switching, while taking into account status, life course, and geographic factors.

The generational comparisons are made to the cohorts born before 1925, and they show that religious switching is relatively stable across

Table 2.8. *Generation and Ethnicity Effects on the Odds of Religious Switching and Apostasy*

|  | Switching logistic | Apostasy |
| --- | --- | --- |
| 1925–1940 cohort | .1% | 80%*** |
| 1944–1955 cohort | −5% | 208%*** |
| 1956–1970 cohort | −9% | 188%*** |
| 1971–1994 cohort | −7% | 315%*** |
| Pre-1925 cohort | Comparison | Comparison |
| Native American | 28%*** | 18% |
| Eastern European | −51%*** | −18%** |
| Asian | −48%*** | −33%*** |
| African American | −20%*** | −43%*** |
| Latin American | −49%*** | −45%*** |
| Western European | Comparison | Comparison |

*Note*: Estimated from a multinomial logistic regression controlling for gender, status differences, life-course factors, and geographic mobility.

* $p < .05$ two tailed, ** $p < .01$ two-tailed; *** $p < .001$ two tailed

generations. The oldest generation is slightly more likely to have made a shift in identification, but its members also had a lot more time to shift their identifications. In contrast, apostasy is significantly higher in the younger generations, even after controls for such factors as educational attainment, income, geographic mobility, and marriage and childrearing. The odds that someone born after 1971 rejected identification are over three times higher than the odds for a person born before 1925. Indeed, the odds of apostasy are 80% higher for those who were born between 1925 and 1940, and the middle generations are about twice as likely to renounce religious identification compared to the pre-1925 cohort. In general, it is quite clear that apostasy is increasing across generations and that there was a sharp spike in apostasy in the baby-boom generation.

For ethnicity, western Europeans were used as the comparison category. Compared to western Europeans, those who claim Native American ancestry are significantly more likely to switch their religious identities. However, western Europeans are significantly more likely to switch identities when compared to all other ethnic groups. Indeed, the differences in the odds are quite substantial, showing that western European Americans are about twice as likely to switch identities when compared to eastern Europeans, Asians, and Latin Americans. African Americans also switch at a significantly lower rate, having 20% lower odds of switching when compared to western European Americans. The same pattern holds for apostasy. Western Europeans have significantly higher rates of apostasy when compared to all other ethnic groups except Native Americans. The Native American finding is interesting and suggests that the Native American experience causes reflection on other identities. Indeed, scholarship on Native American identities suggests that many Americans have embraced Native American ancestry as a choice (Nagel 1996; Thornton 1987).

Overall, these findings show the importance of ethnicity for producing incentives and disincentives for shifting religious identifications. Because western Europeans enjoy considerable social dominance in the United States, they are less subject to normative pressures to conform and more adept at generating social rewards in multiple contexts. Hence, while sectarian groups are seen as lower in status when compared to liberal and moderate Protestant groups, if one is of western

*Table 2.9. Status and Life-Course Effects on the Odds of Religious Switching and Apostasy*

|  | Switching logistic | Apostasy |
|---|---|---|
| Education difference | 3% | 18%*** |
| Income difference | 1% | 3% |
| Married | 62%*** | −33%*** |
| Widowed | 70%*** | −24%*** |
| Divorced | 52%*** | 13%* |
| Never married | Comparison | Comparison |
| Female | 14%*** | −42%*** |
| Number of children | 1% | −9%*** |

*Note:* Estimated from a multinomial logistic regression controlling for generation cohort, ethnicity, and geographic mobility.

\* p < .05 two tailed, \*\* p < .01 two-tailed; \*\*\* p < .001 two tailed

European ancestry, the loss of social status from switching from Methodist to Baptist may be slight. Further, western European sectarians, Lutherans, and Catholics will find it much easier to move "up" in the social hierarchy when compared to people with other ethnic ties, since they will benefit from positive social rewards that easily accrue to members of the dominant ethnic group. The same applies to apostasy: ethnic advantage allows western Europeans the relative freedom to reject religious identities.

Table 2.9 presents the influence of status and life-course factors on religious switching and apostasy. For status factors, it examines a measure of educational attainment using years of education, while income is indicated by a constructed GSS item which converts household income to constant dollars over the cumulative GSS. For our purposes, what matters is the difference in education and income for a respondent compared to the education and income of the average person who grew up in his or her denomination of origin. To do this, the table compares a respondent's education and income to those of peers in the denomination of origin using a z-score, computed by subtracting the respondent's income or education from the average in his or her religious identification of origin and dividing that by the standard deviation for that religious identification. Status differences in education and income do not predict religious switching. However, respondents who attained more education than peers in the denomination of origin were significantly more likely to become apostates—education does lead to the rejection of religious identification. Hence, status mobility is linked to leaving religion, though it does not predict absolute rates of switching. Later, we will assess how status mobility may influence the direction of religious switching.

Life-course events such as marriage, divorce, and childrearing also play a role in motivating religious switching. Married respondents are significantly more likely to have switched religious identities when compared to those who never marry. Widowed and divorced respondents are also more often found among religious switchers. Much of this difference is attributable to intermarriage, which often fosters religious switching and accounts for a sizeable fraction of the switching differences between married and unmarried adults (Sherkat 1991, 2004; Sherkat and Wilson 1995).

Notably, married individuals are less likely to become apostates when compared to those who are not married. In a highly religious country such as the United States, marriage produces a bond which is more likely to be to someone who holds a religious identity, and these ties put social pressure on individuals to maintain religious identities. In contrast, people who are divorced are more likely to become apostates even when compared to those who were never married. Divorce is viewed negatively by most religious traditions—and proscribed for Catholics and members of many sectarian groups—and becoming divorced may conflict with religious identities. Social benefits of religious ties may be less salient or even turn negative for people who have experienced divorce. Having children also lowers the risk of apostasy but has no independent effect on the likelihood of religious switching. Children provide an incentive to retain some religious ties as an example, and religious groups also provide myriad social opportunities for families with children (Sherkat 1998; Sherkat and Wilson 1995).

Geographic mobility is one of the most important sources of shifts in religious identification. People who move to different areas are uprooted from existing social network ties, and this frees them to create new connections which sometimes differ from their former identities (Sherkat 1991; Sherkat and Wilson 1995; Stark and Bainbridge 1980). Mobility is especially important when it crosses large expanses of geographic space and when it involves moves to urban or rural areas. In the United States, the South is a culturally distinctive region, where religion

*Table 2.10. Geographic Mobility Effects on the Odds of Religious Switching and Apostasy*

| | Switching logistic | Apostasy |
|---|---|---|
| Immigrant | −18%** | −25%*** |
| Second-generation immigrant | −23%*** | 2% |
| Urban, non-South, different city and state | 66%*** | 332%*** |
| Urban, South, different city and state | 71%*** | 181%*** |
| Rural, non-South, different city and state | 90%*** | 272%*** |
| Rural, South, different city and state | 75%*** | 124%*** |
| Urban, non-South, different city, same state | 55%*** | 219%*** |
| Urban, South, different city, same state | 61%*** | 88%*** |
| Rural, non-South, different city, same state | 70%*** | 168%*** |
| Rural, South, different city, same state | 23%** | 58%* |
| Urban, non-South, same city | 23%*** | 176%*** |
| Urban, South, same city | 24%*** | 74%*** |
| Rural, non-South, same city | 21%** | 87%*** |
| Rural, South, same city | Comparison | Comparison |

*Note*: Estimated from a Multinomial Logistic Regression controlling for cohort, ethnicity, gender, status factors, and life course factors.

* p < .05 two tailed, ** p < .01 two-tailed; *** p < .001 two tailed

plays a strong role in civic life and communities have a homogeneous, mostly sectarian Protestant religious market (Ellison and Sherkat 1995b, 1999; Hunt and Hunt 1999; Sherkat 2002). In the South, religious participation is expected, and those who fail to retain a religious identity will be held in low social esteem (Ellison and Sherkat 1995b; Sherkat and Ellison 1999).

Table 2.10 examines the impact of international and intranational geographic mobility on religious switching and apostasy (controlling for the factors examined in the previous tables). First, it examines the potential impact of immigration on switching and apostasy. Second, it shows the influence of intranational migration focusing on urban-rural, southern-nonsouthern, and intra- and interstate mobility. The comparisons are made across twelve groups: (1) urban, nonsouthern, living in a different city and state; (2) urban, southern, living in a different city and state; (3) rural, nonsouthern, living in a different city and state; (4) rural, southern, living in a different city and state; (5) urban, nonsouthern, living in a different city in the same state; (6) urban, southern, living in different city in the same state; (7) rural, nonsouthern, living in a different city in the same state; (8) rural, southern, living in a different city in the same state; (9) urban, nonsouthern, living in the same city;

(10) urban, southern, living in the same city; (11) rural, nonsouthern, living in the same city; (12) rural, southern, living in the same city. Lifelong rural southerners who live in their hometown are used as the comparison category.

Immigration to the United States is often linked to varied religious outcomes. It is possible that immigrants will cling to ethnic religion in ethnic communities; however, some immigrants may have moved to the United States to seek refuge from traditional religious expressions in their origin nation, and they may use new religious identities to embrace assimilation (Alanezi and Sherkat 2008; Ebaugh 2003; Sherkat 2010a). Immigrants who identify with Christianity may be particularly likely to use religion to sustain cultural values while at the same time promoting assimilation (Chong 1998; Levitt 2003), and the act of immigration may foster more stability of identification and greater participation (Connor 2008, 2011; Jasso et al. 2004). Table 2.10 shows that net of other factors, immigrants in the first and second generation are significantly less likely to switch religious affiliations. First-generation immigrants are also substantially less likely to reject their original religious identity. Given that the United States is a highly religious and majority-Christian nation, immigrants may use religion as an important resource to provide integration into the United States. Further, immigrants may have elected to migrate to the United States in part because of the presence of religious institutional support. As we saw earlier, about 44% of immigrants are Catholic, and 77% hold Christian identities. Many immigrants grew up Lutheran, Methodist, Adventist, Reformed, or Anglican, and all these religious groups are well supported in the American religious marketplace. At least in the case of U.S. immigrants, the migration experience is not fostering a turn to new religious expressions but instead promotes loyalty to familiar religious identities.

Intranational migration presents a quite different picture, and the odds comparisons presented in table 2.10 show the importance of moving within the United States. Even moving to another rural southern town in the same state significantly increases the odds of religious switching by 23% and of apostasy by 58%. Urban-rural differences are also apparent, since urban southerners who have not moved show 24% higher odds of switching and a 74% greater risk of rejecting religious identification. Regional variations in mobility and switching are also visible, with rural, stable nonsoutherners having a 21% greater chance of switching and 87% higher odds of apostasy when compared to their southern counterparts. Regional differences in switching rates are not apparent among nonmobile urban residents; however, stable, urban nonsoutherners are significantly more likely to become apostates when compared to stable, urban southerners.

Across all classes of mobility, rates of apostasy are higher outside the South and in urban areas. People who move out of state to urban areas are particularly likely to reject religious identifications, even after controlling for status and life-course factors. In contrast, rates of switching are actually highest among migrants in rural areas outside the South. This is likely a function of higher levels of religious diversity in the non-South, combined with a general expectation in rural areas that people maintain some religious identification. In the South, even interstate mobility to a rural area is likely to place a person in a religious market similar to the one found in the migrant's hometown.

## Switching Distance

Beginning with Weber and Troeltsch, sociologists have long thought about the relative similarity of religious expressions along social, theological, and ecclesiastical foundations (Babchuk and Whitt 1990; Kluegel 1980; Newport 1979; Troeltsch 1931). In the United States, this similarity has often been linked to a status ordering of religious groups, yet those status orderings appear to have become more fluid in the past several decades (Sherkat 2001b; Sherkat and Wilson 1995; Wuthnow 1988). While the status ordering of religious groups may have shifted, this has not appreciably influenced the density of switching across similar religious identities. Studies consistently show that most people switch to denominations similar to the ones in which they grew up. It is relatively easy and common to find people switching from Baptist to Methodist and vice versa, but it is relatively uncommon to see Muslims becoming Baptists or Catholics joining sectarian Protestant groups (Kluegel 1980; Newport 1979; Roof and McKinney 1987; Sherkat 2001b).

Because of the diversity of religious identities in the United States, analyzing switching across them is a formidable venture, particularly when you add the complexity of generational and ethnic differences.

*Table 2.11. Association Parameters for Row ($\mu_i$)*
*and Column ($\nu_j$) Effects on Religious Mobility*

| Identification | Cohort distance parameter | Ethnic distance parameter |
|---|---|---|
| Liberal Protestant | −.06 | −.20 |
| | (5) | (3) |
| Episcopalian | .08 | −.03 |
| | (8) | (5) |
| Moderate Protestant | −.24 | −.41 |
| | (3) | (2) |
| Lutheran | .05 | −.47 |
| | (7) | (1) |
| Baptist | −.44 | −.03 |
| | (1) | (4) |
| Sectarian Protestant | −.39 | −.02 |
| | (2) | (6) |
| Mormon | .02 | .23 |
| | (6) | (11) |
| Other Protestant | −.18 | .03 |
| | (4) | (8) |
| Catholic | .19 | .02 |
| | (11) | (7) |
| Jewish | .68 | .70 |
| | (12) | (12) |
| Other religion | .14 | .06 |
| | (9) | (9) |
| None | .16 | .11 |
| | (10) | (10) |

*Note*: Rank of scale in parentheses.

New statistical techniques for examining movement across categories allow a scaling of religious groups on the basis of their rates of mobility to and from one another. The models also provide an indication of how ethnicity and generations play a role in structuring the distance between religious identities.

Table 2.11 presents the statistical parameters showing the relative distance between identifications by generation and ethnicity. In the cohort model, the identity at one pole (the negative pole, though the sign is arbitrary) is Baptist, followed by sectarian Protestant, moderate Protestant, and other Protestants. Episcopalians and Lutherans are scaled more in the middle and are notably "closer" to people who reject religious identification and to Catholics. This indicates that the heaviest switching occurs between denominational groups with similar values on the association parameters. Jews have the highest positive association parameter—thus showing that the least common switch in identification is from Jewish to Baptist, or vice versa.

The association parameters for the ethnic model are aligned differently, indicating that when we take into account ethnicity, the rates of exchange between religious groups shifts. In the ethnic model, the negative pole is occupied by Lutherans—a largely white ethnic denomination—and moderate Protestant denominations, many of which are also majority white and ethnic. The 20th century saw considerable movement across these identifications, as Lutherans lost their distinctive ethnic flare and intermarriage and migration spurred shifts in identification. Liberal Protestant groups are scaled next to the moderates, while Episcopalians, Catholics, sectarian Protestants, and Baptists locate in the middle of the scale. Jewish identifications occupy the far positive pole, furthest of all from Lutherans and moderate Protestants.

The association models not only provide a scale of the relative attractiveness between different religious identities but also provide an estimate of how "close" these measures are for different cohort or ethnic groups. Figure 2.1 presents these "intrinsic association" parameters for the generational model. These parameters show that the relative "distance" between groups was highest for people born before 1925, so moving across any group was a more distant move in this cohort.

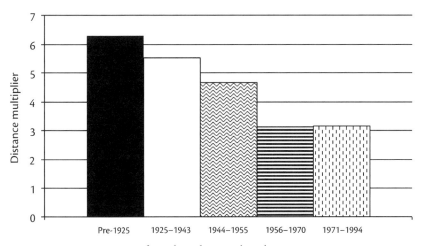

Fig. 2.1. Intrinsic association of switching distances by cohort

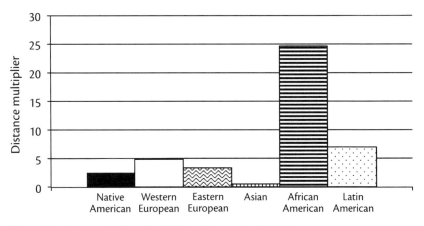

Fig. 2.2. Intrinsic association of switching distances by ethnicity

The intrinsic association declines substantially for the generations born after 1925, indicating that religious mobility is easier in the younger cohorts. The intrinsic association is about the same for people born between 1956 and 1970 and those born from 1971 to 1994 and is less than half that found in the pre-1925 cohort. Religious mobility has become much more common across cohorts, but the relative attractiveness of the different identities has been stable across cohorts.

Figure 2.2 shows that the intrinsic association between religious identities varies quite substantially by ethnicity. African Americans have much higher intrinsic association parameters, making a switch across any of the categories a more distant move. Latin Americans have the next-highest values, while Asians have the lowest intrinsic association of religious identities. Native Americans and eastern Europeans also have relatively small intrinsic associations when compared to western Europeans. These results indicate that Asians and Native Americans are more likely to make uncommon changes in their religious identities. In contrast, bold moves are rare for African Americans and Latin Americans.

Switching distances can be constructed using these models to examine how family, social status, ethnicity, gender, and migration influence how much people changed their religious identity if they made a switch and to discern how these factors predict the direction of religious switching. Because the poles of the association parameters are different

in the ethnic and cohort model, I examine switching distances separately and estimate cohort and ethnic influences in the complemen-
tary models.

Table 2.12 presents estimates predicting switching distances for the
cohort and ethnic models and for the absolute value and direction of
the switching distances. Because the cohort and ethnic models are a
direct function of the specific cohort or ethnicity (which specify the
intrinsic association), cohort effects can only be measured in the ethnic
models, and ethnic effects are only appropriate in the cohort models.
In the cohort models, where the poles of the switching distances are
Baptists and sectarians on one pole and Jews on the opposite pole, there
are several important ethnic effects on both absolute switching distance
and the direction of the distance. Looking at the absolute values, if African Americans, Latin Americans, and Native Americans switch, they
go significantly further than western Europeans, net of other factors. In
the directed models for cohorts, positive parameters indicate switching toward the sectarian pole of the distribution, while negative effects
reflect moving toward the Jewish-none pole. Here, switchers from
eastern European, Asian, and Latin American backgrounds are significantly more likely to switch to the sectarian end of the distribution if
they make a switch. Given that these ethnicities are also associated with

*Table 2.12. Generation and Ethnic Effects on Switching Distances*

| | Cohorts, absolute distance | Cohorts, directed distance | Ethnicity, absolute distance | Ethnicity, directed distance |
|---|---|---|---|---|
| 1925–1940 cohort | — | — | −.03* | .02 |
| 1944–1955 cohort | — | — | −.00 | −.04** |
| 1956–1970 cohort | — | — | −.01 | −.04** |
| 1971–1994 cohort | — | — | −.02* | −.02 |
| Pre-1925 cohort | — | — | Comparison | Comparison |
| Native American | .02** | −.01 | — | — |
| Eastern European | .01 | .06*** | — | — |
| Asian | −.01 | .02** | — | — |
| African American | .02** | −.01 | — | — |
| Latin American | .03*** | .07*** | — | — |
| Western European | Comparison | Comparison | — | — |

Note: Estimated from a multinomial logistic regression controlling for gender, status differences, life-course factors, and geographic mobility.

* p < .05 two tailed; ** p < .01 two-tailed; *** p < .001 two tailed

growing up in Judaism, other religions, no religion, and Catholicism, this makes perfect sense—they have nowhere to go but up.

Looking at the ethnic models, the upper bound of the parameters are Lutherans and other moderate Protestants, and the negative pole is Judaism and nonreligion. With regard to absolute values, the oldest cohort made more distant switches. Respondents born before 1925 made more radical changes in religious identification than did those born between 1925 and 1940 and those born after 1971. This suggests that the religious marketplace defined in ethnic terms was less of a barrier to switching for these early 20th- and late 19th-century cohorts. Looking at the directional differences across generations is also instructive. The 1944–1955 and 1956–1970 cohorts had significantly more negative directed switching—meaning that they were more likely to move to the Jewish-none end of the pole, while the older generations born before 1944 switched in the direction of the moderate Protestant mainline. High rates of apostasy among the younger generations also drive the direction of their switching toward the negative pole.

Table 2.13 presents the effects of status and life-course factors on the absolute and directed switching distances from the cohort and ethnicity models. The models for cohorts show that absolute differences in educational attainment actually promote small shifts in religious identification. Overall, people who have a different level of education from those who were raised in their denomination of origin will seek a "close" substitute identification. Looking at the direction of switching, a more interesting relationship becomes apparent. People who outdistance their peers in the denomination of origin in both educational attainment and income attainment switch in the direction of Judaism and nonidentification and away from Baptist and sectarian denominations. Conversely, people who attain less education and income than their peers in the identification of origin tend to switch toward sectarian identifications. In all, these findings support the expectations of status-based theories of religious switching. Social mobility pushes people away from sectarian identifications, while downward mobility makes people more likely to identify with more sectarian religious groups. In the ethnic models, in which the pole of the switching distance shifts to moderate mainline denominations, the relationship becomes positive for directed switching—exceeding the educational and income attainment of peers in the

*Table 2.13. Social Status and Life-Course Effects on Switching Distances*

| | Cohorts, absolute distance | Cohorts, directed distance | Ethnicity, absolute distance | Ethnicity, directed distance |
|---|---|---|---|---|
| Education difference | −.01* | −.08*** | −.01 | .02* |
| Income difference | .00 | −.06*** | −.01 | .03* |
| Married | −.00 | .13*** | −.15*** | .11*** |
| Widowed | .02 | .02* | −.05*** | .05*** |
| Divorced | .02 | .04*** | −.07*** | .05*** |
| Never married | — | — | — | — |
| Female | −.05*** | .06*** | −.04*** | .05*** |
| Number of children | .04*** | .01 | .05*** | −.04*** |

*Note*: Estimated from a multinomial logistic regression controlling for cohort, ethnicity, and geographic mobility.

* p < .05 two tailed; ** p < .01 two-tailed; *** p < .001 two tailed

denomination of origin increases switching toward mainline Protestantism—as status theories predict (Newport 1979; Roof and McKinney 1987; Stark and Glock 1965).

Marital status also plays a role in the direction and distance of religious mobility. In the cohort models, marriage, widowhood, and divorce are all associated with switching toward the sectarian end of the distribution when compared to people who have never married. Notably, however, rearranging the relationship finds a significantly more sectarian pattern of switching for married respondents when compared to those who are divorced or widowed. Of course, much of the directional pull for those who have never married is leaning them toward apostasy. Aligned with the ethnic distance scale, marriage reduces the absolute value of shifts in affiliation compared to other marital-status groupings. The widowed and divorced also have significantly shorter switching distances when compared to the never married. Marriage also influences the direction of shifts toward the moderate mainline when compared to other groups and especially the never married.

In both the cohort and the ethnic models, women make shorter shifts in identification than men do. Further, women's switching is directed toward the sectarian or mainline poles. Hence, women tend to switch to identifications more similar to those they grew up with, and if they do move, they tend to choose more mainline or sectarian identifications. In contrast, men shift their identifications toward the Jewish/ nonidentification pole, with apostasy and Catholicism being somewhat common shifts for men. Finally, children have a positive impact on the distance of religious switching. If people switch, having children propels them further from their original identities net of other factors. The ethnic models for switching directions reveal that children move identities away from moderate mainline Protestantism.

Geographic mobility is also an important factor influencing the distance and trajectory of religious switching. Table 2.14 shows that first- and second-generation immigrants travel quite distinctive directions in their switching patterns. First, in the cohort and ethnic directed distance models, immigrants are more likely to switch toward the sectarian and Protestant end of the spectrum. Given that immigrants are substantially more likely to originate in religious groups near the Jewish, Catholic, other religion, and nonidentification end of the spectrum, Protestant switching directions seem quite in line with supply-side theories. When Protestantism is what is available, it is an easy and socially acceptable choice. Yet the ethnic absolute distance models also show that immigrants are significantly less mobile across switching distances when compared to other Americans. Immigrants who change their religious identities may tend to pick new identifications up the Protestant end of the spectrum, but they do not go very far.

*Table 2.14. Geographic Mobility and Switching Distances*

| | Cohorts, absolute distance | Cohorts, directed distance | Ethnicity, absolute distance | Ethnicity, directed distance |
|---|---|---|---|---|
| Immigrant | −.01 | .03** | −.06*** | .02* |
| Second-generation immigrant | −.00 | .06*** | −.06*** | .06*** |
| Urban, non-South, different city and state | .04* | −.10*** | −.00 | −.02 |
| Urban, South, different city and state | .04** | −.04** | −.02 | .02 |
| Rural, non-South, different city and state | .01 | −.02* | −.05*** | .02 |
| Rural, South, different city and state | .03** | −.01 | −.04** | .03* |
| Urban, non-South, different city, same state | .01 | −.06*** | −.03 | .01 |
| Urban, South, different city, same state | .02* | −.03* | −.03* | .02 |
| Rural, non-South, different city, same state | .02 | −.02 | −.04** | .02 |
| Rural, South, different city, same state | −.01 | −.01 | −.02* | .02 |
| Urban, non-South, same city | .04* | −.08*** | −.00 | −.00 |
| Urban, South, same city | .02 | −.04** | −.00 | .01 |
| Rural, non-South, same city | .01 | −.04*** | −.03* | .02 |
| Rural, South, same city | Comparison | Comparison | Comparison | Comparison |

*Note*: Estimated from a multinomial logistic regression controlling for cohort, ethnicity, gender, status factors, and life-course factors.

* p < .05 two tailed; ** p < .01 two-tailed; *** p < .001 two tailed

Mobility within the United States also helps structure switching distances and trajectories. In the cohort models, the absolute distance of a switch is magnified by moving to an urban area—or even living in an urban environment without moving. Indeed, switching distances are as high among lifelong residents of urban areas as they are for urbanites who move. Overall, as in the models for switching and apostasy, rural southerners who do not move have the lowest switching distances. However, switching distances are just as low (slightly lower but not significantly different) for rural southerners who move within their home state. Interstate mobility among rural people significantly increases the absolute distance of mobility in the cohort models. Scaling switching distances using the ethnic model dramatically changes the impact of intranational migration on switching distances—making stable rural southerners more mobile across the ethnic spectrum. Part of this is a function of African American population concentrations and their very high intrinsic association parameter in the ethnic model. Additionally, the ethnic models show a stronger southern effect on absolute switching distances, with southerners charting longer shifts in identification. Again, ethnic concentrations play a strong role, with rural southerners being heavily western European, African American, and Latin American—the three groups with the highest intrinsic association parameters.

In the cohort models, intranational migration tends to spur switching toward the nonsectarian end of the distribution. When compared to stable, rural southerners, lifelong residents of other locales tend to switch to a less sectarian identity if they make a change in religious identification. The southern divide is also quite clear. Nonsoutherners tend to switch even further away from the sectarian pole when compared to southerners who made similar moves to a different city and/or state. When scaled on the ethnic model, switching directions for intranational migrants are less substantial. Indeed, compared to stable, rural southerners, only rural, southern interstate migrants are significantly different—and they move toward the mainline end of the distribution.

## The Circulation of the Saints?

Religious switching realigns the religious identifications of about a third of Americans. Yet the patterns of switching are localized, and people tend to move to a religious group similar to their former identity, a pattern which Reginald Bibby and Merlin Brinkerhoff described as the "circulation of the saints" (Bibby 1978; Bibby and Brinkerhoff 1973, 1983). This gives considerable inertia for the dominant identifications—most people retain the identification they were socialized to prefer as children, and if they do shift their religious identities, they pick something quite like what they grew up with. Grand theories positing sectarian dominance in the winners and losers in the religious marketplace (such as those of Iannaccone [1992, 1994] and Finke and Stark [1992]) do quite poorly for predicting rates, patterns, and trajectories of religious switching. Secularization theories may be bolstered by the finding that a growing proportion of shifts in religious identities are to holding no religious identification. Yet the lack of a religious identification in 20% of recent cohorts scarcely indicates a collapse in the importance of religion in the United States, and identification is only one measure of religiosity that could be used to gauge secularity.

Grand theories such as the supply-side model and secularization theory do not get us very far toward explaining the many factors that influence changes in the distribution of religious identities in the United States. This chapter has showed that identities shift in response to social pressures and changes in social environments and that these changes vary across generations and also by ethnicity. Life-course events such as marriage, migration, and socioeconomic mobility push people toward or away from particular religious identities—and they also help to solidify religious identities. Most importantly, the changes in religious identification in the United States over the past four decades and across many generations are a function of the ethnic milieu created by patterns of immigration. Immigrant religion is not simply a sideline. "Real America" is not western European sectarian Protestantism. Real America is defined, produced, and reproduced by waves of diverse immigrant groups assimilating into or accommodating with a broader Anglo-dominated culture.

Religious identifications tell us something about the cultural significance of religion based on the changing structure of those identities in the population. The shifting percentage of people identifying with Baptist and moderate Protestant groups says something about the current and future power of denominations and the stability of their congregations. It also might imply something about a shift in the religious belief structures of Americans, and this religious character of the United States is likely a function more of underlying beliefs than of identifications with particular denominations—even though these denominations may impact those beliefs. More importantly, the strong expansion of religious nonidentification in recent cohorts and in ethnic groups with higher rates of recent immigration suggests that irreligiosity may be growing. The next chapter investigates the connections between religious identification and religious belief.

3

Belonging and Believing

Identifications with religious denominations and traditions are important because they are linked to distinctive beliefs about supernatural rewards and compensators, and they channel religious behaviors. Indeed, when we think about the religious character of the United States, distinctive beliefs, public piety, and private devotion are what mark the exceptional character of American religion. So far, we have focused on identifications with denominational groupings and their contours and dynamics. This chapter demonstrates how these identifications matter for religious beliefs and behaviors. Identification with religious groups indicates that a person has participated to some extent in that religious group and that he or she continues to embrace the distinctive beliefs and practices of that faith. Further, religious identifications indicate a sense of commonality with and connection to others who hold similar identities and commitments. Identifications stem from socialization and social participation, and they provide important anchors for future attachments and commitments.

This chapter explores several important features of religious belief and belonging. First, any discussion of religious participation requires an exploration of how religious commitments are structured by age and life-course factors. Young adults rarely participate in religious groups. This is a long-recognized phenomenon (Hoge, Petrillo, and Smith 1982; Nash 1968; Nash and Berger 1962; Roof and Greer 1993). The development of families of procreation often leads people to return to religious participation and identification (Wilson and Sherkat 1994), and older people are more stable in their social ties and flexible in their work and family obligations—which makes social participation such as religious and political activism increase with age (Strate et al. 1989).

Second, the chapter investigates how identifications structure religious beliefs and religious belonging. While several prominent religious commentators have claimed that denominational factors are no longer important for informing religious beliefs or motivating religious participation (Hunter 1991; Wuthnow 1988, 1993), we will see how and why denominational identifications still matter and investigate whether such influences are shifting across generations. Additionally, it will become clear how ethnicity channels both beliefs and commitments and may also be reshaping the contours of American religion.

Finally, the chapter addresses the popular meme which contends that Americans are increasingly "believers who don't belong." Many scholars have been arguing that this is a growing trend (Davie 1990, 1994; Hout and Fischer 2002; Putnam and Campbell 2012); however, this line of inquiry has largely ignored prior research and theorizing about the relationship between religious beliefs and behaviors. Sociologists have long observed that identification with and participation in religious groups is often not correspondent with the acceptance of religious dogma. Indeed, even in radical, high-cost groups such as the Hare Krishna and the Moonies, people often identify with and participate in the group without accepting the core principles of the religion (Lofland and Stark 1965; Rochford 1985, 2007). With that fact in mind, we will track not only the phenomenon of believing without belonging but also the tendency to belong while not believing—and the growing trend of not believing and not belonging.

## Religious Commitments over the Life Course and across Generations

Religious identifications and participation in religious organizations are both structured by social forces that shift over the life course. Religious socialization is an important part of childhood socialization for people who embrace the supernatural explanations provided by religious firms (Sherkat 1998; Sherkat and Wilson 1995). As chapter 2 showed, religious identifications are relatively stable, and they are a product of early socialization. If people do change identifications, they typically pick one that is similar to their religion of origin in its ritual, theology, and social status. People tend not to choose their religious identifications but instead adopt those of their family of origin. And religious commitments are often influenced by geographic mobility, educational attainment, and career formation—all of which tend to be patterned during the life course.

Young adults find themselves able to make relatively independent religious choices for the first time. Typically, people in their late teens and early twenties are single, childless, and either completing their education or entering the workforce for the first time. The time demands of educational attainment and of early career jobs are not conducive to maintaining ties to religious organizations—even if identifications remain stable (Myers 1996; Stolzenberg, Blair-Loy, and Waite 1995). Further, educational attainment and workforce participation often necessitate geographic mobility, which disrupts social ties supportive of religious participation and often places young people in unfamiliar religious markets (Alanezi and Sherkat 2008; Sherkat 1991; Sherkat and Wilson 1995). As a consequence, young adults are much less active in religious organizations, and they are also more likely to reject religious identification (Roof and McKinney 1987; Sherkat and Wilson 1995).

By the time people reach their mid- to late twenties, the majority of Americans have completed their educational attainment, settled into careers, and married and/or had children. U.S. Census Bureau data show that the median age of marriage in the U.S. increased from about twenty-three years for men and twenty-one years for women in 1972 to twenty-eight years for men and twenty-six years for women in 2010. Similarly, U.S. Vital Statistics show that the age of first birth for women increased from about twenty-one years in 1970 to almost twenty-six years in 2011. These upward shifts may influence cohort patterns of religious disengagement and reengagement. Life-cycle factors also interact with one another to influence religious engagement over the life course. People who have children at a very early age tend to have lower rates of religious participation than those who have more age-normative patterns of marriage and childrearing (Stolzenberg, Blair-Loy, and Waite 1995). Of course, normative patterns of marriage and childrearing are structured by the ages of marriage and first birth prevalent at a given period of time. And people with children under age five are often hard-pressed to engage in social participation of any form.

In cross-sectional data such as the GSS, age and generation are highly correlated, and it is difficult to discern aging effects, which may be closely aligned with life-course events, from cohort effects—which

Table 3.1. *Weekly Church Attendance by Age of Interviewee and Generation*

| Generation | Under 30 | 30–39 | 40–49 | 50–64 | Over 65 |
|---|---|---|---|---|---|
| Pre-1925 cohort | — | — | 31.7% | 36.3% | 40.0% |
| 1925–1943 cohort | 23.3% | 29.0% | 31.8% | 32.8% | 39.0% |
| 1944–1955 cohort | 20.7% | 26.3% | 25.6% | 27.3% | 34.9% |
| 1956–1970 cohort | 19.4% | 22.4% | 25.5% | 27.2% | — |
| 1971–1994 cohort | 16.1% | 20.3% | 23.2% | — | — |

Table 3.2. *Less-than-Yearly Church Attendance by Age of Interviewee and Generation*

| Generation | Under 30 | 30–39 | 40–49 | 50–64 | Over 65 |
|---|---|---|---|---|---|
| Pre-1925 cohort | — | — | 21.2% | 17.5% | 21.9% |
| 1925–1943 cohort | 23.3% | 21.8% | 19.1% | 21.4% | 23.1% |
| 1944–1955 cohort | 25.9% | 22.7% | 25.6% | 27.3% | 38.4% |
| 1956–1970 cohort | 23.4% | 26.3% | 27.9% | 30.3% | — |
| 1971–1994 cohort | 31.7% | 29.3% | 36.2% | — | — |

evidence generational shifts. Tables 3.1 and 3.2 examine rates of weekly and less-than-yearly religious participation by cohort and age. This allows a comparison of how people born in different time periods participate when they are at the same age as people born in other time periods. Of course, nobody in the GSS who was born before 1925 was interviewed when he or she was under thirty-seven, and none of the respondents born after 1970 has been observed past age forty-two.

It is clear from table 3.1 that weekly church attendance is declining across generations, and this is not simply a function of later cohorts being interviewed at younger ages, when participation is always low. Weekly church attendance for people under age thirty declined from 21% in the 1944–1955 baby-boom generation to 16% for respondents born after 1971. For people interviewed when they were in their thirties, weekly attendance decreased from 29% in the 1925–1943 cohort to 19% in the 1971–1994 cohort. Similar patterns are evident across the age ranges—weekly church attendance is declining.

Table 3.2 examines the same patterns for less-than-yearly religious participation. Here, the findings mirror those in table 3.1—at similar ages, later generations are substantially more likely to avoid religious participation. Only 22% of respondents in their thirties from the

1925–1943 cohort participated in religious groups less than once a year, while 29% of people in their thirties who were born after 1970 attended less than yearly.

Religious participation is on the decline in the United States, and members of younger generations are significantly less likely to be regular attenders and substantially more likely to participate less than once a year. Given that the older generations are dying off and being replaced by younger generations who are less active, we can expect to see a fairly sizeable drop in overall religious participation in the coming decades, and decreasing participation is already quite evident.

## Private Devotion and Religious Beliefs across Cohorts

Declining religious identification and diminished participation in religious organizations is a key feature of religious change in the United States in the 21st century; however, many religious commentators claim that these public expressions of religion do not accurately reflect the underlying religiosity of the American populace. Popular pundits and social scientists have promulgated the idea that Americans increasingly "believe but don't belong" (Davie 1990; Putnam and Campbell 2012). Indeed, sociological theorists adhering to supply-side rational-actor models use this notion as a critical assumption of their models, claiming that religious demand is stable and unchanging, while religious activity varies with religious regulation and competition (Iannaccone 1990; Stark and Finke 2000). However, more sociological perspectives on the development and maintenance of preference structures suggest that the desire for supernatural goods may be more fluid, as it is for other cultural goods such as music, art, literature, or sport (Sherkat 1997, 1998; Sherkat and Wilson 1995).

Over the past four decades, private religious devotion and religious beliefs have also shifted. Table 3.3 presents the cohort differences for frequency of prayer, beliefs about god, beliefs about the sacred texts of the dominant tradition, and belief in life after death. Private prayer seems to be falling alongside public expressions of piety; and the two are connected. Prayer in the Abrahamic traditions which dominate the U.S. religious marketplace is often a social event. Prayers are frequently conducted at family meals, events, and meetings and as part

Table 3.3. Religious Devotion and Belief by Generation

|  | Pre-1925 cohort | 1925–1943 cohort | 1944–1955 cohort | 1956–1970 cohort | 1971–1994 cohort |
|---|---|---|---|---|---|
| Less-than-weekly prayer | 1.5% | 3.3% | 4.0% | 4.7% | 12.4% |
| Daily or more prayer | 75.4% | 64.4% | 56.3% | 51.2% | 47.9% |
| Atheist | 2.0% | 2.3% | 2.7% | 2.8% | 3.2% |
| Nontheist | 10.7% | 14.1% | 16.6% | 16.4% | 22.0% |
| Believer with no doubts | 72.0% | 67.9% | 63.2% | 61.7% | 55.4% |
| Biblical fundamentalist | 43.8% | 38.2% | 30.0% | 31.8% | 30.4% |
| Secular Bible beliefs | 11.7% | 14.9% | 18.4% | 16.8% | 20.2% |
| Believe in life after death | 78.1% | 79.3% | 80.2% | 80.8% | 80.9% |
| Definitely believe in hell | 52.8% | 53.6% | 51.6% | 51.9% | 53.1% |

of nighttime rituals for children and family. Indeed, I have frequently been exhorted to participate in Christian prayers at events at supposedly secular, state-supported universities. Such prayers are frequent at sporting events, graduations, city council meetings, and all manner of "nonreligious" voluntary organizations. As a consequence, prayer is only partly private, and it is often engaged in because of social pressures rather than voluntary choice (Sherkat and Cunningham 1998). Praying less than once a week is exceptionally rare among people born before 1925, and the low figure more than triples to nearly 5% among respondents from the 1956–1970 cohort and jumps to over 12% for those born after 1970. Further, daily prayer falls from 75% among those born before 1925 to less than 48% in the latest generation.

Beliefs may be less subject to social approval influences—though intolerance against atheism may cause nonbelievers to falsify their preferences (Edgell, Gerteis, and Hartmann 2006; Kuran 1993, 1995). Indeed, supply-side theorists and religious activists are fond of pointing to opinion polls which show extremely high levels of belief in "god" and stability of those beliefs over time in the United States. However, the GSS asks a much more sophisticated question: rather than a simple binary which forces respondents to choose belief or atheism, the GSS question taps agnosticism, believing in a higher power "but not a god" and varying degrees of doubt in the existence of god (Sherkat 2008). Table 3.3 tracks rates of atheism, nontheism, and belief without doubt across generations. Despite the enormous intolerance toward atheists in the United States, a growing portion of Americans are embracing this as their position on the existence of god. Only 2% of respondents born before 1925 are atheists, but in the youngest cohorts, the figure is 3.2%—a small but growing fraction. Nontheism is indicated by atheism, agnosticism (believing "I don't know whether there is a god, and I don't believe there is any way to find out"), and believing "in a higher power *but not a god.*" Nontheism is much more prevalent than pure atheism is; and even in the oldest cohorts, more than one in ten respondents are nontheists. The proportion of nontheists also increases considerably across cohorts, more than doubling to 22% in the latest cohort. Just as atheism and nontheism have become more prevalent across cohorts, unflinching belief in god has declined. While 72% of respondents born before 1925 believe in god with no doubts, only 55% of the youngest cohort are true believers. Interestingly, research shows that atheism and other religious beliefs are relatively stable with age. People generally do not embrace belief in god as they age (Sherkat 2008).

Fundamentalist beliefs in the inerrancy of sacred texts are the most important religious beliefs for predicting sociological and political out-comes. Fundamentalism is commonly juxtaposed with beliefs that gods inspired the sacred texts and also the belief that the sacred texts of the Abrahamic tradition are "ancient books of fables, legends, history and moral precepts recorded by men." Table 3.3 tracks belief fundamen-talism and secular views of the Bible across generations. The analyses show that belief fundamentalism declined considerably from nearly 44% in the pre-1925 cohort to 30% of the 1944–1955 baby-boom genera-tion. Fundamentalism remains fairly stable around 30% in the cohorts of people born after 1955. Secular views of the Abrahamic sacred texts have increased across generations. Among those born prior to 1925, about 12% viewed the Bible as a book of fables, and this figure increases to over 18% among the 1944–1955 baby boomers. Secular beliefs in the Bible were slightly lower among the 1956–1970 cohorts and rebound to over 20% among those born after 1970. Notably, the increase in secu-lar views is not quite as large as the decrease in fundamentalism, and this implies that the middle position of viewing the Bible as inspired by gods has also become more popular in later generations.

Beliefs in life after death and belief in hell provide curious anoma-lies to the generally secularized beliefs and behaviors found in other dimensions of religiosity. Both beliefs about life after death and belief in hell are remarkably stable across cohorts, and what little movement there is seems to be toward belief in an afterlife, as prior research has shown (Greeley and Hout 1999). About 78% of the oldest cohort believe in life after death, and this figure increases to about 80% in the baby-boom and later cohorts. Belief in hell hovers around 53% with little variation across generations. However, it is difficult to say how Americans, particularly from diverse religious origins, interpret "life after death," and many possible interpretations—such as reincarnation—fly far afield from the Abrahamic interpretations assumed by most people. Hell is less ambiguous and implies that people who engage in proscribed behaviors and/or reject particular beliefs about the supernatural will receive punishment in the afterlife. This is of great importance for more exclusivist traditions, which emphasize that the wicked and nonbelievers will receive eternal torture or some other negative fate from their god.

## Ethnicity, Belonging, and Belief

Religious commitments are structured by ethnic ties and origins, and the changing ethnic composition of the United States will have a profound impact on the religious character of the nation in the coming decades. Table 3.4 shows that religious participation is highest among Americans with African ethnic origins, and African Americans are rarely so disengaged from religion that they attend services less than once a year.

*Table 3.4. Belonging and Believing by Ethnicity*

|  | Native American | Western European | Eastern European | Asian | African American | Latin American |
|---|---|---|---|---|---|---|
| Less-than-yearly religious attendance | 30.1% | 24.6% | 23.9% | 31.2% | 15.2% | 19.9% |
| Weekly or more religious attendance | 22.8% | 28.5% | 28.1% | 27.1% | 30.8% | 26.1% |
| Less-than-weekly prayer | 3.7% | 5.5% | 5.8% | 11.6% | 1.5% | 4.4% |
| Daily or more prayer | 60.5% | 54.2% | 49.3% | 48.5% | 75.4% | 60.1% |
| Atheist | 1.3% | 2.8% | 4.0% | 5.9% | 1.8% | 1.7% |
| Nontheist | 14.6% | 18.6% | 23.5% | 28.2% | 7.9% | 10.0% |
| Believer with no doubts | 66.0% | 58.8% | 48.2% | 50.0% | 80.7% | 73.5% |
| Biblical fundamentalist | 41.7% | 26.9% | 19.1% | 23.8% | 56.1% | 41.6% |
| Secular Bible beliefs | 14.0% | 18.4% | 24.5% | 25.4% | 9.8% | 13.2% |
| Believe in life after death | 86.7% | 81.7% | 69.2% | 74.9% | 78.9% | 72.0% |
| Definitely believe in hell | 69.6% | 49.9% | 35.0% | 43.9% | 67.7% | 52.6% |

While nearly 31% of African Americans report weekly church attendance, only 23% of Native Americans and 26% of Latin Americans participate at this rate. Interestingly, while nearly a third of Asian Americans participate in religion less than yearly, 27% claim to attend weekly. The enormous diversity of Asians is certainly responsible for their polarized rates of participation. For some, religion is a key feature of ethnic communities (Ebaugh 2003; Ebaugh and Chafetz 2000), while for others, immigration to the United States was spurred by secularism (Alanezi and Sherkat 2008; Sherkat 2010a). Latin Americans are also unlikely to be completely disengaged from religious participation, with fewer than 20% attending less than once a year. Yet they are also somewhat less likely than members of other ethnic groups to attend weekly.

Private religious devotion is also stronger among African Americans, who are unlikely to pray less than once a week and three-fourths of whom report daily prayer. In contrast, nearly 12% of Asian Americans pray less than once a week, and less than half of Asians and eastern Europeans report daily prayer. Notably, both Native Americans and Latin Americans report high rates of daily prayer, despite their relative disengagement from public religious participation.

Table 3.4 shows that ethnicity is particularly important for structuring beliefs about god. Atheism is embraced by just over 1% of Native Americans and about 2% of African Americans and Latin Americans. However, much higher proportions of eastern Europeans and Asians are atheists, with over 6% of Asians choosing atheism. Similarly, nontheism is relatively uncommon among Latin Americans (10%) and African Americans (8%), while over a quarter of Asians are atheist, agnostic, or believe in a higher power but not a god. And nearly 24% of eastern Europeans are nontheists, compared to 18% of western Europeans. Not surprisingly, table 3.4 shows that African Americans have the highest rates of belief, with 81% believing in god without a doubt. Uncritical belief in god is also high among Latin Americans, with 74% believing without doubt. In contrast, only 48% of eastern Europeans and 50% of Asians believe without question.

Biblical fundamentalism is most prevalent among African Americans, with 56% believing the Bible is the actual word of god. Latin Americans and Native Americans also tend to embrace fundamentalism, while once again eastern Europeans and Asians tend to shun fundamentalism—and both eastern Europeans and Asians are also are substantially more likely than other ethnic groups to hold secular beliefs about the Bible.

Belief in life after death is more prevalent among Native Americans, at nearly 87%, and nearly 70% believe in hell. In contrast, only 69% of eastern Europeans, 75% of Asians, and 72% of Latin Americans believe in an afterlife. Just 35% of eastern Europeans believe in hell, compared to 44% of Asians and half of western Europeans. Unlike for other beliefs, African Americans are somewhat less likely than western European Americans to believe in life after death. However, African Americans do tend to believe in hell, with 68% embracing the supernatural compensator of eternal punishment for the wicked and nonbelievers. Ethnic variations in many of these beliefs are partly a function of underlying differences in rates of identification with particular religious traditions, and how religious identifications structure religious commitments and beliefs is explored in the next section.

## Religious Identification and Religious Behavior

Religious identifications bring with them expectations for public piety and private devotion. Religious participation is anchored partly in preferences for the supernatural explanations proffered by religious firms to which individuals identify and partly by social rewards and punishments which identifiers may incur as a result of their expressions of public faith (Sherkat 1997, 1998; Sherkat and Wilson 1995). For people identifying with some groups, particularly theologically liberal groups, regular public participation may mean going to services once a month or less. However, for "strict" sectarian religious groups, a higher rate of attendance is expected—or individuals and families will be shunned and shamed (Iannaccone 1994; Sherkat 1997).

Table 3.5 presents the average scores on the GSS church-attendance and prayer items by religious identification. These are ranked by rates of church attendance from highest to lowest. The scales of the two items are different, so the numeric values must be viewed in light of the distributions of the respective measures. Religious identification does not structure prayer as substantially as it does public participation—as theories of social influences on religious choices predict (Ellison and Sherkat

*Table 3.5. Religious Participation and Frequency of*
*Prayer by Religious Identification (Scores on GSS Scale)*

| Identification | Average religious attendance | Average frequency of prayer |
|---|---|---|
| Sectarian Protestant | 5.3 | 5.0 (1) |
| Mormon | 5.2 | 4.9 (2) |
| Catholic | 4.3 | 4.3 (7) |
| Baptist | 4.3 | 4.7 (3) |
| Moderate Protestant | 4.0 | 4.5 (5) |
| Lutheran | 4.0 | 4.3 (9) |
| Liberal Protestant | 3.9 | 4.3 (8) |
| Other Protestant | 3.7 | 4.5 (4) |
| Episcopalian | 3.6 | 4.3 (10) |
| Unitarian | 3.3 | 3.1 (12) |
| Other religion | 3.3 | 4.3 (6) |
| Jewish | 2.7 | 3.2 (11) |
| None | .8 | 2.7 (13) |
| Total | 3.8 | 4.3 |

*Note*: Religious attendance scale: 0 = never, 1 = less than once a year, 2 = once a year,
3 = several times a year, 4 = once a month, 5 = two to three times a month, 6  = nearly
every week, 7 = weekly, and 8 = more than once a week. Frequency of prayer scale: 1 =
never, 2 = less than weekly, 3 = once a week, 4 = several times a week, 5 = daily, 6 =
more than daily. Prayer ranking in parentheses.

1995b; Sherkat 1998; Sherkat and Cunningham 1998). Sectarian Protestants and Mormons have substantially higher rates of religious participation than do members of other groups. Catholics and Baptists fill the
next tier, with moderate Protestants, Lutherans, and liberal Protestants
filling the middle of the distribution. Jews, other non-Christians, Unitarians, and Episcopalians are at the bottom of the participation scale.

Many authors seem to take this ranking of rates of religious participation as an indicator of failure for the organizations at the bottom of
the distribution (e.g., Finke and Stark 1992; Iannaccone 1994). However,
such a view of organizational mobilization rates does not capture the
general sense of religious community sought by nonsectarian organizations. It is important to take note of what the averages mean at the
bottom of the distribution and to reflect on the nature and direction
of social desirability biases and how they might affect those who identify with varied religious traditions. Sectarians and Mormons report
attending church two to three times a month, on average. In contrast,
Jews report attending religious services a bit less than several times
a year, while Unitarians, other non-Christians, and Episcopalians fall

somewhere between several times and year and once a month. Almost-monthly attendance is hardly a demonstration of limited connection to a religious group. Very few people in the United States attend a political meeting every month, and a person who volunteers with a nonprofit organization on a monthly basis would be considered a stalwart sup-porter. The view of liberal Protestants, Jews, and other non-Christians as uncommitted shirkers only holds water if we are to take the hyper-active participation of sectarians and Mormons to be the norm.

Table 3.5 also shows that sectarians and Mormons top the charts on frequency of prayer. However, moderate and liberal Protestants and Catholics have fairly high levels of self-reported prayer, and even Unitarians and Jews report praying more than once a week. An inter-esting shift in the rankings for prayer is found among respondents in the "other religions." Three groups dominate this category: Buddhists, Muslims, and Hindus. Buddhists and Hindus are primarily devotional rather than congregational in their religious participation (Yang and Ebaugh 2001), so it is no surprise that they would have low rates of religious attendance and higher rates of prayer. Muslims are implored by religious prescriptions to pray five times a day. And as supply-side theorists would be quick to point out, all three of these groups may lack religious congregations to enable regular participation. Many Bud-dhists, Muslims, and Hindus travel hundreds of miles to find a temple or mosque fitting their particular interpretation of their faith.

The distributions of both church attendance and prayer are influ-enced heavily by social desirability biases, as people in communities where religion is valued will overreport church attendance just as they overreport voting and other positively valued behaviors (Hadaway, Mar-ler, and Chaves 1993). Indeed, since sectarians and Mormons view reli-gious participation as more of a duty—and one with dire eternal con-sequences—they may be more likely to overreport religious behaviors.

Finally, one group consistently sits at the bottom of both distribu-tions for religious behaviors—people who eschew religious identifica-tion attend church less than once a year, on average, and they pray less than once a week. Nonidentifiers tend not to belong to religious groups or participate in religious activities, and they also tend not to engage in "private" religious devotion. On the latter issue, those who do not iden-tify with a religious group may less often find themselves compelled to pray in social settings. Additionally, those without religious identifications may not believe in a god to which one would be forced to offer devotion, and they may find no value in the supernatural explanations proffered in religious firms. Indeed, rather than nonidentifiers being people who "believe but don't belong," those who reject religious identifications may neither believe nor belong (Aarts et al. 2008; Voas and Crockett 2005).

## Beliefs about God and Religious Identification

Religious groups have different beliefs about gods and what devotees are supposed to believe about them. Not all groups demand that members believe without doubts, and some religious firms present faith as a struggle with doubt and mystery. Still, individuals who identify with a religious tradition may hold beliefs that fly far afield from the official dogma of their religion. Abrahamic religious traditions adhere to a view of god as an active agent, which is commensurate with the sociological definition of gods (Stark and Bainbridge 1987; Stark and Finke 2000)—gods do things, and that matters for the provision of supernatural rewards and compensators for the faithful (and the unfaithful). To the extent that people are certain of the existence of gods, the explanations which promise supernatural compensators and provide supernatural rewards will be more valuable (Stark and Bainbridge 1987; Stark and Finke 2000).

Table 3.6 arrays religious identifications according to their certainty in the existence of a god. Predictably, members of sectarian Protestant groups and Mormons express the greatest certainty in the existence of gods, followed closely by Baptists—and more than 80% of those who identify with these three groups report believing without a doubt. Nondenominational Protestants, moderate Protestants, and Catholics also exceed the national average of 63% in believing without doubts. In contrast, only 12% of Unitarians and 28% of Jews report believing without a doubt, and under half of those with other religious identifications are certain of the existence of a god.

Notably, table 3.6 shows that the ranking of religious identifications on atheism and nontheism mirrors those found for certainty of belief. Very few sectarians, Mormons, or Baptists embrace atheism or believe

*Table 3.6. Beliefs about God by Religious Identification*

| Identification | Believer with no doubts | Atheist | Nontheist |
|---|---|---|---|
| Sectarian Protestant | 85.9% | 1.1% | 3.6% |
| Mormon | 85.3% | 1.8% | 3.1% |
| Baptist | 82.0% | .9% | 4.9% |
| Other Protestant | 70.6% | .8% | 10.0% |
| Moderate Protestant | 68.4% | 1.0% | 9.4% |
| Catholic | 64.5% | .9% | 9.4% |
| Lutheran | 62.4% | .5% | 10.4% |
| Liberal Protestant | 58.5% | 1.6% | 15.6% |
| Episcopalian | 52.7% | 1.2% | 16.3% |
| Other religion | 46.1% | 3.9% | 38.0% |
| Jewish | 28.2% | 3.8% | 36.1% |
| None | 21.7% | 12.5% | 58.6% |
| Unitarian | 12.0% | 12.0% | 64.0% |
| Total | 62.6% | 2.7% | 16.8% |

in a higher power but not a god, while the vast majority of Unitarians, 64%, are nontheists. Indeed, nearly one in ten Americans who identify as nondenominational, moderate Protestant, Catholic, and Lutheran are nontheists—they reject the idea of a god—and nontheism is even more prevalent among liberal Protestants and Episcopalians. Over a third of Jews and other non-Christians also reject belief in a god.

In contrast to the "believing but not belonging" meme, people who reject religious identification tend not to belong to or participate in religious groups (as we saw earlier in this chapter), and they tend to reject religious beliefs. Only 22% of nonidentifiers report certainty in the existence of god, and nearly 13% are atheists. Indeed, 59% of nonidentifiers reject belief in the type of an agentic god which is definitive of the Abrahamic tradition—most people who do not identify with a religious group do not believe in anything remotely resembling the dominant tradition in the United States.

## Fundamentalism, Secularism, and Religious Identification

Fundamentalist beliefs attributing divine authorship of the sacred texts of the Abrahamic tradition are some of the most potent cultural frameworks influencing a variety of social outcomes—from terrorism and patriarchal gender relations to harsh parenting practices and opposition

*Table 3.7. Perspectives on Sacred Texts by Religious Identification*

| Identification | Biblical fundamentalist | Bible is a book of fables |
|---|---|---|
| Sectarian Protestant | 63.1% | 2.8% |
| Baptist | 58.0% | 5.8% |
| Other Protestant | 40.0% | 11.1% |
| Moderate Protestant | 37.2% | 9.6% |
| Mormon | 32.9% | 5.3% |
| Lutheran | 31.8% | 9.7% |
| Liberal Protestant | 22.5% | 13.8% |
| Catholic | 22.7% | 13.5% |
| Other religion | 17.7% | 36.1% |
| Episcopalian | 16.2% | 19.4% |
| None | 10.3% | 53.9% |
| Jewish | 9.0% | 45.5% |
| Unitarian | 4.6% | 66.2% |
| Total | 33.6% | 16.9% |

to civil rights for others. Fundamentalism is rooted in the belief in the inerrant, god-given nature of the sacred texts of a tradition—predominantly the Christian Bible in the United States. Fundamentalism can be juxtaposed with a secular, humanist interpretation of sacred texts as being products of human creation from thousands of years ago.

Not surprisingly, table 3.7 shows that the majority of sectarian Christians and Baptists adhere to a fundamentalist view of the sacred texts of their tradition. However, only about a third of Mormons are fundamentalist—likely revealing their distancing from aspects of the Book of Mormon which have been reinterpreted by LDS prophets. If the LDS sacred texts are literally true, then polygamy and the demonization of nonwhites also must be embraced. There is also a clear gap between sectarian groups and moderate Protestants and Lutherans and between these more moderate groups and liberal Protestants and Catholics. Only 16% of Episcopalians believe in the inerrancy of scripture, and fewer than 10% of Jews and 5% of Unitarians adhere to fundamentalism.

Secular views of sacred texts are dominant among Unitarians, with two-thirds embracing a humanist view. About 46% of Jews and 36% of other non-Christians adopt a secular view of the Bible. Not surprisingly, secular views of scripture are uncommon among sectarians, Baptists, and Mormons. Yet secular views of scripture are embraced by over

19% of Episcopalians, more than 13% of Catholics and liberal Protestants, 11% of nondenominational Protestants, and nearly 10% of moderate Protestants and Lutherans. This shows that many who identify with Christian groups reject any divine influence on the sacred texts of their tradition. Belonging but not believing is fairly common (Francis and Robbins 2007; Marchisio and Pisati 1999). Once again, table 3.7 shows that nonidentifiers tend not to fit the "believing but not belonging" pattern. More than half of nonidentifiers hold secular views of the Abrahamic sacred texts, and only 10% embrace fundamentalism.

## Beliefs about Life after Death and Religious Identification

Belief in life after death is something of a conundrum, since many Abrahamic religious groups think of their supernatural compensators as being beyond life, rather than being life after death. Indeed, the issue of beliefs in life after death has generated considerable controversy among survey researchers (Greeley and Hout 1999, 2001; Stolzenberg 2001). Andrew Greeley and Michael Hout have argued that competition and acculturation processes have driven some religious groups, notably Jews, to embrace a notion of a corporeal afterlife, in contradiction to more orthodox teachings in which the supernatural compensators of the tradition are separate from earthly life. Greeley and Hout's analyses show that both Catholics and Jews have moved to a somewhat more "Protestant" position which amplifies bodily resurrection (Greeley and Hout 1999, 2001), though others dispute these findings (Stolzenberg 2001). Beliefs about supernatural punishment in the form of hell are also not uniformly embraced, since many moderate and liberal groups adhere to universalism—positive supernatural compensators for all—or at least reject divine punishment.

Mormons are quite clear regarding life after death, and their theology paints an afterlife complete with reunited "celestial" families. Not surprisingly, table 3.8 shows that an overwhelming majority of Mormons believe in life after death—95% compared to "only" 85% of sectarians and Baptists. Indeed, Lutherans and moderate Protestants are not far behind Baptists and sectarians, and Catholics' belief in life after death rivals that of liberal Protestants and Episcopalians—very close to the overall sample average of 80%. Sectarian Protestants and Baptists

*Table 3.8. Belief in Life after Death by Religious Identification*

| Identification | Believe in life after death | Definitely believe in hell |
|---|---|---|
| Mormon | 95.0% | 70.7% (3) |
| Sectarian Protestant | 85.3% | 77.7% (1) |
| Baptist | 85.0% | 75.3% (2) |
| Other Protestant | 87.3% | 62.5% (4) |
| Lutheran | 85.4% | 50.5% (6) |
| Moderate Protestant | 84.3% | 55.2% (5) |
| Liberal Protestant | 83.9% | 39.2% (8) |
| Catholic | 79.7% | 47.2% (7) |
| Other religion | 79.9% | 28.9% (10) |
| Episcopalian | 80.6% | 32.1% (9) |
| None | 56.1% | 21.3% (11) |
| Unitarian | 52.3% | 11.1% (12) |
| Jewish | 43.5% | 10.6% (13) |
| Total | 79.9% | 52.4% |

top the charts in embracing a belief in hell, with over three-fourths of their adherents expressing that they definitely believe in hell. Mormons are also fond of the prospect for eternal punishment for nonbelievers and the wicked, with over 70% believing in hell. More than half of moderate Protestants and Lutherans believe in hell, and just under half of Catholics embrace eternal punishment.

Unitarians and Jews are unlikely to believe in life after death, and they resoundingly reject belief in hell. Only 43% of Jews embrace the notion of life after death, while 52% of Unitarians hold this view. Beliefs in hell are even less widely held among these liberal groups, with about 11% of Jews and Unitarians expressing this belief—and their interpretations of "hell" are likely far afield from the fire-and-brimstone conceptions prevalent among sectarians. The majority of liberal Protestants reject belief in hell, and less than one-third of Episcopalians and "other religion" identifiers believe in hell. There is some evidence that later Jewish cohorts are more likely to believe in an afterlife, in contradiction to traditional Jewish theology (Greeley and Hout 1999); however, the basis for cohort comparisons in relatively small groups is weak (Stolzenberg 2001). And, once again, nonidentifiers do not tend to believe in life after death. Only 56% of nonidentifiers believe in an afterlife, and only 21% believe in hell.

## Believing but Not Identifying, and Identifying but Not Believing

Chapters 1 and 2 demonstrated that one of the most striking developments in religion in the United States is the growing proportion of the population that rejects religious identification. Yet many scholars and pundits are somewhat dismissive of trends in disaffiliation as being evidence of growing secularism because, they argue, Americans increasingly believe but do not belong. However, Americans' beliefs are changing as well, as this chapter has shown. And many who do not believe are forced to belong because of social influences on religious commitments. The "believing but not belonging" meme popularized by religious commentators is worthy of some additional scrutiny. Perhaps it is becoming truer that those who reject religious identification—the most rapidly growing religious identification in the United States—are more likely to be believers in later generations. Indeed, nonidentification may be less related to other religious behaviors such as religious participation and prayer.

Table 3.9 explores generational differences in religious behaviors and beliefs among those who have no religious identification. Notably, these results show that the believing-but-not-belonging idea has some merit —in later generations, nonidentifiers are less likely to hold secular views of the Bible and less likely to have nontheistic beliefs or to embrace

*Table 3.9 Belonging and Believing among Nonidentifiers by Generation*

|  | Pre-1925 cohort | 1925–1943 cohort | 1944–1955 cohort | 1956–1970 cohort | 1971–1994 cohort |
|---|---|---|---|---|---|
| Less-than-yearly religious attendance | 84.4% | 79.5% | 76.5% | 74.1% | 70.6% |
| Weekly or more religious attendance | 1.2% | 1.2% | 2.2% | 1.8% | .9% |
| Less-than-weekly prayer | .8% | 1.4% | 1.1% | 1.4% | 3.7% |
| Daily or more prayer | 15% | 25.9% | 18.8% | 18.1% | 31.1% |
| Atheist | 19.2% | 15.7% | 13.7% | 12.5% | 9.4% |
| Nontheist | 63.5% | 65.0% | 61.2% | 56.4% | 54.7% |
| Believer with no doubts | 25.0% | 19.3% | 19.4% | 22.4% | 23.8% |
| Biblical fundamentalist | 8.9% | 11.1% | 7.1% | 11.4% | 11.9% |
| Secular Bible beliefs | 57.4% | 61.9% | 56.6% | 50.5% | 49.9% |
| Believe in life after death | 26.3% | 34.3% | 44.2% | 50.3% | 50.3% |
| Definitely believe in hell | 14.3% | 15.9% | 14.9% | 18.2% | 30.3% |

atheism. In the oldest generation, nearly one in five nonidentifiers was an atheist, while in the youngest cohort, fewer than one in ten are atheists. However, undoubting belief in god is also slightly more popular in the oldest cohorts of nonidentifiers than among younger generations who reject a religious identification. Beliefs in life after death are dramatically higher among younger generations of nonidentifiers. Only 26% of nonidentifiers born before 1925 believed in life after death, and this figure rises steadily to just over 50% in the cohorts born since 1956. Similarly, belief in hell is much more prevalent in the youngest cohorts of respondents who reject a religious identity. While only 14% of nonidentifiers born prior to 1925 embraced a belief in hell, this figure grows to 30% in the cohort born after 1970.

Not only are nonidentifiers in the younger cohorts more likely to hold religious beliefs than are nonidentifiers in earlier cohorts, they also are less likely to be completely disengaged from religious participation. While 84% of nonidentifiers in the oldest cohorts report attending religious services less than once a year, this figure drops to 71% among those born after 1970. Daily prayer also varies across cohorts, but it is substantially higher for nonidentifiers born after 1970: nearly a third report daily prayer.

The analyses in table 3.9 suggest that those who do not identify are more likely to believe and even to engage in religious behaviors. In some sense, there is an increase in "belonging" in tandem with a rejection of religious identification. Notably, in the younger cohorts, nonidentifiers are less likely to have rejected a religion in which they were raised. Instead, they are more likely to have been raised without a religious identification when compared to nonidentifiers in earlier cohorts. And many of these differences may reflect an underlying preference for religion among people who were not raised in a faith.

But is "believing and not belonging" really a definitive feature of religion in the United States? Sociological studies of conversion and religious belief note that believing and belonging are often decoupled. What are the trends in believing but not belonging? How about the trend in belonging but not believing? And, importantly—the question which has largely gone unexplored—what proportion in each generation neither believes nor belongs? Table 3.10 explores these questions and looks at nontheism and secular views of the Bible as indicators of unbelief.

*Table 3.10. Believing and Identification by Generation*

|  | Pre-1925 cohort | 1925–1943 cohort | 1944–1954 cohort | 1956–1970 cohort | 1971–1994 cohort |
|---|---|---|---|---|---|
| Believe in God, don't identify | 1.5% | 2.5% | 4.7% | 6.1% | 10.2% |
| Don't believe in God, don't identify | 2.7% | 4.4% | 7.3% | 8.1% | 13.4% |
| Don't believe in God, identify | 7.9% | 9.7% | 9.2% | 8.3% | 8.5% |
| Believe Bible, don't identify | 1.6% | 2.4% | 5.0% | 6.8% | 11.0% |
| Don't believe Bible, don't identify | 2.2% | 3.9% | 6.6% | 7.2% | 11.8% |
| Don't believe in Bible, identify | 9.5% | 11.0% | 11.7% | 9.7% | 8.4% |

Table 3.10 shows that in the earlier generations, people who do not believe were forced by social pressures to nonetheless identify with some religious group. Close to 10% of the generations born before 1944 were nontheists who nonetheless identified with a religious group, and similar results are found for holding secular views of the Bible. That far exceeds the minuscule proportions of those generations who believe in a god or the divine inspiration for the Bible but do not identify with a faith. Only in the generation born after 1970 does the proportion of believers who do not identify exceed the share of religious identifiers rejecting the belief in a god or the divine inspiration for the Bible. Further, a greater percentage in each generation rejects belief and religious identification—lack of identification is most often coupled with unbelief. Not believing and not belonging is on the rise, and in the youngest generation, disengagement and rejection of theism describes over 13% of respondents.

Another interesting issue regarding belief and identification is how ethnicity may play a role in these patterns of commitment. Earlier in this chapter, we saw that African Americans, Native Americans, and western Europeans were substantially more likely to believe in god and hold that the Bible is a sacred text when compared to other ethnic groups, and in chapters 1 and 2, we also saw that nonidentification was lower among African Americans and Latin Americans but substantially higher among Asians. On both measures of religious beliefs, table 3.11 shows that belief is more often present among nonidentifiers for Native Americans, African Americans, and Latin Americans. In contrast, for western and eastern Europeans and Asians, the rejection of religious identification is linked to nonbelief. Among Asian respondents, over 15% are nontheists who also renounce religious identification, while

*Table 3.11. Believing and Identification by Ethnicity*

|  | Native American | Western European | Eastern European | Asian | African American | Latin American |
|---|---|---|---|---|---|---|
| Believe in God, don't identify | 7.3% | 4.7% | 5.0% | 7.2% | 7.4% | 6.6% |
| Don't believe in God, don't identify | 5.9% | 9.4% | 8.7% | 15.3% | 3.1% | 3.2% |
| Don't believe in God, identify | 8.8% | 9.2% | 14.9% | 12.8% | 4.8% | 6.8% |
| Believe Bible, don't identify | 7.8% | 5.1% | 4.6% | 9.5% | 6.2% | 6.0% |
| Don't believe Bible, don't identify | 5.8% | 7.8% | 7.5% | 12.0% | 2.3% | 3.3% |
| Don't believe in Bible, identify | 8.1% | 10.6% | 16.9% | 13.4% | 7.5% | 9.9% |

less than half that proportion reject an identification yet believe in god. Similar patterns are found for beliefs about the divine inspiration of the Bible.

The lack of religious belief is often found among those who maintain a religious identification for eastern Europeans; nearly 15% are nontheists who hold an identification, and 17% hold a secular view of the Bible and still maintain a religious identity. About 13% of Asians also show this pattern of continued identity along with rejection of belief. Much of this finding could be a function of a high proportion of non-Christians in those ethnic groups. Among eastern Europeans, secular Jews often continue to identify as Jewish, even though they no longer believe. For Asians, particularly Buddhists, Hindus, Taoists, Jainists, and Sikhs, the rejection of the divine authority of the Abrahamic Bible is an orthodox religious view—and the image of the divine in Buddhism, Hinduism, Jainism, and Taoism is much more like "a higher power but not a god."

The cohort findings help make sense of the trends in believing and identification. Figures 3.1 and 3.2 chart the proportion of GSS respondents who (1) identify but do not believe, (2) believe but do not identify, and (3) do not believe and do not identify. Figure 3.1 examines the trend in nonbelief in god, while figure 3.2 presents nonbelief in the Bible as a divine book. Overall, nontheism is becoming more prevalent, with nonbelief increasing from 13% to 20% between 1988 and 2012. There are two types of nonbelievers, those who claim a religious identification and those who do not. The percentage of respondents who hold a religious identification yet do not believe in a god hovered around 10% of GSS respondents in the early 1990s, but their proportions declined slightly to 8.2%. Believing but not identifying increased from 3.6% in 1988 to 7.4% in 2012. But the largest gains were among those who do

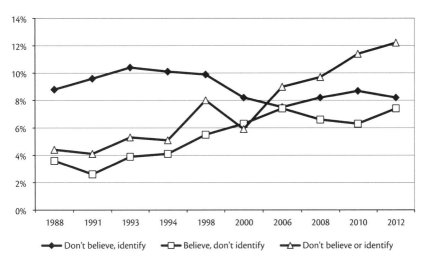

Fig. 3.1. Trend in belief in god by identification

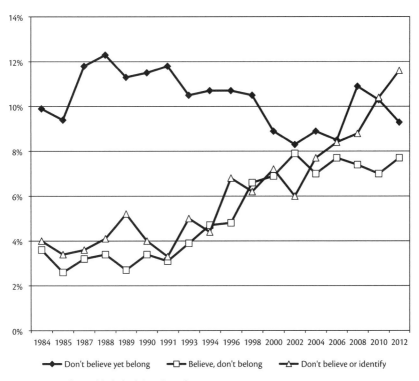

Fig. 3.2. Trend in Bible beliefs by identification

not believe and do not belong, which went from 4.3% of the sample in 1988 to 12.2% in 2012. In figure 3.2, in which beliefs in the divine origin of the Bible are considered, there are similar results. Identification without belief stays around 10% from 1984 to 2012. Believing in the divine inspiration of the Bible but not belonging to a religious group increases from 3.6% to 7.7%, while not believing and not belonging rises from 4% to 11.6%.

## Religious Identities, Religious Mobilization, and Religious Beliefs

This chapter has detailed the continuing importance of denominational identities for structuring religious belonging and religious beliefs. Public religious commitments are not necessarily driven by a desire for the supernatural rewards and compensators sold at religious firms, as supply-side theorists claim. Instead, public piety is often motivated by a desire to garner connections in the community, status, friendship, and social interaction. Yet religious denominations induce these rewards and punishments in different ways, and their varied theological orientations also prompt participation. Norms of religious behavior vary across religious traditions and for denominations within religious traditions; and the hyperactive mobilization of sectarian Christians and Mormons contrasts with the staid, regular involvement of liberal and moderate Protestants, Jews, and Unitarians. Further, religious beliefs and social influences on religious participation vary substantially across ethnic groups. What is important to remember is how trends in affiliation created by differential birth rates, immigration, and religious switching will redirect religious participation and restructure religious beliefs in the coming decades.

Sectarian Protestants, Baptists, and Mormons make up an increasing share of the population that continues to hold religious identities; however, as chapter 2 showed, sectarian religion is not growing in the overall population. High birth rates have ensured that these groups have maintained their proportion in the population, while more moderate and liberal Protestant groups have a declining share of the religious market, and Catholics cling to market share because of an infusion of immigrants. The "growing" categories for identification are nondenominational Protestants (who tend to rank somewhere with moderate Protestants in terms of beliefs but are less active in religious organizations), other religious traditions (whose growth is enhanced by Asian immigration), and nonidentification. What this means is that *among those who are religious*, an increasing fraction are prone to high rates of religious participation, fundamentalist beliefs, an embrace of eternal punishment for others, and a strong faith in positive supernatural compensators in the form of an afterlife. Among those who cling to religious identities in the United States, a decreasing proportion identify with groups characterized by regular, respectable participation which would not interfere with other civic and social engagements; and fewer Americans who hold a religious identity embrace doubt about their gods, temper their beliefs about the divine sanction of the sacred texts, or embrace universalism instead of exclusivism regarding an afterlife and divine retribution. While the United States is not becoming more sectarian—in contrast to the common myth—American Protestantism is becoming more sectarian, more fundamentalist, and more exclusivist.

This chapter has shown that across five broad birth cohorts in the United States, religious participation, identification, and belief are on the wane. Fewer individuals are identifying with religious groups and participating in religious organizations, and it is not because they "believe but don't belong." Quite on the contrary, fewer Americans believe in the central tenets of the Christian tradition, which has dominated the American religious marketplace. An increasing proportion of Americans do not believe in a god, and younger cohorts are also more likely to see the Bible as a book of fables. Religious skepticism has always been present in the United States; however, it was hidden from view. Few skeptics had the courage to admit that they did not believe in the Bible or in god, and the vast majority of nonbelievers in older cohorts were compelled through social pressures to identify with (mostly Christian) religious groups and to participate in religious organizations. However, this situation has changed, and younger cohorts are freer to choose their attachments and to make their religious commitments fit their religious preferences. Believers will tend to retain the religious identities they forged in childhood socialization, but those whose preferred understandings of the supernatural do not fit the explanations sold by mostly Christian religious firms will defect. People who reject fundamentalism may find a home in a denomination which has less extremist interpretations of the faith, and people who no longer subscribe to beliefs in the supernatural will be free to exit the religious marketplace by rejecting religious identification.

There are three key trends impacting the future of religion in the United States: (1) the sectarianization of Protestantism, (2) the growth of nonidentification, and (3) the flowering of non-Christian religion. We have seen how these three trends influence religious behaviors and beliefs, and the next two chapters will show how religious identifications and beliefs influence other realms of social life, including family and sexuality, social stratification, and political commitments.

# 4

## Faith, Family, and Fortune

Religion and family are intimately connected in American society. Religious congregations and denominations rely on families for participation and to provide the next generation of members, while families enjoy the multigenerational context of congregations and the mutual reinforcement of diverse values and beliefs related to family and religion. Religion is a valued part of culture for many Americans, and families socialize children into religious beliefs and identifications and reinforce these commitments through multigenerational interactions (Sherkat 1998, 2003). Religious prescriptions and proscriptions, often enforced by tightly knit communities, influence how individuals and families generate their children's desire for supernatural goods, and religious organizations help mold the type of supernatural explanations that children find valuable. Religious movements make demands on those who bear their identities, and these demands influence sexual behavior, family formation, fertility, and childrearing. Further, the expectations placed on those who embrace religious identities often create conflicts with personal interests, which can have varied results. Religious influences on family are consequential for informing both family relations and stratification outcomes, such as educational and economic achievement. Indeed, religious factors play a strong role in the stratification of American society, and the values and commitments forged in the family channel the fortunes of adherents of the varied faiths (Darnell and Sherkat 1997; Fitzgerald and Glass 2008; Glass and Jacobs 2005; Keister 2003, 2007, 2008, 2011; Lehrer 1995, 1999a, 1999b; Read and Oselin 2008; Sherkat and Darnell 1999; Stryker 1981; Wilder and Walters 1998).

Conservative Christian commentators often amplify the "family values" embraced by members of exclusivist religious groups, and the values they identify as being "pro-family" advocate female subordination in family relations (W. B. Wilcox 2004), discourage nonmarital sex, and extoll the virtues of early marriage and high fertility (Regnerus 2009; Regnerus and Uecker 2011). Conservative Christians tend to present patriarchy as a solution to discordant family relations, to magnify the importance of incessantly monitoring children's activities to ensure obedience, and to maintain the necessity of using corporal punishment to ensure compliance with the will of the male-headed family (Bartkowski and Wilcox 2000; Ellison and Sherkat 1993a, 1993b; W. B. Wilcox 2004). Much of the authoritarian parenting style of conservative Christians increases the parental demands for women—who are typically charged with the task of monitoring and disciplining children. The end goal of this style of parenting is to shelter children from secular influences—directing children's cultural preferences, choices, and social networks (C. Smith 2003).

In contrast, secular people and universalistic religious organizations tend to amplify the value of egalitarianism in families—in which parents and children negotiate family relations. For universalistic religious groups, sexuality is usually viewed as a private concern between mutually supportive partners, and issues of sexuality and family life are governed by ethical principles, rather than being defined through the lens of ancient religious prescriptions and proscriptions. Religious liberals and secular people are thus more likely to support teaching young people about contraception and delaying marriage until people are old enough to enter into mature egalitarian relationships. Childbearing and sex are not strictly confined to marriage for individuals identifying with universalistic religious groups, and in the 21st century, most liberal Protestant denominations are comfortable with responsible premarital sex, including homosexuality. Divorce is also less stigmatized in universalistic denominations, and single-parent families are more welcome in universalistic religious groups. Of particular concern for secular people and those holding liberal religious identities is that marriage and childbearing should be delayed until after the completion of education and the attainment of employment. In more universalistic religious groups, education and employment are advocated for both men and women, rather than confining women to household tasks. Children are encouraged to think for themselves and to develop autonomy from parental direction (Ellison and Sherkat 1993b; Starks and Robinson 2005). And people of more universalistic religious identifications tend to eschew the use of violence as a childrearing technique (Ellison and Sherkat 1993a). These differences in childrearing orientations are a product of divergent views of human nature. While sectarians tend to view human nature as inherently corrupt and in need of monitoring and correction, religious liberals tend to view humans as basically good and capable of making the correct choices through their own free will (Ammerman 1997; Edgell 2005; Ellison and Sherkat 1993b).

Family factors have long-term consequences for life-course development and for status attainment. While conservative Christian commentators have argued that early marriage and wifely submission result in positive material benefits (Regnerus and Uecker 2011; W. B. Wilcox 2004), sociological studies consistently show that early marriage, female labor-force withdrawal, and high rates of fertility create friction within families and prevent individuals from attaining higher education, professional occupations, and robust household incomes (Booth and Edwards 1985; Cherlin 1992; Smock, Manning, and Gupta 1999). Faith impacts fortune in large part by influencing family and the management of sexuality (Civettini and Glass 2008; Fitzgerald and Glass 2012; Fitzgerald and Glass 2008; Glass and Nath 2006; Keister 2011; Lehrer 2004; Lehrer and Chiswick 1993).

## First Comes Sex: Religious Identification and Sexuality

Conservative Christian pundits are fond of amplifying the benefits of marriage and giving marriage primacy as a starting point for human intimate behavior. But in reality, most Americans have sex before they are married, and most Americans have sex with several different partners before settling into relatively monogamous relationships. Table 4.1 examines patterns of nonmarital sexual behavior by religious identification when growing up (origin) and current religious identification. Premarital sex is indicated by the proportion of never-married respondents who reported at least one sex partner in the past year—and overall, 75% of unmarried Americans had sex during the past year. There are substantial differences in rates of premarital sex by origin and current religious identification. People raised as Mormon or in other (non-Christian) religions have the lowest rates of premarital sex (though still

*Table 4.1. Sexual Behaviors by Origin and Current Religious Identification*

| Identification | Pre-marital sex, origin ident. | Pre-marital sex, current ident. | Extra-marital sex, origin ident. | Extra-marital sex, current ident. | Homo-sexual sex in past 5 years, origin | Homo-sexual sex in past 5 years, current |
|---|---|---|---|---|---|---|
| Mormon | 60.3% | 40.3% | 15.3% | 14.8% | 4.9% | 2.5% |
| Other religion | 65.1% | 70.8% | 12.7% | 21.1% | 3.4% | 8.4% |
| Liberal Protestant | 66.9% | 65.7% | 19.4% | 16.1% | 3.5% | 2.3% |
| Sectarian Protestant | 68.5% | 66.2% | 16.9% | 15.1% | 4.0% | 3.5% |
| Episcopalian | 69.1% | 71.8% | 18.0% | 17.5% | 5.7% | 7.4% |
| Lutheran | 68.6% | 68.6% | 16.8% | 14.1% | 4.1% | 3.2% |
| Moderate Protestant | 74.7% | 75.0% | 17.5% | 16.0% | 3.6% | 2.8% |
| Other Protestant | 77.0% | 69.8% | 20.1% | 20.6% | 4.9% | 3.5% |
| Catholic | 76.7% | 75.4% | 16.6% | 15.3% | 4.3% | 3.6% |
| Unitarian | 77.8% | 71.4% | 28.0% | 26.8% | 12.5% | 10.5% |
| Baptist | 78.2% | 78.7% | 19.5% | 19.3% | 3.6% | 2.7% |
| None | 78.8% | 80.6% | 19.2% | 25.0% | 4.7% | 7.0% |
| Jewish | 83.3% | 88.1% | 15.1% | 15.3% | 3.2% | 3.8% |
| Total | 75.1% | 75.1% | 17.7% | 17.7% | 4.1% | 4.1% |

over 60%), while those raised Jewish or without an identification have the highest rates (more than 83%). Current Mormons have the lowest rates of premarital sex (40%) and are the only identification for which less than half of unmarried respondents report having had sex in the past year.

Notably, sectarian Protestants are not particularly averse to having premarital sex—about two-thirds of unmarried sectarians report having had sex in the past year—and liberal Protestants are somewhat less likely to have had premarital sex than are sectarians and especially Baptists. However, the higher rates of premarital sex among Baptists are partly a function of high proportions of African Americans holding Baptist identification. Still, 70% of unmarried white Baptists report having sex in the past year, which is higher than the 65% found among white liberal Protestants. More than three-quarters of unmarried Catholics also report having had sex in the past year, and unmarried white Catholics were not substantially different from Catholics from other ethnicities, with about 74% reporting premarital sex in the past year.

Nearly 18% of married GSS respondents report having had sex with

someone other than their spouse while married. Religious identifications also seem to influence rates of extramarital sex, with Unitarians,
nonidentifiers, and people from other religions having higher rates of
extramarital sex. Lutherans, Mormons, sectarians, and Catholics have
the lowest rates of extramarital sex; however, growing up with those
identifications has less of an impact on marital infidelity. Respondents
raised with non-Christian identifications have the lowest rates of extramarital sex. People who originated in sectarian groups were about
average in their rates of marital infidelity, while Baptists were above
the mean.

The GSS also taps the sex of respondents' sex partners in the past five
years, and cross-classifying this statistic with respondents' sex enables
an estimate of rates of homosexual sex. Overall, 4.1% of GSS respondents report having had sex with someone of the same sex in the past
five years. Indeed, looking at religious identification at age sixteen, only
Unitarians stand out as having higher rates of homosexuality, at over
12%. Current identifications are quite different, with many LGBT people likely switching out of sectarian groups and Mormons and joining
more tolerant and affirming groups or rejecting religious identification.
While nearly 5% of respondents who grew up Mormon report having
had same-sex relations, only 2.5% of currently identified Mormons report homosexual behavior.

In contrast to the equivocal relationships between religious identifications and sexual behaviors, beliefs about sexuality follow a more familiar script—with sectarians, Baptists, and Mormons viewing nonmarital
sex as always wrong and Unitarians, nonidentifiers, Jews, and Episcopalians viewing nonmarital sexuality in a less harsh light (see table 4.2).
Since most people remain in their denomination of origin, values in
table 4.2 are presented for current religious identification. Only 28% of
Americans view premarital sex as always wrong, while more than half
of sectarians and Mormons think premarital sex is always wrong—even
though most unmarried sectarians and Mormons have had premarital
sex. In contrast, only 2% of Unitarians think premarital sex is wrong,
and less than 10% of Jews and those who have no religious identification
do. Indeed, only 21% of Catholics think premarital sex is always wrong.
Notably, since 1973, the proportion of Americans who view premarital

*Table 4.2. Sexual Attitudes by Religious Identification*

| Current identification | Premarital sex always wrong | Homosexual sex always wrong | Extramarital sex always wrong |
|---|---|---|---|
| Mormon | 57.2% | 85.5% | 91.2% |
| Sectarian Protestant | 55.1% | 87.4% | 88.9% |
| Baptist | 39.0% | 82.2% | 82.3% |
| Other Protestant | 32.9% | 66.3% | 80.8% |
| Moderate Protestant | 29.1% | 73.4% | 78.7% |
| Lutheran | 24.6% | 67.9% | 78.9% |
| Other religion | 21.4% | 47.7% | 66.1% |
| Liberal Protestant | 21.4% | 61.5% | 72.9% |
| Catholic | 20.9% | 61.4% | 76.2% |
| Episcopalian | 13.4% | 50.3% | 66.1% |
| Jewish | 9.4% | 27.7% | 52.6% |
| None | 6.8% | 33.2% | 57.1% |
| Unitarian | 2.3% | 11.2% | 39.4% |
| Total | 27.5% | 65.8% | 76.2% |

sex as always wrong has declined from 37% to 22% in 2012. Yet, in the GSS findings since 2010, 69% of Mormons, 53% of sectarians, and 38% of Baptists still regard premarital sex as always wrong.

Americans tend to disapprove of extramarital sex, and 76% of GSS respondents believe that extramarital sex is always wrong. Still, Mormons, sectarians, and Baptists are even more disapproving than other Americans, while Unitarians, nonidentifiers, Jews, and Episcopalians are less inclined to believe extramarital sex is always wrong. Unlike attitudes toward premarital sex, Americans' views on extramarital sex have not changed systematically over the nearly forty years of GSS data.

Religious differences are even larger for disapproval of homosexual sex, with over 82% of sectarians, Baptists, and Mormons saying that homosexuality is always wrong, while only 11% of Unitarians view homosexuality as always wrong. About half of Episcopalians and "other religion" identifiers think homosexuality is always wrong, while 33% of nonidentifiers and 28% of Jews hold this view. On average, 66% of GSS respondents regarded homosexuality as always wrong; however, this average is for the 1973–2012 cumulative data over time—in 1973, 73% of respondents believed homosexuality to be always wrong, while in 2012, this figure was down to 45%. Yet even with that trend, sectarians, Baptists, and Mormons remain distinctive (Loftus 2001; Sherkat et al. 2011). Indeed, for GSS respondents interviewed since 2010, 68% of Baptists,

78% of sectarians, and 70% of Mormons believe that homosexuality is always wrong, compared to 45% for other Americans.

Taken together, the findings from tables 4.1 and 4.2 reflect the considerable tension between exclusivist sectarian religiosity and the norms of sexuality in American society. Exclusivist identifications are not strongly associated with nonmarital sexual behaviors—premarital sex is very common for sectarians, Baptists, and Mormons, and they are about as likely as others to have extramarital affairs or sex with partners of the same sex. However, sectarian identifications are more tightly linked to holding moral approbation toward nonmarital sexuality—more than half of sectarians and Mormons view premarital sex as always wrong, even though more than half of the unmarried in these groups report having had sex in the past year. Further, as more and more Americans come to view premarital sex and homosexuality as unproblematic, exclusivist sects find themselves increasingly at odds with the prevailing moral sentiments of other Americans.

## Then Comes Marriage: Religious Identification and Marriage

Marriage is the social and political recognition of the bond between people which is part of what sustains and defines family. Religious groups have long held a formal stake in the definition of marriage and in granting formal recognition of family status—indeed, the definition of marriage and who may marry whom are potent political issues, as will be discussed in the next chapter. Most people marry, and religion often helps direct the choice of marriage partners (Sherkat 2004). Marriage across different faiths is fairly common in the United States; however, GSS respondents from nearly all religious identifications are more likely to marry someone who grew up in their own religious identification than to marry someone with a different identification (Sherkat 2004). Previous research has shown that the highest rates of religious homogamy are found among Jews, Catholics, Lutherans, and Baptists, while nonidentifiers, sectarians, and "other Protestants" have lower rates of religious homogamy (R. Johnson 1980; Sherkat 2004). Unfortunately, the GSS has not collected data on spouses' religious origins since 1994, so new insights regarding the structuring of intermarriage are unavailable.

*Table 4.3. Age of First Marriage by Gender and Religious Identification*

| Identification | Men, origin religion | Women, origin religion | Men, current religion | Women, current religion |
|---|---|---|---|---|
| Other religion | 26.5 | 22.7 | 25.1 | 21.9 |
| Jewish | 25.8 | 22.3 | 25.7 | 22.3 |
| Unitarian | 25.1 | 22.4 | 24.5 | 22.8 |
| Episcopalian | 25.0 | 22.0 | 25.3 | 22.0 |
| Lutheran | 24.4 | 21.6 | 24.3 | 21.6 |
| Catholic | 24.1 | 21.7 | 24.2 | 21.7 |
| Liberal Protestant | 24.0 | 21.6 | 24.0 | 21.9 |
| Moderate Protestant | 23.7 | 20.9 | 23.6 | 20.9 |
| None | 23.6 | 20.6 | 23.8 | 21.4 |
| Other Protestant | 23.3 | 20.7 | 23.6 | 20.7 |
| Baptist | 22.7 | 20.0 | 22.7 | 19.9 |
| Sectarian Protestant | 22.5 | 20.0 | 22.9 | 19.9 |
| Mormon | 22.3 | 20.1 | 22.4 | 20.3 |
| Total | 23.7 | 21.0 | 23.7 | 21.0 |

Religious identifications also help to determine the timing of marriage. Conservative Christians often amplify a "pro-family" message which advocates early marriage in order to prevent nonmarital sex (Regnerus and Uecker 2011). In contrast, secular people and more universalistic religious groups see mutual fulfillment and mature egalitarian relationships as being the goal of marriage, and such unions are often seen as impossible early in the life course as people strive to complete education and begin careers. Table 4.3 tracks the age of first marriage for men and women by religious identifications. Once again, the uniqueness of exclusivist sectarian identifications is manifest, with Mormons, sectarians, and Baptists having the youngest ages of marriage for both men and women. Indeed, the average sectarian and Baptist woman married as a teenager, while the average age is about twenty-two for most of the more universalistic groups. A similar pattern holds for men, with sectarians marrying before age twenty-three, while Jewish, other non-Christian, and Episcopalian men marry at age twenty-five or over on average. Notably, Catholic men and women marry at ages quite similar to what is found among liberal and moderate Protestants, with men marrying at twenty-four and women marrying at twenty-two.

The average age of marriage is not a very useful statistic when using cross-sectional data since it lumps together respondents of varied ages, some of whom have not yet married (and some who never will).

Further, different ethnicities have varied propensities toward marriage, and the age of marriage has also increased across cohorts. To take these factors into account, models can estimate the effect of religious identifications on the rate of marriage while controlling for ethnicity, gender, and cohort (see table 4.4). The effects of identifications are compared to the rate of marriage found among people with no religious identification, and the ordering of these rates reflects how much higher the rate of marriage is for people who identify compared to those who do not. Marriage rates for people growing up sectarian are 52% higher than for people who had no identification at age sixteen, while the rates are 68% higher for Baptists and 75% greater for Mormons. The differences are even more pronounced when estimates are based on current identifications—Mormons have nearly double the rate of marriage when compared to nonidentifiers, and the rate of marriage for Baptists is 95% higher. In any given year, sectarians are also 87% more likely to marry than are people with no religious identification. All the religious identifications have a significantly higher rate of marriage when compared to current nonidentifiers, though growing up without an identification slows marriage rates less. Rates of marriage are roughly similar for Catholics, Episcopalians, and liberal Protestants. Jews, Unitarians, and other non-Christians have lower rates of marriage than do most religious groups.

*Table 4.4. Marriage Rate by Religious Identification*

| Identification | Marriage rate, origin religion | Marriage rate, current religion |
|---|---|---|
| Mormon | 1.748 | 2.205 |
| Baptist | 1.682 | 1.954 |
| Sectarian Protestant | 1.519 | 1.869 |
| Lutheran | 1.474 | 1.807 |
| Moderate Protestant | 1.435 | 1.666 |
| Liberal Protestant | 1.421 | 1.677 |
| Unitarian | 1.385 ns | 1.358 |
| Other religion | 1.364 | 1.294 |
| Episcopalian | 1.352 | 1.624 |
| Catholic | 1.322 | 1.606 |
| Jewish | 1.175 | 1.445 |
| Other Protestant | 1.098 | 1.449 |
| None | 1.000 | 1.000 |

ns = not significant at .05 level, two tailed

### Maybe with Children: Religious Identification and Fertility

Virtually all the major religious traditions can be interpreted as having a pronatalist message, and a family consisting of a heterosexual couple with several children is touted as the traditional ideal by conservative Christians, who tend to dominate American religious discourse on the family (Edgell 2005; W. B.Wilcox 2004). Religion plays a strong role in structuring fertility expectations and outcomes (Lehrer 1996, 1999a, 2004; Pearce 2002, 2010); Pearce and Thornton 2007; Sherkat 2010c), and table 4.5 examines how religious identifications influence family size and the rate of first births—the age at which people first start having children. To get a more accurate picture of the relationship between family size and religious identification, it is useful to examine the total number of children for women age forty-five and older. This gives a more accurate picture with cross-sectional data, since younger respondents may not have completed their fertility at the time of interview.

Mormon women are tops in total fertility, averaging nearly four children for both origin and current Mormons. Indeed, Mormons even outdistance Baptists and other sectarians by a full child, and the

Table 4.5. Completed Female Fertility and Rates of First Birth by Religious Identification

| Identification | Number of children, origin religion | Number of children, current religion | Rate of first birth, origin religion | Rate of first birth, current religion |
|---|---|---|---|---|
| Mormon | 3.8 | 3.7 | 1.32 | 1.78 |
| Baptist | 2.8 | 2.9 | 1.33 | 1.64 |
| Sectarian Protestant | 2.7 | 2.9 | 1.39 | 1.71 |
| Catholic | 2.6 | 2.7 | 1.02 | 1.28 |
| Moderate Protestant | 2.6 | 2.5 | 1.10 | 1.38 |
| None | 2.5 | 1.9 | 1.00 | 1.00 |
| Other Protestant | 2.5 | 2.4 | 1.12 | 1.31 |
| Lutheran | 2.4 | 2.5 | .99 | 1.31 |
| Liberal Protestant | 2.3 | 2.3 | .92 | 1.16 |
| Episcopalian | 2.2 | 2.2 | .73 | .99 |
| Other religion | 2.2 | 2.1 | .88 | 1.01 |
| Unitarian | 2.1 | 1.9 | .93 | .92 |
| Jewish | 2.0 | 2.0 | .70 | .92 |
| Total | 2.6 | 2.6 | — | — |

Controlling for ethnicity, rural, Southern, and cohort.

completed fertility for current Mormons is nearly *twice* that of Jews, Unitarians, nonidentifiers, and other non-Christians. Fertility plays a profound role in the growth of the Latter-Day Saints, and it also contributes substantially to the growth of other exclusivist sects. Both Baptists and sectarians have a greater-than-average number of children, while Catholic fertility is average. Episcopalians and liberal Protestants have lower rates of fertility than average. Interestingly, growing up with no religious identification has no real impact on women's subsequent fertility; however, women with no current religious identification have substantially fewer children than average.

Number of children is one way of looking at fertility, but the timing of childbirth is also important. People who have children when they are young are more likely to fail to attain higher education, they are more likely to obtain manual or unskilled jobs, and they are less likely to be able to take advantage of economic opportunities (Keister 2011). Further, studies consistently show that younger parents have more stress and fewer resources, produce poor childrearing outcomes, and are more likely to divorce (Booth and Edwards 1985; Card and Wise 1978; Cherlin 1992). Table 4.5 shows that Mormons, Baptists, and sectarians have the highest rates of first birth (calculated as the age at first birth in years, relative to nonidentifiers, with respondents with no children censored in the proportional hazards model), even after controls for gender, ethnicity, cohort, region, and residential size. Respondents who grew up with no religious identification actually have higher rates of first birth when compared to many of the universalistic religious groups. Indeed, respondents who grew up Jewish are 41% less likely to have a birth in a given year when compared to nonidentifiers. This changes when we examine rates for people with no current identification, who have basically the same rate of first birth as Episcopalians, Unitarians, Jews, and other non-Christians. Catholics have their first children on par with moderate Protestants and Lutherans. Notably, as is the case with most of the family indicators, there is a perceptible "middle" of the demographic distribution which is filled by Catholics, Lutherans, and moderate Protestants—more universalistic groups have lower fertility and later ages of marriage, while more exclusivist sectarian groups have more children and have children at earlier ages.

*Table 4.6. Age at First Birth by Gender and Religious Identification*

| Identification | Men, origin religion | Women, origin religion | Men, current religion | Women, current religion |
|---|---|---|---|---|
| Baptist | 23.7 | 21.3 | 23.9 | 21.3 |
| Sectarian Protestant | 24.3 | 21.7 | 24.5 | 21.6 |
| Mormon | 24.2 | 21.7 | 24.1 | 22.0 |
| Other Protestant | 25.0 | 22.4 | 25.1 | 22.9 |
| None | 25.4 | 22.2 | 25.3 | 22.4 |
| Moderate Protestant | 25.7 | 22.6 | 25.3 | 22.6 |
| Lutheran | 26.1 | 23.2 | 26.2 | 22.9 |
| Catholic | 25.8 | 23.4 | 25.9 | 23.5 |
| Liberal Protestant | 26.5 | 24.4 | 27.1 | 24.6 |
| Unitarian | 27.6 | 25.9 | 27.6 | 25.8 |
| Other religion | 27.7 | 24.0 | 26.4 | 23.2 |
| Episcopalian | 27.9 | 24.6 | 27.6 | 24.6 |
| Jewish | 29.3 | 26.3 | 29.2 | 25.9 |
| Total | 25.4 | 22.7 | 25.4 | 22.7 |

Table 4.6 separates men and women to examine the age of first birth controlling for cohort, region, rural residence, and ethnicity. In general, the findings mirror those in table 4.5, with exclusivist groups having children early in the life course and universalistic groups postponing childrearing. It is notable that the difference between sectarians and more universalistic respondents in the timing of first births encompasses crucial ages for educational and occupational attainment, particularly for women. On average, liberal Protestants, Jews, other non-Christians, Unitarians, and Episcopalians are having children in their late twenties for men (twenty-seven to twenty-nine) and in the mid-twenties for women (twenty-four to twenty-six). In contrast, Mormons, sectarians, and Baptists are having children when they are about twenty-four for men and under twenty-two for women. The average woman who grew up in or currently identifies with an exclusivist sect has a child by the time she turns twenty-two—the conventional age of college graduation. In contrast, the average Jewish or Unitarian woman has her first child at twenty-six, a year after the conventional age for graduating from law school.

Another distinctive trait of exclusivist religious groups is their advocacy of unyielding obedience, aversion to free thinking, and embrace of physical violence to enforce their will. The family is the arena where this characteristic of exclusivist religious identifications plays out most prominently. Exclusivist religious groups amplify the value of obedience in children, while downplaying the desire for children who think for themselves (Ellison and Sherkat 1993a, 1993b; Starks and Robinson 2005). Table 4.7 shows that over 30% of sectarians and 28% of Baptists value obedience in children over all other values. In contrast, only 9% of nonidentifiers, 7% of Jews, and less than 2% of Unitarians give primacy to obedience. Similarly, while over 60% of Episcopalians, Jews, liberal Protestants, and nonidentifiers rank "thinking for yourself" the most valuable trait in children, only 40% of Baptists and 37% of sectarians valued this most highly—well below the average of 50% for all Americans.

Not only do exclusivist sectarians demand obedience in children, but they also believe that obedience should be enforced through physical punishment: 39% of Baptists and sectarians strongly believe that "sometimes a child needs a good hard spanking." This figure is substantially higher than the national average of 27%, and less than 8% of Unitarians and 15% of Jews hold this view. Notably, Catholics and Mormons are below the national average in support for corporal punishment, with 22% and 21%, respectively, supporting violent correction—nearly the same as liberal Protestants, nonidentifiers, other non-Christians, Lutherans, and Episcopalians.

*Table 4.7. Childrearing Orientations by Religious Identification*

| Current identification | Obey first | Think for self first | Strongly favor spanking |
|---|---|---|---|
| Sectarian Protestant | 30.2% | 37.5% | 38.9% |
| Baptist | 28.0% | 40.0% | 38.6% |
| Moderate Protestant | 20.5% | 49.8% | 31.1% |
| Mormon | 17.4% | 46.5% | 21.3% |
| Other Protestant | 17.4% | 49.1% | 29.2% |
| Catholic | 15.8% | 48.4% | 21.5% |
| Lutheran | 15.4% | 57.1% | 20.7% |
| Other religion | 13.5% | 52.4% | 21.8% |
| Episcopalian | 12.4% | 64.1% | 18.5% |
| Liberal Protestant | 12.4% | 61.1% | 21.2% |
| None | 9.0% | 59.5% | 21.2% |
| Jewish | 7.0% | 67.2% | 14.5% |
| Unitarian | 1.6% | 73.8% | 7.8% |
| Total | 18.5% | 49.5% | 27.2% |

## Until We Part: Religious Identification and Divorce

Divorce is the social and political recognition of the dissolution of a marriage. Most religious traditions are quite uncomfortable with marital dissolution, and it is proscribed for members of many exclusivist sects and for Roman Catholics who wish to hold fealty with the church. Divorce rates have declined in the United States over the past three decades, after a surge of divorce in the previous two decades in the mid-20th century. Still, one in five GSS respondents report that they have been divorced or separated, and religious identification plays an important role in the structuring of divorce.

Table 4.8 presents the percentage of respondents in each religious identification who have ever had a divorce, by origin and current identification. Looking first at identifications growing up, Unitarians have the highest rate with 29% (though there were only thirty-eight respondents who were raised Unitarian who were asked this particular question); Baptists and sectarians follow close behind with over a quarter of respondents who grew up Baptist experiencing divorce and 24% of other sectarians. Other non-Christians and Jews have the lowest rates of divorce, at 12% and 14%, followed by Catholics at 16%. For current

*Table 4.8. Rate of Divorce and Marital Happiness by Religious Identification*

| Identification | Ever divorced, origin religion | Ever divorced, current religion | Divorce rate, origin religion | Divorce rate, current religion | Marital happiness |
|---|---|---|---|---|---|
| Unitarian | 29.0% | 19.4% | 2.306 | .740 | 65.0% |
| Baptist | 25.6% | 24.9% | 1.567 | 1.124 | 63.0% |
| Sectarian Protestant | 23.9% | 23.4% | 1.413 | 1.052 | 64.2% |
| Other Protestant | 22.8% | 26.4% | 1.166 | .976 | 64.7% |
| None | 22.6% | 25.4% | 1.000 | 1.000 | 57.5% |
| Moderate Protestant | 22.2% | 21.3% | 1.225 | .848 | 64.5% |
| Episcopalian | 21.1% | 21.1% | 1.194 | .863 | 67.9% |
| Mormon | 20.0% | 19.5% | 1.162 | .955 | 69.4% |
| Liberal Protestant | 18.0% | 16.8% | .951 | .680 | 68.3% |
| Lutheran | 16.9% | 17.8% | .861 | .739 | 62.8% |
| Catholic | 15.8% | 13.8% | .757 | .521 | 62.7% |
| Jewish | 13.6% | 14.5% | .680 | .527 | 68.7% |
| Other religion | 12.4% | 21.1% | .689 | .883 | 63.2% |
| Total | 20.2% | 20.1% | — | — | 63.5% |

identifications, the picture looks much the same, except for the lower rate of divorce among Unitarians (likely because of the larger pool of respondents) and an increasing proportion of divorced and separated respondents among non-Christians. Notably, the divorce rate among current Catholics is under 14%—reflecting the defection of divorced respondents from Catholicism.

Because these proportions are systematically related to the age of individuals (many married people or unmarried people will eventually divorce, and younger respondents have not been observed for the same amount of time as older respondents), proportional hazards models are estimated both to take into account the duration of observation and to control for generations, gender, ethnicity, region, and rural residence. The ordering of the rate of divorce, relative to nonidentifiers, is remarkably similar to what we find with the simple proportions, with Jews and Catholics having substantially lower rates than people with no religious identification, while sectarians and Baptists have higher rates of divorce than people with no religious affiliation. Net of ethnicity and other controls, Baptists are 12% more likely than nonidentifiers to divorce in a given year, while other sectarians have a 5% greater risk of divorce. All other current religious identifications have lower rates of divorce than the nonidentifiers (or Baptists and sectarians).

Conservative Christian activists often claim that there is a "civilizing" influence of religion on marital relations and argue that clearly defined gender roles create happy marriages through the generation of an "enchanted sense of gratitude" in marital relations (W. B. Wilcox 2004), but careful analyses of high-quality data show otherwise. Exclusivist religious traditions generate marital conflict through their inegalitarian marital relations, and when combined with early marriage, high fertility, and economic insecurity, this is often a recipe for divorce (Keister 2011). Further, despite the claims of blissful patriarchal marriages, sectarian Christians do not report having happier marriages —despite the strong social-desirability biases that should make them more likely to report happy marriages than people with more universalistic identifications are. Indeed, religious identifications are mostly unrelated to marital happiness, as table 4.8 shows. Only 0.3% of the variation in marital happiness is explained by religious identification, and a careful inspection of the relationship shows that most of this is a function of nonidentifiers tending to say they are "pretty happy" with their marriages instead of "very happy."

## Teach Your Children? Well . . .

Families socialize children to fulfill social roles according to the cultural expectations of parents and important others connected to them in social groups. These connections are structured by a variety of factors, including social class, region, linguistic communities, and religion. Religious identifications matter for structuring commitments to the development of human capital and to how human capital should be used (Darnell and Sherkat 1997; Keister 2003, 2007, 2011; Sherkat and Darnell 1999). In the United States, exclusivist sectarian religious groups have encouraged particular patterns of life-course development, childrearing orientations, opposition to education, and aversion to many lucrative occupations. American Catholics and Jews also hold particular orientations toward both family relations and educational attainment and occupational advancement. As we have seen, sectarian Christians value obedience in children over autonomy, and they reinforce this orientation with harsh parenting practices, in contrast to more universalist groups, which value autonomy and teach children to think for themselves (Ellison and Sherkat 1993a, 1993b; Starks and Robinson 2005). These orientations have consequences, as cultural preferences come to structure a variety of network entanglements and intersect with family trajectories to help structure the most important variable aspect of status attainment—educational achievement.

Religious opposition to secular education has been a longstanding issue; however, until the mid-20th century, the fights were purely internecine—with Catholics, Jews, Mormons, and some other sects fighting it out with liberal Protestant elites for control over what were often blatantly Protestant curricula promulgated by public schools. The Catholic solution was to create a separate school system and to counter Protestant dominance with an explicitly Catholic education. On the whole, this effort was quite successful, and Catholic schooling continues to be a springboard for status attainment (Keister 2007, 2011). More recently, in response to the elimination of Christian themes in public education in the 1960s and to mandatory racial integration, sectarian Christians have also begun to develop a network of alternative schools from kindergarten through graduate school. However, sectarian private schools are not on the same plane as the Catholic school system, and their development requires considerable resources from the families of students and other coreligionists. In families with few resources and many children, sectarian Christian private schooling is unattainable. Many activists now tout "homeschooling" as an alternative to public or religious schools (Kunzman 2009), yet few devotees who desire such educational instruction for their offspring are qualified to teach their children well.

Religious identifications have strong influences on educational attainment and particularly postsecondary educational attainment (Darnell and Sherkat 1997; Sherkat and Darnell 1999). Across generations, the impact of exclusivist Christianity often led sectarians to eschew all but primary school education—which also fit their modal occupational trajectory as unskilled agrarian workers (Sherkat 2012). During the 20th century, formal requirements for education through high school were implemented, the agricultural sector became more mechanized, and even unskilled occupations began to require a high school diploma as evidence of basic knowledge and devotion to tasks. High school graduation rates for sectarian Christians rose markedly in the late 20th century—67% of Baptists and other sectarians failed to graduate from high school in the generations born prior to 1925, and this figure improves to just 15% for Baptists and 20% for other sectarians in the more recent cohorts. Some commentators claim that educational attainment among sectarians is on the rise and that differences have disappeared (Beyerlein 2004); however, more systematic analyses reveal that sectarians and Baptists have considerable deficits when compared to people who hold other religious identifications (Massengill 2008; Sherkat 2010c). Research has also shown that sectarians tend to track themselves into vocational and technical curricula in high school and to avoid coursework which provides a foundation for postsecondary attainment (Darnell and Sherkat 1997; Sherkat and Darnell 1999). As a consequence, while college-degree attainment has become more common for many Americans, sectarians have been left behind.

Figure 4.1 presents the proportion of college graduates by religious identification and gender, controlling for cohort, ethnicity, region, and rural residence. The contrasts at the poles of the figure are striking: over

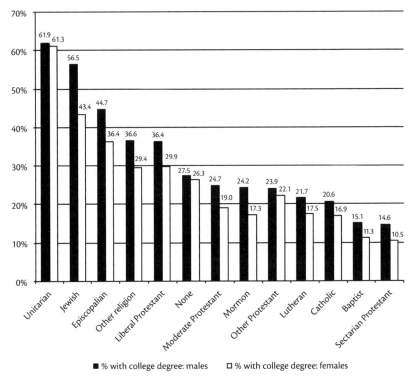

Fig. 4.1. Adjusted proportion of college graduates by gender and religious identification

61% of Unitarian men and women are college graduates—nearly six times higher than the rate of attainment for sectarian women (10.5%) or Baptist women (11.3%) and four times as high as is found among sectarian and Baptist men.

Religious identifications influence gender differences in educational attainment, and while contemporary studies show that women are now outpacing men in college-degree attainment, for most GSS respondents, this was not true in their generation or when they were interviewed. Religious identifications with high rates of college-degree attainment have a larger gap between men and women, favoring men. The exceptions are among Unitarians and the nonidentifiers, for whom there are only slight gender differences in degree attainment. The gender gap in college attainment for Jews is over 13%, which is higher than the total graduation rate for Baptist and sectarian women. Gender gaps are around 8% for Episcopalians and about 7% for Mormons, other non-Christians, and liberal Protestants, and they are somewhat smaller for moderate Protestants, Lutherans, and Catholics. While gender gaps in education may be higher among some of the more universalistic religious groups, educational attainment for women is substantially higher when compared with more exclusivist sectarian groups. While only 11% of Baptist and sectarian women hold a college degree, 30% of women who identify with liberal Protestant groups and 36% who embrace an Episcopalian identification hold college degrees; 61% of women who identify as Unitarian hold college degrees, as do 43% of Jewish women.

Overall, it is clear that there are substantial differences in educational attainment across religious identifications, but many commentators have claimed that the status ordering of denominations is becoming more fluid (Beyerlein 2004; Hunter 1991; Wuthnow 1988). Table 4.9 presents college-degree attainment across generations and religious identification. Overall, rates of college graduation rates were much lower in the generations born prior to 1925, and only Unitarians are over 50%. Notably, Jews from this generation fall behind Episcopalians and nonidentifiers in their rates of college graduation—likely because of recent immigration and discrimination against Jews for admission to college. Under 5% of Baptists and sectarians born prior to 1925 hold a

Table 4.9. College-Degree Attainment by Religious Identification and Generation

| Current identification | Pre-1925 cohort | 1925–1943 cohort | 1944–1955 cohort | 1956–1970 cohort | 1971–1994 cohort |
|---|---|---|---|---|---|
| Unitarian | 60.0% | 71.4% | 66.7% | 66.7% | — |
| Episcopalian | 26.9% | 41.4% | 50.0% | 54.0% | 55.6% |
| None | 23.3% | 33.0% | 38.6% | 30.3% | 29.5% |
| Jewish | 23.2% | 54.4% | 70.4% | 67.2% | 72.2% |
| Liberal Protestant | 19.3% | 36.4% | 40.7% | 45.5% | 48.9% |
| Mormon | 16.7% | 18.8% | 27.8% | 28.5% | 25.6% |
| Other religion | 11.1% | 34.7% | 45.9% | 36.2% | 48.7% |
| Moderate Protestant | 10.8% | 18.2% | 28.1% | 27.7% | 35.4% |
| Other Protestant | 10.7% | 20.0% | 28.0% | 29.0% | 28.8% |
| Catholic | 7.7% | 17.9% | 26.8% | 27.4% | 30.5% |
| Lutheran | 7.5% | 17.2% | 26.7% | 30.0% | 42.5% |
| Baptist | 4.8% | 9.2% | 14.9% | 15.1% | 21.1% |
| Sectarian Protestant | 3.5% | 10.1% | 12.3% | 17.4% | 16.4% |
| Total | 10.2% | 19.7% | 27.8% | 27.3% | 30.1% |

college degree. In the generations since the baby boom, Jewish attainment exceeds even Unitarians and is over 72% among those born after 1970 (considering only respondents who were over age twenty-five at the time of interview in this cohort). While Baptists and sectarians have increased their rates of college attainment, the progress has been slow. Only 21% of Baptists and 16% of sectarians born after 1970 hold a college degree—compared to 49% of liberal Protestants and 56% of Episcopalians. While some scholars have argued that the "middle" has collapsed in American Protestantism (Sullins 1993), the GSS data show that once again moderate Protestants and Lutherans do indeed constitute a distinctive "middle class" between low-achieving sectarians and high-achieving liberal Protestants. Catholic attainment is somewhat lower than what is found among moderate Protestants and Lutherans —and we will see later in this chapter that ethnicity plays a strong role in the positioning of Catholics in the status hierarchy.

Notably, the educational stratification of religious identifications cuts across ethnicity. While many researchers lump together all African American Protestants, table 4.10 demonstrates why that strategy is ill suited to understanding the impact of religious identifications. Across all ethnicities, sectarian Protestants and Baptists have lower rates of college-degree attainment than do liberal Protestants, Episcopalians, nonidentifiers, Jews, other non-Christians, and even moderate Protestants and Lutherans. Ignoring African American Protestant diversity is particularly problematic. In chapter 1, we saw that almost 19% of African Americans identify with moderate Protestant groups (most of them being Methodists); African Americans who identify with these groups have almost double the rate of college graduation when compared with sectarians, and their rate of degree attainment is almost 50% higher than the rate charted by Baptists. Differences are even greater for the 3% of African Americans identifying with the liberal Protestants, Episcopalians, and Lutherans—taken together, a quarter of the African American respondents from these identities hold college degrees, compared to less than 7% for African American sectarians and under 9% of African American Baptists. Table 4.10 shows that African American sectarians are more educationally disadvantaged relative to both African American liberal Protestants and moderate Protestants than are western European sectarians. Among African

*Table 4.10. College-Degree Attainment by Religious Identification and Ethnicity*

| Current identification | Native American | Western European | Eastern European | Asian | African American | Latin American |
|---|---|---|---|---|---|---|
| Unitarian | 0% | 65.4% | 12.5% | 0% | 50.0% | 0% |
| Jewish | 50.0% | 46.6% | 49.3% | 38.5% | 5.9% | 44.4% |
| Episcopalian | 6.7% | 42.2% | 40.5% | 50.0% | 27.4% | 33.3% |
| Liberal Protestant | 22.5% | 34.6% | 27.8% | 55.6% | 23.7% | 23.1% |
| Other religion | 17.0% | 33.5% | 36.3% | 56.7% | 14.5% | 28.6% |
| None | 5.9% | 31.7% | 39.3% | 59.5% | 10.5% | 11.5% |
| Other Protestant | 7.8% | 25.3% | 32.0% | 56.4% | 19.9% | 13.3% |
| Moderate Protestant | 9.7% | 23.7% | 22.7% | 50.0% | 12.4% | 9.5% |
| Mormon | 14.3% | 22.8% | 14.3% | 40.0% | 7.1% | 14.3% |
| Catholic | 8.9% | 22.3% | 18.4% | 42.5% | 16.3% | 8.9% |
| Lutheran | 8.6% | 19.7% | 15.6% | 18.8% | 20.8% | 11.8% |
| Baptist | 5.3% | 14.5% | 14.7% | 32.4% | 8.6% | 12.1% |
| Sectarian Protestant | 7.0% | 13.1% | 22.0% | 34.1% | 6.6% | 6.0% |
| Total | 7.8% | 23.8% | 27.6% | 50.2% | 10.9% | 9.7% |

Americans, the odds of having a college degree are 3.6 times higher for liberal Protestants and 1.9 times higher for moderate Protestants when compared to sectarians, while among western Europeans, the odds are 2.6 times greater for liberal Protestants and 1.8 times higher for moderate Protestants.

Asians' and Latin Americans' educational achievements also suffer when they adhere to sectarian and Baptist religious identities. While of 50% of Asian respondents hold a college degree, only 34% of Asian sectarians and 32% of Asian Baptists are college graduates. Almost 60% of Asians who do not hold a religious identification are college graduates. This statistic conflicts with the commonly articulated narrative that Asian American Christians are academically superior and that religion plays a role in their assimilation and success (Busto 1996; Park and Ecklund 2007). Latin American Catholics have lower rates of educational attainment than do most Protestants—the exception being sectarians —and nearly 10% of Latinos hold sectarian identifications.

Overall, for college-degree attainment, the GSS data show that the stratification hierarchy of American religion is relatively unchanged across generations, despite overall increases in degree attainment. Further, the GSS data show that religious identifications operate in a similar fashion across varied ethnic groups.

## Religious Identification, Occupational Attainment, and Intergenerational Mobility

Attaining a college degree enables people to obtain employment in occupations which tend to have higher remuneration and benefits, greater job security, and safer and more comfortable working conditions. Because occupations are radically diverse in modern societies, sociologists often focus on two classes of occupations—professional occupations (medicine, law, management, education, finance, technology, and the like) and nonprofessional occupations (clerical, manual, agrarian, and such). Presented alongside professional careers is labor-market exit, which can disrupt career trajectories leading to promotion, income growth, and job stability (Keister 2011; Sherkat 2012). The most prominent form of labor-market exit is housewifery, which has been linked strongly to religious identifications (Lehrer 1999a, 2004; Sherkat 2000, 2012).

Figure 4.2 charts the proportion of respondents who hold professional occupations and the proportion of women who report being housewives by current religious identification. Not surprisingly, the proportion of respondents who hold professional occupations follows the religious profile found for college-degree attainment—since most professional occupations require members to hold a college degree. Nearly two-thirds of Unitarians and Jews and 56% of Episcopalians hold professional occupations—and about half of those who hold liberal Protestant identifications or who identify with other non-Christian groups are in professional jobs. In contrast, only 30% of Baptists and sectarians work in professional occupations. There is also a substantial "middle" stratum of religious identifications where between 44% and 36% hold professional occupations, and these include nonidentifiers, other Protestants, moderate Protestants, Lutherans, Mormons, and Catholics.

Figure 4.2 also shows that women's housewifery increases as professional employment decreases. The adjusted proportions for professional occupational attainment take into account gender differences, so differences across identifications are not simply a function of differential rates of female labor-force exit. In general, rates of housewifery are not as different across religious identifications, ranging from 20% of

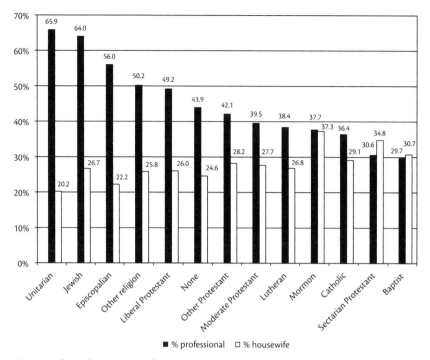

Fig. 4.2. Adjusted proportion of respondents in professional occupations and women who are housewives by current religious identification

Unitarian women to about 38% of Mormon women. What seems most interesting in figure 4.2 is that more exclusivist religious groups have a smaller gap between the proportion of respondents holding professional occupations and the proportion of women who are housewives. For nearly all religious identifications, there are more professionals than the proportion of housewives; however, for Mormons, the proportion is roughly the same, and both Baptists and other sectarians have proportionately more housewives than professionals. Notably, sectarians and Baptists are not appreciably different in their rates of housewifery when compared to Jews, other non-Christians, other Protestants, moderate Protestants, or Catholics. What seems likely, however, is that the rationale for labor-force exit differs across religious identifications. Among people with more universalistic religious identifications, women may exit the labor force because their partner earns a substantial income from professional employment, thus allowing them to invest in child care (Lehrer 1999a, 2004). In contrast, women holding more exclusivist religious identifications are implored to shun careers because of their interpretations of sacralized gender roles in the family, and labor-force exit is not offset by high levels of resources available to the family—as will be shown later by examining household income.

Stratification is connected to family in large part because parents pass on resources of income, wealth, and education which enable children to attain similar standards of living as their parents. Much of the sociological literature on stratification concerns itself with mobility —moving up or down compared to one's upbringing. The GSS enables some investigation of this phenomenon, though sample sizes and the limitations of occupational data across the four decades of the GSS requires some lumping together of religious identifications and a focus on father-to-son mobility.

Figure 4.3 summarizes GSS findings on upward and downward mobility by comparing origin religious identifications to white men who grew up with sectarian Protestant identifications, with Baptists and other sectarians considered together (for a more detailed analysis of occupational attainment and mobility by religious identification, see Sherkat 2012). We focus here on two oppositional processes—upward mobility, defined as a man whose father held a nonprofessional occupation attaining a professional job, and (2) downward mobility, when a man whose father held a professional occupation holds a nonprofessional occupation. Perhaps not surprisingly, given sectarian Protestants' low rates of educational attainment, they are the least likely to be upwardly mobile when compared to all other religious identifications. Catholic men with fathers in manual occupations are 36% more likely to become professionals when compared to sectarians, and similar differences are found for moderate Protestants (combining Lutherans with other moderates), "other religion" identifiers, and nonidentifiers. In general, men who identify as sectarian Protestants are more than 40% more likely to be stuck in manual occupations if they grew up in working-class families. Upward mobility is substantially higher for liberal Protestants (combining Episcopalians and other liberals) and especially Jews. Men who grew up in working-class liberal Protestant families are nearly three times as likely to hold professional occupations when compared to men who grew up in sectarian families—and for Jewish men,

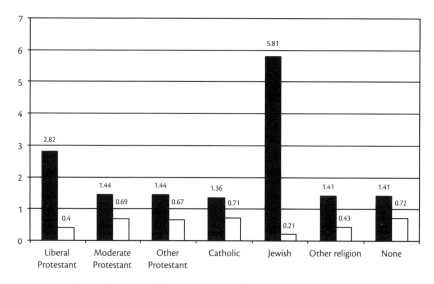

Fig. 4.3. Intergenerational occupational mobility by religious identification for white men

the rate of upward mobility is nearly six times higher than for sectarian men.

Downward mobility is an understudied process in sociology, particularly since current estimates show that downward mobility is 31% more common than upward mobility is (Sherkat 2012). Conservative Christian commentators often dismiss claims about the negative stratification consequences of exclusivist religion by pointing to the fact that sectarians very often come from hardscrabble backgrounds (Smith and Emerson 1998). However, figure 4.3 shows that even when white sectarian men grow up in households where the father holds a professional occupation, they are substantially less likely to join the ranks of professionals as an adult. The odds of downward mobility are 30% higher among sectarian men than among men who grow up identifying as moderate Protestant, other Protestant, or Catholic or who had no identification. Compared to liberal Protestants and other non-Christians, sectarian men have 60% greater odds of downward mobility. Put another way, sectarian men are more than twice as likely to fall out of the professional occupational class as are liberal Protestants and non-Christians. Jewish men with professional fathers are unlikely to join the ranks of clerical and manual workers, and they are roughly five times less likely to be downwardly mobile when compared to sectarian men.

## The Meek Shall Inherit Nothing: Religious Identification and Income

Occupations matter in part because they pay different salaries. Income is strongly related to a variety of positive outcomes, including life satisfaction, happiness, and marital stability (Dynan and Ravina 2007; Easterlin 2001; Frijters, Haisken-DeNew, and Shields 2004; Tzeng and Mare 1995), and figure 4.4 shows that religious identifications help to structure income stratification as well. Figure 4.4 limits the analyses to married respondents and present household incomes in constant 2012 dollars. Because religious factors are tied to fertility and therefore household size, it is instructive to look at income stratification per member of the household as well as total household earnings, which are also charted in figure 4.4.

Not surprisingly, religious identifications pattern the distribution of income in much the same way that they do educational and occupational attainment—with Unitarians, Jews, Episcopalians, and liberal Protestants having the highest income, while sectarians, Baptists, and Mormons have the lowest household incomes for married families. Household incomes for sectarian married couples are slightly more than half that found among Unitarians, and Unitarian households enjoy more than twice as much income per member when compared to sectarians or Baptists. The household incomes of married Episcopalians, liberal Protestants, and nonidentifiers give them between $880 to $355 more income *per month per household member* when compared to sectarians, and the difference is slightly larger for Baptists. This is a very sizeable gap in the availability of resources for family members. Indeed, another very interesting finding in figure 4.4 is that Catholics, and to a lesser extent Lutherans, have relatively high incomes per family member. While Catholics lag behind liberal Protestants in total household income by almost $10,000 per year, they are virtually even in their incomes per household member. This helps explain why Catholics have achieved parity with mainline Protestants with regard to wealth accumulation (Keister 2007, 2011).

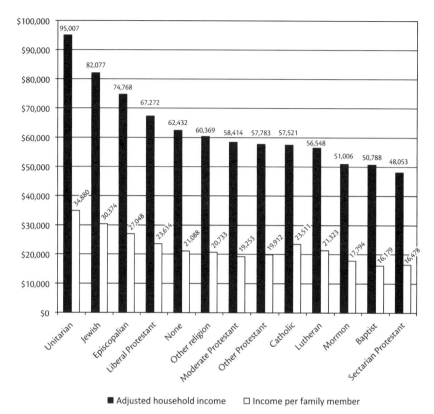

Fig. 4.4. Adjusted household income and income per family member by religious identification

Income stratification by religious identification is equally evident in table 4.11 for unmarried men and women and for divorced men and women. Across nearly all religious identifications, unmarried men earn more than unmarried women do. The only exception is among Unitarians, for whom women's incomes exceed men's. Liberal Protestants and other Protestants also have relatively low male-female income ratios for unmarried respondents.

Of particular note is the gender disparity in per-member household income for divorced respondents, evidencing the well-known disadvantage facing divorced women, who are generally responsible for children. Across most religious identifications, divorced men enjoy roughly twice the income per household member when compared to divorced women. The burden of divorce falls hardest on women with sectarian,

*Table 4.11. Adjusted Income per Household Member by Religious Identification and Marital Status*

| Current identification | Income per member, unmarried men | Income per member, unmarried women | Male/ female ratio | Income per member, divorced men | Income per member, divorced women | Male/ female ratio |
|---|---|---|---|---|---|---|
| Jewish | $32,892 | $25,406 | 1.29 | $58,538 | $29,039 | 2.02 |
| Episcopalian | $30,040 | $24,337 | 1.23 | $40,314 | $24,857 | 1.62 |
| Unitarian | $25,990 | $30,785 | .84 | $36,778 | $28,994 | 1.27 |
| Liberal Protestant | $23,714 | $20,415 | 1.16 | $37,421 | $18,669 | 2.00 |
| None | $22,985 | $16,588 | 1.39 | $32,246 | $20,844 | 1.55 |
| Moderate Protestant | $22,644 | $17,062 | 1.33 | $32,219 | $16,236 | 1.98 |
| Catholic | $22,523 | $17,198 | 1.31 | $28,262 | $15,696 | 1.80 |
| Other Protestant | $22,316 | $18,904 | 1.18 | $26,577 | $16,758 | 1.59 |
| Other religion | $21,954 | $17,975 | 1.22 | $31,247 | $23,849 | 1.31 |
| Lutheran | $21,042 | $16,919 | 1.24 | $30,548 | $16,730 | 1.83 |
| Baptist | $20,017 | $15,690 | 1.28 | $25,077 | $14,029 | 1.79 |
| Sectarian Protestant | $19,602 | $14,654 | 1.34 | $25,852 | $13,312 | 1.94 |
| Mormon | $19,070 | $14,542 | 1.31 | $36,264 | $11,967 | 3.03 |

Baptist, and Mormon identifications, whose families must subsist on less than half the income per member enjoyed by divorced women from more universalistic traditions. Gender disparities in income among the divorced are lowest for Unitarians, nonidentifiers, and non-Christians.

Ethnicity and religious identification also intersect to help explain income stratification. Generally, the patterns found in the full sample controlling for ethnicity hold for specific ethnic groups—with sectarians on the bottom and universalistic groups on the top (see table 4.12). Sectarian and Baptist identifiers earn significantly less than do people with other religious identifications across all the ethnic categories, and the differences are quite substantial. The salience of differences in attainment across religious identifications is of particular importance for African American Protestants, who are often grouped together in contemporary schemes of classification. Also of note is the relative disadvantage of Latin American Catholics, whose household incomes per member are lower than all but Latin American sectarians. The high incomes of Asians per household member is another important finding, particularly given their high concentrations of nonidentifiers and those who identify with other religions. While the relatively small numbers call for caution, there is considerable stratification among these "other religion" identifications. GSS data show that Hindu respondents have substantially higher household incomes ($67,500) than do Buddhists ($58,200) or Muslims ($40,600), and their earnings are in line with their attainment of college education. Nearly 78% of Hindu respondents have a college degree, while the figures are 52% for Buddhists and 35% for Muslims. Notably, a recent study of immigrant Americans' attainments shows that Muslim attainment is driven down by African American converts, and Buddhists occupy the middle rung among the three major non-Christian faiths (Amin and Sherkat 2014).

## So Shall Ye Reap

Conservative commentators have long held that family factors have a strong influence on stratification outcomes, and pundits have increasingly pointed to heterosexual marriage as the panacea for mitigating rising inequality (Murray 2012; Wilcox et al. 2012). It is true that family factors have a profound influence on stratification outcomes; however, in this chapter, we have seen that the solutions proposed by conservative Christian commentators (chastity and early marriage) are precisely what is driving deprivation among those who adhere to the tenants of exclusivist Christianity. While conservative pundits praise early marriage and condemn nonmarital sex, conservative Christians continue

*Table 4.12. Household Income per Member by Religious Identification and Ethnicity*

| Current identification | Native American | Western European | Eastern European | Asian | African American | Latin American |
|---|---|---|---|---|---|---|
| Unitarian | $8,997 | $35,004 | $24,955 | $37,763 | $18,971 | $12,129 |
| Jewish | $11,375 | $34,490 | $33,293 | $22,117 | $10,057 | $25,556 |
| Episcopalian | $10,106 | $30,381 | $31,085 | $27,694 | $17,525 | $31,234 |
| Liberal Protestant | $20,653 | $26,041 | $19,714 | $31,802 | $20,355 | $24,381 |
| None | $16,384 | $25,110 | $27,699 | $29,423 | $15,722 | $14,914 |
| Other religion | $12,532 | $24,346 | $23,688 | $23,666 | $15,505 | $13,594 |
| Other Protestant | $14,098 | $22,466 | $20,244 | $25,792 | $19,813 | $13,921 |
| Moderate Protestant | $17,637 | $22,272 | $19,276 | $22,876 | $14,077 | $16,571 |
| Catholic | $16,098 | $22,215 | $20,578 | $21,133 | $15,001 | $12,665 |
| Lutheran | $16,744 | $20,203 | $20,919 | $25,025 | $16,541 | $19,348 |
| Baptist | $14,514 | $18,695 | $20,672 | $23,426 | $12,472 | $14,479 |
| Sectarian Protestant | $14,035 | $17,517 | $16,030 | $16,205 | $12,630 | $11,084 |
| Mormon | $19,709 | $16,918 | $17,585 | $6,750 | $6,609 | $19,264 |
| Total | $15,275 | $22,157 | $23,471 | $24,127 | $13,764 | $13,124 |

to engage in premarital sex (often without contraception), marry early (often as a "solution" to an unplanned pregnancy), and then find themselves adrift with minimal education, dead-end jobs, and low incomes.

Thus, sexuality and family are negotiated differently across religious identifications. Exclusivist religious groups abhor all forms of nonmarital sexuality, yet members of those groups have high rates of premarital sex and are just as likely as other Americans to be gay, lesbian, or bisexual and to have extramarital affairs. Contrary to the claims of conservative Christian commentators, Americans from more universalistic religious traditions do not eschew marriage—they simply do it later. And religious liberals and moderates are no more likely than sectarians to have premarital, homosexual, or extramarital sex. Fertility is substantially higher among sectarians, and their age of first birth is much lower. Exclusivist Christians often find themselves married and raising children long before they could have completed a college education.

This family situation usually requires abandoning the pursuit of post-secondary educational attainment (especially for women) and obtaining a job which does not require a college degree—almost uniformly in the nonprofessional sectors of the economy. High rates of fertility and patriarchal gender roles often dictate labor-force exit for women, and this further reduces the resources available to large, sectarian Christian families. Children raised in those families suffer from low levels of educational attainment in the household and from authoritarian parenting, which stifles autonomy and enforces obedience with violence. It is little wonder that sectarian Christians tend to do poorly in modern educational and occupational settings which require independent thought and creativity. Indeed, given that large pluralities of Americans embrace sectarian Christianity—particularly large segments of the African American population—religious exclusivism plays a substantial role in anchoring individuals and families in the bottom rung of American society.

5

# Religious Identification and Politics in the United States

Politics is the process of engaging the state to try to obtain collective goods or to seek the mitigation of collective harms (Sherkat 2006), and in the United States, political activity occurs at municipal, state, and federal levels through party and nonpartisan electoral activity in the representative process of the democratic system. Beliefs and values are key schemata informing the valuation of collective goods generated by the state, and religiously inspired understandings can profoundly influence the value of collective goods—with some religious values turning what many people see as a collective good into a collective bad, and vice versa. Religious institutions and beliefs can produce distinctive preferences, and religious organizations provide institutional and cognitive support for engaging in political collective action.

In the United States, religious factors have always played a key role in politics, despite the formal separation of religious firms from the state. Yet the disestablishment of religious groups in several states was not completed until the early 19th century (Finke and Stark 1992). In the 19th century, most political mobilizations pitted the Anglo-Protestant majority against more recent Catholic immigrants—focusing on issues such as the legal status of alcohol and on Protestant curricula and religious clothing in public schools. While some minority religious groups were generally tolerated, such as the Jews, others such as the Mormons suffered terrorist attacks which were supported or ignored by municipal, state, and federal authorities. Indeed, the Mormon practice of polygamy was banned by the federal government, forcing many families to flee the United States (Palmer 1994) and the LDS to change its practices in 1890. Of course, indigenous religious beliefs and practices were brutally repressed, and the federal government enabled Protestant and Catholic religious authorities to forcibly Christianize the subjugated indigenous populations well into the 20th century (Harrod 1995; Nagel 1996; Thornton 1987).

The penetration of other non-Christian religions into the United States was largely halted by anti-immigrant political movements that instituted the various "exclusion" acts into U.S. immigration policy in the late 19th and early 20th centuries. These guidelines effectively prevented Buddhists, Hindus, Muslims, Sikhs, Jains, Zoroastrians and others from moving to the United States, and it was not until the lifting of these acts in 1965 that the U.S. saw significant growth in those faiths (Alanezi and Sherkat 2008; Ebaugh 2003; Ebaugh and Chafetz 2000; Sherkat 2010a). Politics influences religious markets, and religious institutions and beliefs also impact politics. Religious factors continue to play a role in a vibrant anti-immigrant movement in the United States, and in the past decade, opposition to Islam has been a focal part of these mobilizations. And, of course, white sectarian Christianity played a substantial role in political movements seeking to implement and sustain "Jim Crow" laws and to prevent the political and social elevation of African Americans (Aho 1995; Barkun 1997; C. Wilcox 1996; Wilcox and Wilcox 1992)—even as African American sectarian movements from the same denominational families militated for civil rights (Morris 1986).

Catholics and Anglo-Protestants battled in the 19th and early 20th centuries over the nature and content of public education—a struggle largely won by Protestantism, which imposed antigarb laws that prevented members of Catholic religious orders from teaching in public schools, while maintaining curricula tinged with Protestantism (D'Antonio and Hoge 2006). As we have seen, with public schools being seen by Catholics as a collective bad which would socialize their children away from Catholicism, the Catholic Church forged an alternative school system and has ever since tried to garner some form of federal or state funding through tax credits, vouchers, or other mechanisms. Interestingly, the growth of exclusivist Protestant schools following racial integration of public schools (Andrews 2002) and the secularization of public schools in the 1950s and 1960s has led many exclusivist Protestants to embrace Catholic political movements seeking to use public funding to finance religious education (Deckman 2002). Conflicts over education shifted focus in the 20th century, and as public schools secularized their curricula, religiously inspired political movements rooted in exclusivist Protestantism sought to resacralize public school curricula and eliminate the teaching of evolution and literary works deemed salacious or blasphemous (Berkman, Pacheco, and Plutzer 2008; Deckman 2004).

Anglo-Protestant political movements also sought to regulate product markets for alcohol and for entertainment, art, and literature. The Prohibition movements of the 19th and early 20th centuries were incredibly successful, eventually culminating in the 1919 passage of the 18th Amendment to the Constitution, which made alcohol production and sales illegal throughout the nation (Gusfield 1986). The sale of alcohol remains illegal in many U.S. counties and municipalities, and Protestant-inspired "blue laws" prevent the sale of alcohol on the recognized Christian holy day (Sunday, for all but a handful of sects). Although the 18th Amendment was repealed in 1933, it had a devastating impact on the development and trajectory of the mostly Catholic- and ethnic-Protestant-owned alcohol industries. Many Catholics and ethnic Lutherans lost their businesses, and the developing wine and beer industries in the United States have yet to recover from the impact of this religious political movement—in large part because sectarian Protestants continue to militate for extreme regulation of the alcohol industry. In the late 20th century, these religious movements turned their sights on the regulation of marijuana and other drugs, leading to the "War on Drugs" prosecuted by the Reagan administration.

Religious movements have also been critical for motivating the political regulation of books, images, music, and now the Internet—arguing that commercial production and private consumption of cultural products which violate religious tenets on sexuality or which blaspheme and profane religion should be prohibited. The success of the crusades against pornography was only broken in the late 1950s with an organized industry confronting regulation. The religious sources of political regulation have not been lost on those who produce these products—and sexual-expression-industry figures such as Larry Flynt and Hugh Hefner forged movements to strike back at conservative Christian activists such as Jerry Falwell and Catholic clergy (who joined with Protestants in opposition to displays of sexuality and the regulation of speech deemed blasphemous). The rise of modern contraception invigorated religious political movements seeking to regulate sexuality, and the legalization of abortion in 1973 further fueled conservative religious movements seeking to regulate sexuality and helped coalesce movements of conservative Protestants and Catholics opposed to nonmarital sexuality. Notably, however, liberal religious movements were pivotal in advocating for contraception and the legalization of abortion (Luker 1985). More recently, the regulation of sexuality has begun to focus on opposition to civil rights for gays, lesbians, bisexuals, and transgendered people. This follows a long history of Christian mobilization against civil rights for communists, atheists, and homosexuals (Edgell, Gerteis, and Hartmann 2006; Stouffer 1992).

This chapter examines how religious identities remain an important feature of American politics, influencing political beliefs and commitments on a variety of issues and helping to structure partisan identities and voting behavior. Where relevant, it also examines how ethnicity intersects with religious identification to influence political values and commitments. And it explores how religious identification and ethnicity help explain shifting patterns of partisanship in the United States.

## Religious Identification and the Regulation of Sexuality

The state is responsible for meting out laws regulating sexual behavior, determining how sexual imagery is regulated, who can be taught about sex and when, who can have sex with whom, and who can marry and divorce. Religious groups have long used their influence to tip the state to favor some forms of sexual expression over others. Religiously motivated movements are most readily evident on issues regarding sexuality, and the most prominent among these have tilted toward maintaining or increasing government control over sexual imagery and sexuality and toward enforcing exclusivist Christian hegemony, particularly in the face of opposition from secularists (Edgell, Gerteis, and Hartmann 2006).

Table 5.1 presents GSS totals for several indicators of sexual regulation, with predictable patterning by religious identification. Looking first at the regulation of sexual imagery, more than 62% of Mormons and 57% of sectarian Protestants believe that pornography should be illegal, and Baptists are next in line at 45%. In contrast, only one in five

*Table 5.1. Sexual Regulation and Religious Identification*

| Identification | Pornography illegal | No sex education | No contraception for teens | Oppose abortion for rape | Oppose abortion for choice |
|---|---|---|---|---|---|
| Mormon | 62.2% | 25.4% | 58.3% | 24.0% | 80.8% |
| Sectarian Protestant | 57.1% | 25.0% | 55.3% | 36.4% | 79.6% |
| Baptist | 44.9% | 17.9% | 48.1% | 22.8% | 69.8% |
| Moderate Protestant | 43.5% | 13.0% | 43.8% | 13.6% | 59.1% |
| Liberal Protestant | 42.5% | 10.4% | 43.3% | 8.0% | 49.9% |
| Lutheran | 41.1% | 11.7% | 45.5% | 10.3% | 57.0% |
| Other Protestant | 40.7% | 16.6% | 44.6% | 22.5% | 59.7% |
| Catholic | 36.6% | 11.5% | 42.4% | 22.0% | 64.3% |
| Episcopalian | 35.5% | 8.2% | 35.4% | 5.6% | 38.9% |
| Other religion | 32.2% | 13.3% | 35.8% | 11.1% | 42.7% |
| Jewish | 20.1% | 5.1% | 22.8% | 2.6% | 22.0% |
| None | 17.7% | 5.8% | 23.4% | 7.3% | 34.0% |
| Unitarian | 13.5% | 2.5% | 18.3% | 1.0% | 18.7% |
| Total | 39.5% | 13.6% | 42.0% | 18.2% | 59.5% |

Jews support strict regulation, and even fewer Unitarians and nonidentifiers support these proscriptions. Notably, however, moderate and liberal Protestants and Lutherans are not far behind Baptists in their support for making pornography illegal, while Catholics, Episcopalians, and "other religion" identifiers are more wary of regulating the pornography industry.

Next, table 5.1 explores how religious identifications inform beliefs about teaching sex education in public schools and about the legality of making contraception available for teenagers. The GSS question about sex education taps a rather binary response of favoring or opposing "sex education in public schools." The content of such education is not specified, and as a result, the vast majority of Americans agree with the basic public good of providing education about sexuality. Yet a quarter of sectarian Protestants and Mormons are opposed to any sex education, and nearly 18% of Baptists oppose all forms of sex education. Notably, this opinion sets them quite apart from all other religious groups. Only 13% of moderate Protestants and even fewer Lutherans, liberal Protestants, and Catholics are opposed to sex education, though, quite interestingly, nearly 17% of the "other Protestants" are opposed to teaching kids about sexuality. Catholic support for sex education is quite notable. Many pundits and activists assume that because the Catholic hierarchy militates against nonmarital sexuality, lay Catholics in the United States follow suit—however, this is not the case by any measure, as will be seen on other issues as well.

The issue of abortion has been the most pivotal political issue mobilizing religious constituencies to political action in the United States during the four decades since the *Roe v. Wade* Supreme Court decision which legalized abortion in 1973. Polarization on the issue of abortion has pitted religious universalists—who were key political actors in the legalization of abortion (Luker 1985)—against conservative Catholics and sectarians. Since *Roe v. Wade*, religious political mobilization against abortion has yielded considerable success for limiting access to abortion, making it virtually unavailable in many regions of the United States, particularly for poor women. Beliefs about the legality of abortion usually fall into two camps: when there are "extreme circumstances" versus when the abortion is a matter of a woman's decision not to carry a pregnancy to term. Two items which are representative of these two positions are whether respondents think abortion should be legal if the pregnancy was caused by rape and whether abortion should be legal "for any reason."

Nearly one in five GSS respondents believe that abortion should be illegal even if the pregnancy was caused by rape, and opposition to legal abortion is heavily influenced by religious identification. Indeed, over 36% of sectarian Protestants oppose legal abortion for rape victims, and 24% of Mormons, 23% of Baptists, and 22% of Catholics and other Protestants are also opposed to legal abortion for rape victims. In contrast, only 8% of liberal Protestants would deny legal abortion to rape victims, and the percentage is even lower for nonidentifiers, Episcopalians, Jews, and Unitarians. Religious polarization over abortion in extreme cases has increased over the four decades of the GSS—mainly because sectarian Protestants have radicalized their opposition to abortion. In the 1970s, opposition to legal abortion in the case of rape was 31% among sectarian Protestants and under 23% for Baptists, while in GSS data collected since 2010, opposition has increased to 46% among sectarian Protestants and over 27% for Baptists.

The legality of abortion "for any reason" comes closest to the pure prochoice position advocated by many feminist groups; however, the majority of GSS respondents, nearly 60%, reject allowing abortion to be legal for any reason. Once again, religious identifications play a crucial role in structuring support for legal abortion, with about 80% of sectarians and Mormons rejecting the prochoice perspective and nearly 70% of Baptists and 64% of Catholics. In contrast, 39% of Episcopalians believe that the legality of abortion should be limited, and 34% of nonidentifiers oppose the prochoice perspective. Opposition to the prochoice position is even lower for Jews (22%) and Unitarians (19%). Prochoice opposition fell from 65% in the 1970s to 56% after 2010.

Marriage is the legal recognition of coupling and intimacy, providing people with myriad benefits, from reduced taxation to insurance discounts to privileged access to partners' persons and property when they are sick or die. The modern nation-state grants people the right to marry and officially acknowledges who may or may not receive these benefits. Religious groups have long challenged the legitimacy of secular marriages and have sought to make marriage rights conform to religious prescriptions and proscriptions. Nowhere is the conflict between religion and the state in more stark relief than in contemporary controversies over granting marriage rights to same-sex couples.

Table 5.2 presents opposition to same-sex marriage by religious identification in the 2006–2012 General Social Surveys. Opposition to same-sex marriage has decreased considerably since the survey first tallied perceptions in 1988—when over 72% of respondents reported being opposed or strongly opposed to same-sex marriage (Sherkat et al. 2011). By 2012, opposition to same-sex marriage in the general population had declined to under 39%. The 2006–2012 data are grouped together to better discern differences across religious identifications. Predictably, sectarian Protestants, Mormons, and Baptists are most opposed to granting marriage rights to same-sex couples: over 72% of sectarians oppose marriage rights for same-sex couples, while opposition is at 68% for Mormons and 62% for Baptists. In contrast, only 39% of Catholics oppose same-sex marriage, and opposition is even lower for Episcopalians (35%). Less than 23% of nonidentifiers oppose same-sex marriage, and only one in five Jews would withhold the right to marry for same-sex couples. None of the Unitarians interviewed since 2006 were opposed to same-sex marriage, which is not surprising given that the Unitarian Universalist Association began marrying same-sex couples in 1996 (Unitarian Universalist Association of Congregations 2013). It is

*Table 5.2. Marital Regulation and Religious Identification*

| Identification | Oppose same-sex marriage | Make divorce harder | Whites who support laws against interracial marriage |
|---|---|---|---|
| Sectarian Protestant | 72.2% | 62.4% | 38.3% |
| Mormon | 67.6% | 58.4% | 17.9% |
| Baptist | 61.8% | 51.1% | 45.0% |
| Moderate Protestant | 53.3% | 52.9% | 33.5% |
| Other Protestant | 52.0% | 52.0% | 17.4% |
| Lutheran | 48.1% | 58.5% | 24.8% |
| Liberal Protestant | 45.8% | 51.6% | 23.1% |
| Catholic | 39.2% | 51.7% | 19.1% |
| Episcopalian | 34.9% | 45.6% | 14.8% |
| Other religion | 28.4% | 43.1% | 9.8% |
| None | 22.7% | 30.0% | 11.1% |
| Jewish | 19.6% | 32.5% | 9.0% |
| Unitarian | 0% | 24.4% | 5.1% |
| Total | 45.5% | 50.1% | 25.7% |

quite interesting that LGBT activists and many opponents of marriage rights for same-sex couples often assume that Catholics are at the fore-front of opposition given that the Catholic Church hierarchy has made opposition to same-sex marriage a priority in its political activism. Yet the majority of Catholics support the extension of marriage rights to same-sex couples. Indeed, Pope Francis's call to refrain from political activism to deny civil rights based on sexuality seems in concert with the views of the majority of American Catholics.

As same-sex marriage has become a key issue in contemporary politics, some conservative Christian commentators have argued that sectarian Christians are not substantially different from other Americans on sexuality issues and LGBT rights; however, that is not the case. In contrast to the claims of Christian activist scholars, younger sectarians are actually more different from their cohort peers than are older cohorts of sectarian Protestants (Baunach 2011; Sherkat et al. 2011). Indeed, GSS data show that young sectarians are more opposed to same-sex marriage than are liberal Protestants from the World War II generation. Further, on the issue of same-sex marriage, there were no significant differences across religious identifications in 1988—the first year for which we have GSS data—and all the religious variation evident in more recent data has been a result of rapid changes in opinion among more universalistic religious groups (and the nonreligious), combined with very small shifts in beliefs about marriage rights among sectarian Protestants and Baptists. Notably, the religious structuring of beliefs about marriage rights for same-sex couples also holds for African Americans (Sherkat, de Vries, and Creek 2010).

Divorce is a hot-button political issue in many nations from varied religious traditions, and the liberalization of divorce laws in the United States led to a brief increase in rates of divorce during the first decade of the GSS (Cherlin 1992). Indeed, table 5.2 shows that concern about high rates of divorce has led a bare majority of Americans to believe that laws should be designed to make divorce more difficult. And, as usual, people who identify with more exclusivist religious groups are more likely to think that divorce should be made more difficult, while respondents from more universalistic traditions are less likely to want the government to make divorce harder to obtain. Interestingly, Catholics are only just above the mean, at 52%, favoring stricter divorce laws, despite strong proscriptions against divorce in the Catholic Church. In contrast, over 62% of sectarian Protestants and 58% of Mormons want divorce to be more difficult to obtain, while only 24% of Unitarians, 30% of nonidentifiers, and 33% of Jews (the group with the lowest divorce rate) think that divorce should be thwarted by political policy.

Whom you marry and whether you can dissolve a marriage are not the only political questions regarding state recognition and regulation of sexual intimacy; laws against interracial marriage have been at the core of the white-supremacist system of segregating African Americans from whites, and not only in the South, the historical cradle of slavery and segregation. Indeed, across the GSS, table 5.2 shows that 26% of white respondents favor laws against interracial marriage—more than one in four. Predictably, white Baptists, who form the core of white, southern, exclusivist Christianity, are most in favor of laws against interracial marriage, with 45% advocating denying the right of interracial couples to marry. Sectarian Protestants are not far behind, with 38% supporting such laws, and such laws have the support of over a third of moderate Protestants (many of whom are Southern Methodists, who were the elite bulwark of the Jim Crow South). Unitarians, Jews, and other non-Christians are most opposed to laws against interracial marriage. Opposition to interracial marriage has declined over time; however, the religious differences reported in the full sample persist. The question about interracial marriage has only been asked twice in the 21st century (in 2000 and 2002), and in those years, over 25% of white Baptists and 21% of white sectarians favored laws against interracial marriage.

The issue of interracial marriage segues directly into how religious identifications may influence other indicators of politicized racial and ethnic antipathy. A vast body of research has demonstrated that religious exclusivism fuels prejudice and discrimination against those who are not in the majority, and the findings are quite consistent across varied cultural environs (Emerson and Smith 2000; Hunsberger 1995; Hunsberger and Jackson 2005; Tolsma, De Graaf, and Quillian 2009). In the United States, the principal ethnic fault lines have been between African Americans and whites. Table 5.3 first presents data from only white respondents regarding whether they believe that whites should be able to segregate neighborhoods and whether they would vote for an African American for president. Notably, each of these items shows a substantial liberalizing trend in the GSS; however, the religious differences are relatively invariant to this trend—universalistic identifiers had less racist responses in the 1970s, and they continue to be ahead of more exclusivist groups in the early 21st century.

Not surprisingly, white Baptists are at the forefront of racial animosity in the United States. Baptists are heavily concentrated in the South, where people of African descent were enslaved for over two centuries and racial antipathy has remained high since emancipation. Whites who identify with other exclusivist sects are also more likely to support segregation, with nearly a third agreeing that whites should be able to keep African Americans out of their neighborhoods. Moderate Protestant groups show the next-highest level of support for racial segregation—no doubt owing to the large concentrations of white Methodists, who also supported segregation and opposed the civil rights movement. Catholics, Lutherans, and liberal Protestants fall just below the mean on the segregation issue, while Unitarians, Jews, other non-Christians, and nonidentifiers are substantially less supportive of segregation than are other Americans. Interestingly, Mormons and Episcopalians score similarly on all the racial politics items, and they chart fairly liberal positions. Most of the GSS data were collected after the 1978 declaration (Official Declaration 2) of racial equality for membership and the priesthood

*Table 5.3. Ethnic Politics and Religious Identification*

| Identification | Whites should be able to segregate (white respondents only) | Would not vote for a black president (white respondents only) | Immigrants can't become fully American (all respondents) |
|---|---|---|---|
| Baptist | 37.4% | 26.1% | 66.2% |
| Sectarian Protestant | 32.0% | 20.9% | 65.1% |
| Moderate Protestant | 29.8% | 18.4% | 60.6% |
| Liberal Protestant | 26.9% | 13.6% | 54.2% |
| Lutheran | 25.7% | 13.1% | 55.6% |
| Catholic | 25.0% | 11.4% | 58.1% |
| Other Protestant | 22.7% | 12.9% | 56.2% |
| Episcopalian | 19.7% | 12.6% | 46.2% |
| Mormon | 19.3% | 10.8% | 47.1% |
| Jewish | 17.6% | 8.7% | 42.2% |
| None | 16.0% | 9.5% | 50.9% |
| Other religion | 15.2% | 8.7% | 41.8% |
| Unitarian | 10.7% | 3.2% | 50.0% |
| Total | 26.8% | 15.2% | 57.3% |

in the Church of Latter-Day Saints, and it appears that most Mormons took this declaration to heart in their responses on racial politics.

Table 5.3 finds a similar religious structuring for the item tapping whether a white respondent would vote for an African American for president. Over one-fourth of white Baptists and more than one in five white sectarian Protestants admit to an interviewer that they would not vote for an African American for president. Moderate Protestants are not far behind, with over 18% rejecting a candidate based on race. Notably, this is substantially below the proportion found among liberal Protestants, Lutherans, and Episcopalians—and further amplifies why we cannot consider white "mainline" Protestants to be monolithic. Catholics and Mormons are also much more receptive of the possibility of voting for an African American president when compared to all varieties of Protestants. Across the nearly forty years of the GSS, under 10% of Jews, other non-Christians, nonidentifiers, and Unitarians report that they would not vote for an African American for president. Of course, with the candidacy and presidency of Barack Obama, many people have reconsidered this possibility, and cohort replacement has altered the racial climate over these four decades. Since 2008, just under 6% of white GSS respondents admit they would not vote for an African American—but even after 2008, 10% of white Baptists and over 8% of white sectarians admitted to an interviewer that they would not vote for an African American for president.

Anti-immigrant movements have been an important force in American politics since the 19th century, and religious factors have loomed large in the justification for limiting immigration and for subjecting immigrants to Anglo-Protestant cultural domination. Indeed, anti-immigrant movements in the 21st century have fueled substantial legislative success, as well as terrorist activities including several murders and assassinations of public officials (J. Johnson 2011; Wright 2009). Contemporary anti-immigrant sentiment has focused on whether immigrants are "real Americans," echoing the "100% Americanism" of the Ku Klux Klan and the Know-Nothing Party. In 1996 and 2004, the GSS tapped a similar sentiment, asking whether immigrants could ever be "fully American." Indeed, 57% of GSS respondents reported thinking that immigrants could never be fully American. Predictably, exclusivist Protestants with Baptist or other sectarian identifications were substantially more likely to hold this view, with about two-thirds in each group doubting that immigrants could be real Americans. Jews and other non-Christians were least likely to deny American status to immigrants, with just over 40% saying that immigrants could not be real Americans. Curiously, 58% of Catholics said they believe that immigrants cannot become fully American, despite the relatively high proportion of Catholics who are first- or second-generation immigrants (indeed, there is no substantial difference between Catholic immigrants and other Catholics on this item).

## Religious Identification and Politicized Patriarchy

Most religious traditions amplify a gendered separation of social roles that denies women control over collective resources in the state— women's place is seen to be in the home and not in the public sphere (Palmer 1994). Religious arguments from the Protestant Christian perspective were long used to justify denying women the right to vote, with many people arguing that Catholic women would blindly vote with their husbands, thus giving Catholics two votes (Marshall 1985, 1986, 1991). The patriarchal impulse in politicized Christianity remains quite strong, particularly among exclusivist Protestants and conservative Catholics—but it is unclear whether the average member of these groups embraces the view that women should be excluded from political leadership. Figure 5.1 examines how religious identification influences politicized patriarchy using two items: (1) the belief that women's place is in the home, not running the country, and (2) unwillingness to vote for a qualified woman from one's own party for president.

Overall, 24% of GSS respondents report that women's place is in the home, not running the country, and over 13% would not vote for their own party's candidate if a woman was nominated. Not surprisingly, sectarian Protestants and Baptists have the highest rates of politicized patriarchy—with 38% of sectarians and 33% of Baptists believing that women should run the home and not the nation. Nearly 22% of sectarians and 18% of Baptists would not vote for a woman for president. Identifiers with more universalistic religious groups and respondents who reject religious identification are far less likely to support politicized patriarchy. No Unitarians report that they would not vote for a woman for president, and only 5% of Jews and 7% of nonidentifiers would fail to support a female candidate from their own party. Liberal Protestants, "other religion" identifiers, and Episcopalians are roughly half as likely as sectarians and Baptists to support either indicator of politicized patriarchy. Notably, Mormons are more similar to moderate Protestants and Lutherans on these politicized indicators of patriarchy, and Catholics are even more liberal than moderate Protestants are—contrary to the patriarchal orientation of many conservative Catholic political and religious leaders.

## Religious Identification and Civil Liberties

In the United States, citizens are supposed to enjoy the right to speak freely, to choose how or whether to view or revere the supernatural, and to pursue happiness unfettered by discrimination based on religion, race, or political commitments. Of course, the history of the United States has rarely matched this ideal, and large pluralities of Americans oppose the extension of civil rights to people who differ from themselves. Religious factors play a strong role in how Americans see civil liberties, particularly for minorities such as atheists, communists, and LGBT people. Further, while many Americans believe that the state

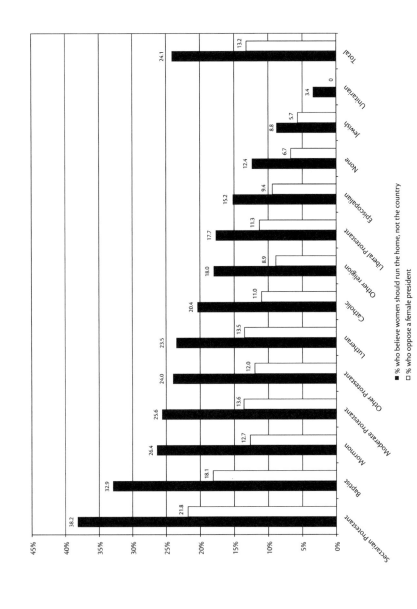

Fig. 5.1. Religious identification and politicized patriarchy

■ % who believe women should run the home, not the country
□ % who oppose a female president

| | % believe women should run home | % oppose female president |
|---|---|---|
| Sectarian Protestant | 38.2 | 21.8 |
| Baptist | 32.9 | 18.1 |
| Mormon | 26.4 | 12.7 |
| Moderate Protestant | 25.6 | 13.6 |
| Other Protestant | 24.0 | 12.0 |
| Lutheran | 23.5 | 13.5 |
| Catholic | 20.4 | 11.0 |
| Other religion | 18.0 | 8.9 |
| Liberal Protestant | 17.7 | 11.3 |
| Episcopalian | 15.2 | 9.4 |
| None | 12.4 | 6.7 |
| Jewish | 8.8 | 5.7 |
| Unitarian | 3.4 | 0 |
| Total | 24.1 | 13.2 |

should not promote an established religion, others claim that America is a distinctively Christian nation and that the promotion of Christianity does not violate the establishment clause of the Constitution or infringe on the rights of people who are not Christian (or Christians who differ in their interpretation of that tradition).

Since the work of Sam Stouffer (1992) in the 1950s, social scientists examining American political opinion have often used critical questions about whether civil rights should extend to minority groups —and particularly to minorities which large pluralities find objectionable. These sets of items are often described as indicators of "tolerance" toward minorities. The GSS asks respondents whether they believe civil rights should apply in a variety of settings and across several different groups. Table 5.4 presents two iconic questions on civil liberties—freedom of speech and employment security for teachers—to see how religious identities structure the extension of civil liberties to three groups: (1) atheists, (2) homosexuals, and (3) communists. Notably, across all the civil liberties measures, Americans are least likely to grant basic civil rights to atheists—who are more unpopular than communists, homosexuals, and racists (Edgell, Gerteis, and Hartmann 2006). However, groups fare differently on the specific civil liberties in question.

*Table 5.4. Opposition to Civil Liberties and Religious Identification*

| Identification | Oppose right of atheists to speak | Oppose right of homo-sexuals to speak | Oppose right of communists to speak | Fire atheist teacher | Fire homo-sexual teacher | Fire communist teacher |
|---|---|---|---|---|---|---|
| Sectarian Protestant | 42.3% | 40.7% | 51.2% | 61.5% | 50.9% | 58.4% |
| Baptist | 42.1% | 37.1% | 49.9% | 60.5% | 46.3% | 58.1% |
| Moderate Protestant | 33.5% | 26.9% | 42.4% | 55.7% | 37.3% | 54.3% |
| Lutheran | 27.6% | 21.3% | 35.3% | 49.4% | 30.7% | 47.9% |
| Catholic | 27.1% | 19.2% | 35.6% | 45.5% | 26.3% | 45.0% |
| Liberal Protestant | 23.5% | 19.8% | 29.9% | 47.5% | 30.7% | 46.2% |
| Other Protestant | 22.2% | 19.6% | 29.3% | 39.7% | 27.3% | 41.5% |
| Other religion | 21.0% | 18.2% | 22.3% | 35.9% | 24.0% | 30.0% |
| Mormon | 18.9% | 23.6% | 30.1% | 40.9% | 33.8% | 46.6% |
| Jewish | 16.5% | 8.3% | 16.5% | 34.3% | 10.1% | 30.2% |
| Episcopalian | 15.7% | 11.3% | 23.3% | 37.9% | 21.3% | 37.8% |
| None | 11.0% | 10.1% | 16.8% | 21.6% | 14.4% | 25.2% |
| Unitarian | 6.1% | 1.1% | 5.2% | 12.4% | 4.3% | 16.5% |
| Total | 29.2% | 24.1% | 36.7% | 47.8% | 32.3% | 46.9% |

Overall, 29% of GSS respondents would deny atheists the right to speak, which is lower than the 37% who would deny communists the right to speak—though Americans are more likely to favor firing atheist teachers than communist teachers. About one-fourth of GSS respondents would deny homosexuals free-speech rights. Once again, rejection of civil rights for minorities is higher among people from exclusivist sects—with 42% of sectarians and Baptists rejecting free speech for atheists and about half denying free speech for communists. Large pluralities of sectarians (41%) and Baptists (38%) also would deny free speech for homosexuals. Interestingly, Mormons' experience of persecution has apparently tempered their views on civil liberties —only 19% of Mormons would deny free speech for atheists—though they are a bit more harsh on homosexuals and communists. Jews, Episcopalians, nonidentifiers, and Unitarians are much more supportive of civil liberties when compared to other GSS respondents. The items tapping the willingness to fire teachers who are atheist, homosexual, or communist mirror those for free speech. However, it is notable that the rate of intolerance is higher for each of these items. Over 60% of sectarians and Baptists would fire an atheist teacher, and nearly that percentage believe that communist teachers are unfit. Atheist teachers are viewed in a particularly harsh light, with nearly half of GSS respondents calling for their jobs—indeed, even more than one in five respondents with no religious identification advocated dismissal for atheist teachers.

In the early 1960s, the U.S. Supreme Court handed down critical decisions about school prayer, *Engel v. Vitale* in 1962 and *Abington School District v. Schempp* in 1963. These decisions largely removed teacher-initiated Christian prayers from public school classrooms (though in many schools, mandatory Christian prayers are commonplace, in violation of the rulings). The GSS has long tapped support for "Bible based" prayer in public schools, and a majority of GSS respondents support mandatory Christian prayers—with 60% favoring establishing Christianity in public schools. Figure 5.2 shows that enthusiasm for "Bible" prayers is far lower among Unitarians (12%) and Jews (18%)—who probably suspect that the prayers may not reflect their own commitments to the supernatural. Still, 31% of nonidentifiers are supportive of mandatory prayers to the god of the Christian Bible. On the upper end, exclusivist sects are at the forefront of support for Christian prayers in

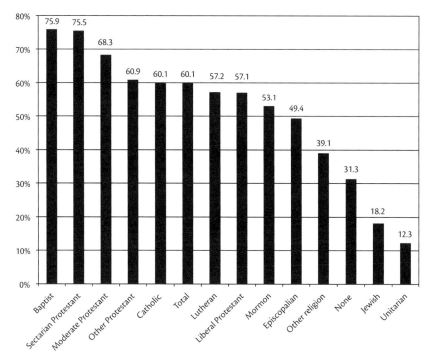

Fig. 5.2. Support for school prayer by religious identification

public schools, with over three-quarters favoring school prayer. Once again, Mormons are below the mean at 53%—lower than moderate and even liberal Protestants—reflecting, perhaps, their circumspection regarding civil liberties.

## Religious Identification, Crime, and Punishment

Religious traditions call for the state to regulate behaviors by making them contrary to secular law and enforcing punishment on offenders. The sacred texts in the Abrahamic tradition are quite elaborate in directing authorities to mete out sanctions against all manner of behaviors and prescribe often barbaric punishments to those who violate religious proscriptions. The politicization of crime and punishment in the United States has a marked racial component, with African Americans suffering from both the brunt of victimization and a legal and judicial

*Table 5.5. Crime and Punishment and Religious Identification*

| Identification | Support capital punishment, whites | Support capital punishment, blacks | Support gun laws, whites | Support gun laws, blacks | Legalize marijuana, whites | Legalize marijuana, blacks |
|---|---|---|---|---|---|---|
| Mormon | 88.5% | 81.8% | 60.1% | 50.0% | 13.5% | 33.3% |
| Baptist | 82.5% | 48.8% | 67.9% | 81.6% | 17.7% | 24.0% |
| Moderate Protestant | 80.6% | 51.7% | 73.3% | 82.6% | 20.9% | 24.4% |
| Lutheran | 79.8% | 72.5% | 75.7% | 79.3% | 22.4% | 37.0% |
| Other Protestant | 78.8% | 40.1% | 66.9% | 89.1% | 31.1% | 26.5% |
| Liberal Protestant | 77.0% | 46.8% | 77.8% | 87.0% | 23.1% | 47.4% |
| Episcopalian | 76.5% | 62.9% | 80.1% | 87.0% | 30.2% | 15.6% |
| Sectarian Protestant | 76.0% | 42.3% | 70.7% | 82.3% | 14.9% | 14.9% |
| Catholic | 74.7% | 54.5% | 82.5% | 83.5% | 25.5% | 30.3% |
| Jewish | 71.0% | 50.0% | 93.5% | 81.8% | 46.9% | 25.0% |
| None | 69.5% | 45.5% | 75.2% | 76.4% | 56.6% | 46.1% |
| Other religion | 66.8% | 47.1% | 79.0% | 79.8% | 43.8% | 39.1% |
| Unitarian | 51.7% | 50.0% | 89.0% | 100.0% | 52.0% | 33.3% |
| Total | 76.8% | 48.7% | 75.7% | 82.0% | 26.9% | 25.8% |

system which creates harsh laws targeting African Americans and other minorities and metes out punishment more severely on minorities. The GSS does not provide an elaborate array of indicators about crime and punishment, but three items are quite revealing: beliefs about capital punishment, views on gun control, and support for the legalization of marijuana. Table 5.5 examines how religious identification structures these opinions quite differently for whites and African Americans. On these issues, Europeans of all types hold similar responses by religion, and for the sake of parsimony, the analyses are presented for whites and African Americans.

Among white Americans, support for capital punishment is exceptionally strong (nearly 77%), and table 5.5 shows that Mormons are most enthusiastic in their support for capital punishment—with over 88% supporting state-sanctioned killing. Baptists and moderate Protestants are next highest, with over 80% supporting capital punishment. Interestingly, sectarian Protestants are slightly below the mean, perhaps driven by official opposition in some sects such as the Jehovah's Witnesses and Adventists. Despite the Catholic Church's opposition, nearly three-fourths of white Catholics support capital punishment. Nonidentifiers are below the mean at less than 70%, while two-thirds of "other religion" identifiers support capital punishment. Indeed, even more than half of white Unitarians sanction execution.

In contrast, the majority of African Americans oppose capital punishment, and the traditional African American Baptist and Methodist identifications help drive that opposition. The contrast between white and African American Baptists, moderate Protestants, and sectarians is considerable—more than a 30% gap between white Baptists and African American Baptists and nearly that for moderate Protestants. African American Catholics are also more likely to side with the church in opposing capital punishment; however, African American Catholics are more supportive of the death penalty than are "black mainline" Baptist and Methodist respondents. African American sectarian Protestants are among the least supportive of capital punishment, with only 42% favoring state-sanctioned killing. Asians are somewhat less enthusiastic about capital punishment compared to Europeans, with about 70% support, in part because of large proportions of nonidentifiers who reject capital punishment at the same rate as European nonidentifiers. And Asian Catholics are more likely than European Catholics to follow the Catholic Church in opposition to execution—with 67% supporting the death penalty. Latin Americans are also less supportive of capital punishment at 61%, in large part because of high concentrations of Catholics and low support among sectarians; 63% of Latin American Catholics support the death penalty, and only 46% of Latin American sectarian Protestants are in favor of capital punishment.

Despite the profound political clout held by lobbying organizations militating to eliminate laws controlling the sale, transportation, and use of guns, most Americans favor stricter gun-control laws—and African Americans are more enthusiastic about regulating weapons than are whites. The GSS asked respondents whether they favor gun registration permits. And, much like on capital punishment, religious identifications structure beliefs about gun control quite differently for whites and African Americans. For both groups, Mormons are the least favorable toward gun registration—though the majority of Mormons favor gun permits. Among whites, Baptists, sectarians, and other Protestants are less enthusiastic about gun registration—while among African Americans, these groups strongly favor gun permits. Breaking down the data across western and eastern Europeans does not change the

relationships, but eastern Europeans are more supportive of gun registration, in large part because they are more Jewish and more Catholic.
The racial gap among other Protestants is 22%, and for Baptists, it is
14%. A double-digit racial difference is also found for sectarian Protestants, and the difference is nearly that among moderate and liberal
Protestants. In contrast, there are no racial differences in support for
gun control among Catholics or nonidentifiers. Latin Americans also
support gun registration at high rates, with 84% supporting gun permits, and Catholic identifications play a role in Latin American support—84% of Latin American Catholics support gun registration. Similarly, Asians are quite comfortable with increased gun regulation, and
much of that support comes from the majority of Asians who are nonreligious or adhere to a non-Christian faith; 86% of Asian nonidentifiers support gun registration, while 92% of Asians with a non-Christian
identification want guns to be registered.

The "war on drugs" has long been directed primarily against African
Americans and other minorities, yet African Americans have also suffered from high rates of drug abuse in their communities, and antidrug
sentiment runs high (Meares 1997). Overall, there are no substantial
racial differences in support for legalizing marijuana—however, there
are racial differences in how religious identifications structure support
for legalization. In general, support for legalization is highest among
nonidentifiers, Jews, other non-Christians, and Unitarians. Mormons,
sectarians, and Baptists report low levels of support for legalization.
Support for marijuana legalization is higher among African Americans
compared to whites in the "black mainline" Baptist and moderate Protestant groups and among Catholics, Lutherans, and liberal Protestants.
But support for legalization is identical for whites and African Americans who identify with other sects. African American nonidentifiers are
less favorable toward legalizing marijuana than are white nonidentifiers. Indeed, the same is true for Asian and Latin American nonidentifiers—only 41% of Asians and Latin Americans who reject religious
identification support legalization. Asians from other religions also are
quite conservative on marijuana legalization, with only 19% supporting legalization. And table 5.5 shows that African Americans who identify as other Protestant and Episcopalian are less supportive of legalization than are whites with those identifications. Overall, connections

to more liberal religious groups and to the historical core of the black mainline boost support for ending the war on drugs, but in the absence of those ties, African Americans are more conservative than are their white counterparts.

## Religious Identification and Mainstream Politics

Ultimately, the religious structuring of political understandings will serve to influence how people interact with political resources—directing voting, party identification, and general political identification. Mainstream politics in the United States is heavily influenced by race and ethnicity—with ethnic minorities tending not to vote for conservative candidates, being less likely to identify with the Republican Party, and holding less conservative political identifications. Recent research has shown quite persuasively that religion plays a strong role in mainstream politics and that trends in religious identification help shape voting patterns because of two key trends—increasing Republican identification among sectarian Protestants and among Catholics (Brooks and Manza 2004; Manza and Brooks 1997). Using GSS data, we can usefully examine how religious identification influences presidential voting, Republican Party identification, and self-identified political conservatism across the ethnic divisions. By examining these relationships by ethnicity, we will see how the trends in partisanship and voting behavior are largely a function of growing Republicanism among European Catholics and sectarians.

Table 5.6 examines how religious identification and ethnicity influence voting for a conservative presidential candidate in the presidential election prior to the GSS interview. Most of these candidates were from the Republican Party, but there have also been conservative third-party candidates who garnered a substantial plurality of votes (particularly Ross Perot in 1992 and 1996). Overall, western European respondents had a much more conservative voting record, with 63% voting for the conservative candidate in the previous election, compared to 52% for eastern Europeans. For the non-European ethnicities, only about 18% of African Americans and 43% of Latin Americans reported voting for the conservative candidate, while the figures were 48% for Native Americans and 47% for Asians.

*Table 5.6. Voting for a Conservative Presidential Candidate by Religious Identification and Ethnicity*

| Identification | Western European | Eastern European | African American | Latin American | Native American | Asian |
|---|---|---|---|---|---|---|
| Mormon | 83.3% | 75.0% | 33.3% | 68.8% | 64.3% | 100.0% |
| Sectarian Protestant | 75.6% | 80.4% | 23.2% | 57.1% | 74.4% | 80.6% |
| Baptist | 73.2% | 79.5% | 16.1% | 50.8% | 74.5% | 41.2% |
| Other Protestant | 68.8% | 62.8% | 21.7% | 55.3% | 76.4% | 63.4% |
| Moderate Protestant | 68.3% | 58.2% | 14.3% | 37.9% | 60.0% | 71.4% |
| Liberal Protestant | 65.9% | 75.0% | 29.4% | 63.6% | 48.3% | 44.4% |
| Lutheran | 64.9% | 60.0% | 28.6% | 53.8% | 81.8% | 83.3% |
| Episcopalian | 62.2% | 63.2% | 19.1% | 50.0% | 66.7% | 25.0% |
| Catholic | 61.2% | 58.2% | 21.8% | 40.1% | 46.2% | 52.3% |
| None | 46.5% | 39.1% | 23.3% | 38.0% | 52.1% | 35.9% |
| Other religion | 43.4% | 50.0% | 19.2% | 44.4% | 53.8% | 36.5% |
| Jewish | 32.7% | 27.4% | 30.8% | 66.7% | — | 44.4% |
| Unitarian | 32.0% | 0% | 0% | 100.0% | 0% | 100.0% |
| Total | 63.4% | 52.2% | 18.5% | 43.4% | 65.4% | 46.8% |

Religious identifications are particularly important for influencing presidential voting for most ethnic groups—though less so for African Americans, who overwhelmingly reject conservative presidential candidates. Mormons are particularly fond of conservative presidential candidates, and 83% of western European and 75% of eastern European Mormons reported voting for a conservative in the last election, and Mormons have the highest rates of conservative voting across all ethnic groups. European sectarians and Baptists tend to vote for conservative candidates; about 80% of eastern European sectarians voted conservative (slightly higher than among western European sectarians and Baptists). Asian sectarians are also very conservative in their voting behavior, with nearly 81% voting conservative. Latin American Baptists and sectarians are more likely to vote for conservative politicians than are Latin Americans who identify with moderate Protestant groups or the dominant Catholic Church. However, African American Baptists and sectarians overwhelmingly reject conservative presidential candidates—as do African American moderate Protestants. Indeed, European sectarians and Baptists are more than three times as likely to vote conservative compared to their African American counterparts. Among whites, Jews and Unitarians have the least conservative voting records, followed by adherents of other religions and nonidentifiers (less than half of whom voted conservative in the previous election).

While Catholic voting has traditionally tended to favor Democrats (Jennings and Niemi 1981; Nie, Verba, and Petrocik 1979), table 5.6 shows that since the 1976 presidential election (GSS data cover back to the 1968 election, but the ethnicity measure came later), 61% of western European Catholics and 58% of eastern European Catholics voted for a Republican or independent conservative. African American Catholics are somewhat more conservative than are African Americans in the Baptist and moderate Protestant churches, but only 22% voted for a conservative in the last election. Latin American Catholics also avoid voting for conservatives (40%). Asian Catholics have voting records that are more conservative than is the average Asian respondent's, with 52% reporting a conservative vote.

Nonidentifiers tend not to favor conservative presidential candidates across all the ethnic groups; however, African American nonidentifiers were somewhat more conservative in their voting patterns than were other African Americans, and they are substantially more conservative than are African Americans who identify with the traditional Baptist and Methodist denominations. Asians' voting is rooted firmly in their tendency to reject religious affiliation, and fewer than 36% of Asian nonidentifiers reported voting conservative in the last election; the large contingent of Asians who adhere to other religions also rarely vote conservative (37%).

The traditional political conservatism of the European Protestant mainline is also evident. Among western European GSS respondents, almost two-thirds of respondents who identify with liberal Protestant groups voted for conservatives in the last presidential election, while a higher percentage (68%) of white moderate Protestants voted for conservative candidates. Indeed, eastern Europeans who adhere to liberal Protestant and moderate Protestant identities were even more likely to vote for conservatives—contrary to the old assumption of white Anglo-Saxon conservatism. Eastern Europeans appear more politically liberal because many of them are Catholic or Jewish. Episcopalians and Lutherans were less likely to vote conservative than were moderate Protestants or liberal Protestants—once again showing that the amalgamated "mainline Protestant" classification used by many researchers masks considerable diversity.

Party identification is an important source of political cues and of connections to the political system, guiding perspectives about political issues and directing political activism and voting. Religious identifications have long been a source of connections to political parties, and table 5.7 examines how religious identifications and ethnicity influence identification with the Republican Party. Historically, the Republican Party embraced a strong, probusiness orientation, tinged with a substantial opposition to communism. That orientation attracted members of the upper classes and made the party a favorite among "white Anglo-Saxon Protestants" from the liberal and moderate traditions. Overall, identification with the Republican Party is heavily western European, and in the cumulative GSS, nearly 43% of western Europeans identify as Republican or "strongly Republican," while only 28% of eastern Europeans identify with the Republicans. Less than 9% of African Americans identify as Republican, half the rate found among Latin Americans (18%), while about a third of Native Americans and 27% of Asians identify as Republican.

Among Europeans, Asians, and Latin Americans, religious identification is strongly associated with political identification, while African

Table 5.7. Republican Identification by Religious Identification and Ethnicity

| Identification | Western European | Eastern European | African American | Latin American | Native American | Asian |
|---|---|---|---|---|---|---|
| Mormon | 68.8% | 25.0% | 28.6% | 52.2% | 42.9% | 80.0% |
| Liberal Protestant | 57.0% | 52.7% | 6.5% | 21.4% | 30.2% | 27.8% |
| Episcopalian | 54.5% | 36.8% | 7.2% | 25.0% | 46.7% | — |
| Moderate Protestant | 50.8% | 33.0% | 8.1% | 34.9% | 38.4% | 42.1% |
| Lutheran | 48.3% | 38.5% | 15.2% | 10.5% | 41.2% | 56.2% |
| Other Protestant | 48.2% | 34.5% | 8.9% | 30.5% | 41.0% | 40.0% |
| Sectarian Protestant | 47.0% | 43.4% | 8.7% | 18.3% | 38.3% | 44.7% |
| Baptist | 44.9% | 45.7% | 7.9% | 25.0% | 35.9% | 35.7% |
| Catholic | 35.6% | 29.3% | 11.0% | 16.5% | 26.3% | 33.6% |
| Unitarian | 32.1% | 12.5% | — | — | — | 100.0% |
| Other religion | 25.4% | 26.4% | 9.8% | 21.4% | 16.9% | 20.6% |
| None | 25.1% | 18.2% | 9.2% | 11.3% | 20.9% | 14.5% |
| Jewish | 21.2% | 17.8% | 5.3% | 33.3% | — | 7.7% |
| Total | 42.8% | 28.0% | 8.5% | 17.8% | 33.5% | 27.0% |

Americans' political alignments hold less variation—with the exception of higher rates of Republican identification among African American Mormons (29%). The lingering influence of social-class stratification is readily apparent—while Mormons have the highest rates of Republican identification, over half of western European liberal Protestants, Episcopalians, and moderate Protestants identify as Republican, and Lutherans are not far behind. The majority of eastern European liberal Protestants hold a Republican identification, but while other eastern European Protestants have tended to vote conservative in presidential elections, they have not shifted political identities to the Republican Party. Western and eastern European sectarians and Baptists may vote Republican at very high rates, but western European sectarians and Baptists are scarcely above average on Republican Party identification, though eastern European Baptists and sectarians are far more likely to be Republicans than are other eastern Europeans. This is largely because of the high concentration of Catholics and Jews among eastern Europeans, and under 30% of eastern European Catholics and 18% of eastern European Jews identify as Republican (21% for western European Jews). Western European Catholics are less Republican than are other western Europeans (36%), and under a third of western European Unitarians identify as Republican (29%); the figure is under 13% for eastern Europeans. Nonidentifiers have very low rates of Republican identification across all ethnic groups.

Republican identification is also connected to moderate Protestant identification among Asians and Latin Americans, but not among African Americans. And African American and Latin American Catholics are even less likely to identify as Republican than are their European counterparts. Non-Christians from all ethnic groups also tend to reject Republican identification, and this is particularly important among Asians—for whom those religious identities are quite prevalent.

Beginning in the 1950s, the anticommunist stripe in the Republican Party brought in many Americans from the more sectarian Protestant segments of the religious market—and this attraction has continued. In the past five decades, there has been a considerable shift in party identification among whites, particularly in the South, where the collapse of the whites-only, one-party, Democratic monopoly has led to substantial growth in Republican identification (Carsey and Layman 2006; Giles

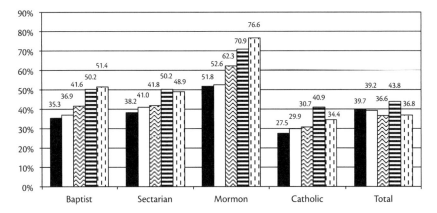

■ Pre-1925 cohort   ☐ 1925–1943 cohort   ⊟ 1944–1955 cohort   ⊟ 1956–1970 cohort   ⊡ 1971–1994 cohort

Fig. 5.3. Surging Republican identification among conservative Christians by generation

and Hertz 1994; Layman 2001; Layman, Carsey, and Horowitz 2006). Richard Nixon's "Southern Strategy" deliberately targeted whites to recruit them to the Republican Party, and the vast majority of these white southerners were Baptists, Methodists, or sectarian Protestants. During the period covered by the GSS, the Republican Party abandoned its traditional libertarianism on civil rights, gender, and sexuality and embraced a social conservatism which was attractive to many sectarians as well as to more conservative Catholics.

Figure 5.3 examines how Republican identification has shifted across generations by religious identification. Notably, overall, identification with the Republican Party has decreased from about 40% of GSS respondents in the oldest cohorts to 37% in the youngest cohorts. However, the peak of Republican identification is among respondents born from 1956 to 1970—likely caused by the "Reagan Revolution." In contrast, for four religious identifications, the overall trend is almost uniformly positive—Baptists, sectarians, Mormons, and Catholics all show increased identification with the Republican Party across generations. In the pre-1925 cohort, only 35% of Baptists identified as Republican, while over half of Baptist respondents in the post-1955 generations identify as Republican. The trend among sectarians matches that found among Baptists; and among Mormons, the shift is even more dramatic —going from 52% in the oldest cohorts to 77% in the latest cohorts.

Catholics have been less attracted to the Republican Party; however, while only 28% of Catholics born before 1925 identify as Republican, that percentage increases to nearly 41% in the large 1956–1970 cohort, before dipping to 34% for Catholics born after 1970.

Another way that Americans identify politically is in general conceptual terms as liberals or conservatives. Table 5.8 shows how religious identifications and ethnicity help structure political conservatism. Here, the GSS asks respondents to answer the question of their political liberalism or conservatism on an ordinal scale, and we focus on the distinctiveness of respondents who identify as "conservative" or "very conservative." Interestingly, while western Europeans are more likely to report being conservative than are most other ethnicities, the difference is not very large, and Native Americans and Asians are both more likely to report being conservative than are western Europeans. African Americans and Latin Americans are the least likely to report being conservative.

Mormons have the highest rates of political conservatism, followed by sectarians, other Protestants, and Baptists. Contrary to much popular discussion, Catholic respondents are relatively unlikely to self-identify as conservative. And liberal and moderate Protestants do not differ in their conservatism among whites. Nonidentifiers are substantially less

*Table 5.8. Conservative Political Identification by Religious Identification and Ethnicity*

| Identification | Western European | Eastern European | African American | Latin American | Native American | Asian |
|---|---|---|---|---|---|---|
| Mormon | 37.5% | 25.0% | 20.0% | 30.0% | 16.7% | — |
| Sectarian Protestant | 30.7% | 31.9% | 17.0% | 18.4% | 29.7% | 18.4% |
| Baptist | 27.3% | 30.0% | 14.1% | 20.2% | 23.0% | 14.7% |
| Other Protestant | 24.9% | 23.9% | 16.4% | 19.8% | 19.1% | 21.2% |
| Liberal Protestant | 19.8% | 20.9% | 6.2% | 16.7% | 19.0% | 22.6% |
| Moderate Protestant | 19.5% | 17.8% | 13.9% | 17.9% | 13.2% | 19.4% |
| Episcopalian | 19.3% | 17.2% | 10.5% | — | 7.1% | — |
| Lutheran | 17.9% | 12.7% | 7.7% | 5.6% | 25.8% | 28.6% |
| Catholic | 15.9% | 16.7% | 9.7% | 13.4% | 15.1% | 15.7% |
| Other religion | 13.7% | 15.3% | 8.8% | 29.2% | 14.0% | 6.3% |
| Jewish | 8.0% | 7.2% | 30.8% | 14.3% | — | 9.1% |
| None | 7.8% | 8.9% | 9.7% | 10.1% | 10.2% | 12.9% |
| Unitarian | 2.0% | — | — | — | — | 10.3% |
| Total | 19.3% | 15.0% | 13.6% | 14.4% | 19.7% | 22.6% |

likely to identify as conservative across all ethnic groups—and very few Unitarians or Jews identify as conservative.

## Religion, Politics, and Polarization

Religious divisions in the United States are heavily politicized, and religious institutions forge identities which leave an indelible mark on political beliefs and commitments. The regulation of sexuality, ethnic politics, education, civil liberties, and crime and punishment are all strongly impacted by religious commitments—and these religiously inspired political beliefs impact political identifications and behaviors, such as voting and other political activities. In this chapter, we have seen how religion influences these beliefs and how these religious influences vary across ethnic groups. We have also seen how the political distinctiveness of some ethnic groups—particularly eastern Europeans, Asians, and Latin Americans—is in large part a function of religious identification. Given the shifts in religious identifications over time and across cohorts and the importance of ethnicity and immigration for those changes, our current state of political polarization seems inevitable. In the mid-20th century, American Christianity was dominated by relatively universalistic moderate and liberal Protestantism, along with a large contingent of sectarian groups and a diverse ethnic Catholic Church which condoned and supported Anglo-assimilation. Few people failed to embrace a religious identity, and they were certainly not numerous enough to mount political struggles. Fast-forward to the first decade of the 21st century, and American Protestantism is more driven by European sectarian Protestant groups, African American Protestants with quite different political orientations toward their faith, and an ethnic Catholic Church dominated by newer ethnic groups and controlled by a conservative Anglo-dominated hierarchy.

But Catholics no longer differ as substantially from liberal and moderate Protestants on social and political issues. Even on issues such as abortion and same-sex marriage, contemporary Catholics are not distinctive from the liberal and moderate mainline Protestant groups and are often more liberal (particularly on same-sex marriage), and the growing category of Protestant with no particular denomination also holds a political middle ground. The "new middle" seems to be the nonsectarian Protestants and Catholics. But the big story for religion and politics for the coming decades is the growth of non-Christian America. Increasing proportions of Americans reject religious identification or identify with non-Christian groups, and by 2012, these non-Christians and nonidentified Americans were more numerous than Baptists and sectarian Protestants—24.8% versus 22.9%. As we have seen, non-Christian Americans are consistently the most liberal in their political commitments, while exclusivist Christians have a strong impulse to use the state to regulate behaviors they consider to be against the will of their god, and they support conservative political organizations and candidates to further this goal.

Notably, the nexus between religion and politics in the United States is primarily about the regulation of social and sexual behaviors. Religious identifications do not seem to generate substantial political mobilizations for economic policies, in contrast to the way religion influences politics in many nations such as India, Turkey, and El Salvador. Playing politics is always dangerous for religious groups, because the winners and losers in politics do not neatly conform to religious cleavages. In the United States, politicization of religious groups may be helping the spread of secularism (Hout and Fischer 2002), as people decide not to identify with religious groups that are actively seeking to limit civil liberties or that are pushing for political positions favorable only for some people. The "white hot" religious mobilizations in the past forty years have been forged in the crucible of exclusivist Christianity—sectarian Protestantism and conservative Catholicism (Zald 1982). These movements seek to mold laws in a way that will limit access to contraception and abortion, deny women and ethnic minorities rights, force others to pray to their god, and condemn and stigmatize all manner of nonmarital sexuality while preventing same-sex couples from marrying. For an increasing number of Americans, the stridently exclusivist orientation of politicized Christianity is not simply not their cup of tea—it is a nefarious political opponent seeking to destroy the core values of America.

# Conclusions

## *Making Sense of Shifting Identities and Their Influence*

This book has presented analyses of forty years of GSS data to examine the distribution and dynamics of religious identifications and to show how these identifications influence religious beliefs and behaviors, family values and commitments, stratification outcomes, and political beliefs and behaviors. We have seen that religious diversity is a product of distinctive identifications with sets of denominations and traditions and that this religious diversity is indelibly influenced by ethnicity. This book has provided several key insights about patterns and trends in religious identification and how these identifications matter. First, we have seen that grand theories of religious change do a poor job of explaining the dynamics of religious identification, because they fail to grapple with how family processes, stratification, ethnicity, and even political factors influence and are influenced by religious identification. Second, this book has focused on the impact of religious identifications on social phenomena across ethnic groups, highlighting the importance of the connections between ethnicity and religious identifications. And, finally, it has shown that dynamics of religious identification are helping to drive increasing polarization in American politics.

Religious identification remains robust and salient. While we have seen that one of the most substantial trends over time and across generations is the rejection of religious identification, 80% of Americans still identify with a religious tradition or denomination. And those identifications remain quite influential across a variety of social domains. While many scholars have argued that the influence of religion is decreasing or that only exclusivist religion is consequential, this book has shown that the impact of religious identifications is evident across the spectrum of religious identities and that the impact of religious identification is often dependent on ethnicity. We have seen that the impulse to dichotomize religious orientations into competing camps of "orthodox and progressive" (Hunter 1991) or "mainline versus evangelical" (Wuthnow 1988, 1993) hinders our understanding of how and when religious identifications matter—and identifications with specific denominations remain consequential.

We have seen in the previous chapters that there is no uniform "mainline" Protestantism—liberal Protestants differ from Episcopalians, and moderates Protestants are not the same as Lutherans. People who identify as Baptist also differ from other sectarian Protestants—particularly for African Americans and people with other non-European ethnicities. For individuals, religious identification means more than the theological commonalities amplified by ecumenical organizations such as the National Council of Churches or the National Association of Evangelicals. Indeed, even within a given religious identity, such as Catholicism, ethnicity and nativity matter for how Catholic identity works to impact both religious commitments and other social outcomes. Religious identities are rooted in family and ethnicity, and they will continue to influence many aspects of American life.

## Beyond Winners and Losers:
## Taking Religious Diversity Seriously

The study of American religion has long suffered from a majoritarian complex—the impulse to imply that the future of religious institutions and religious influence is going to follow the lead of the religious groups with the largest plurality in the religious market. Bigger is assumed to be better, and from the staid tomes of liberal Protestant scholars to the deductive models of supply-side economists, there has been an assumption that something about particular types of religious beliefs and practices explains the proportion of Americans who identify with specific religious groups. Liberal Christian scholars (both Catholic and Protestant) have assumed that people flock to religious groups that provide meaning and relevance to their lives in the modern world. Supply-side theorists contend that exclusivist religious doctrines tip the advantage to sectarian religious groups rather than more universalistic religious denominations. Yet most contemporary sociological research and theorizing emphasizes the primacy of demographic processes, and sociologists amplify the importance of social ties and normative constraints for learning religious explanations, participating in religious organizations, and identifying with religious groups (Hout, Greeley, and Wilde 2001; Sherkat 2010a). From the sociological perspective, the relative size and influence of religious groups is more a function of immigration, fertility, and mortality than it is of the religious products of the various denominations.

Catholic and liberal Protestant religious commentators began amplifying the importance of the relevance of religion for modern life in response to growing secularism in Europe and in reaction to fundamentalism in the United States (Butler, Wacker, and Balmer 2007; Marty 1999; Marty and Appleby 2004). Indeed, much of the rationale for the reforms of Vatican II were based on the perceived need to make the Catholic Church more relevant for the modern world and to increase the voluntary participation of the laity in church affairs (Finke and Stark 1992; Taylor and Heft 1999). Similarly, the deliberate dissociation of liberal Protestant theology from otherworldly religious narratives was predicated on the belief that modernity would lead to the rejection of otherworldly religion—and churches would be left empty if they failed to acknowledge the consciousness reformation forged in modern secular society (Bellah 1970, 1976, 2008; Glock, Bellah, and Alfred 1976; Wuthnow 1976). In this view, capturing the majority for the faith requires attention to what "everyone" wants from religion.

Interestingly, supply-side theories of religious action were forged on the notion that "everyone" does not have a specific preferred type of religion, and original formulations by Laurence Iannaccone (1991) and Roger Finke and Rodney Stark (1988, 1992) argued that religion flourishes where there are diverse religious options. Indeed, supply-side theorists assume that preferences for religious explanations are inherently diverse because of social differentiation and that homogeneous religious "production" can only occur when the state regulates religious markets and prevents competition. Yet some additional theorizing by Iannaccone (1992, 1994) led to a supply-side teleology with less diverse market outcomes. Iannaccone argued that religious groups which are more exclusive produce more valuable religious goods, and therefore exclusivist sects are argued to have better "religious production." In contrast, ecumenical religious groups with more universalistic perspectives on religious rewards and punishments, and less vividly otherworldly religious explanations, are expected to decline—because their religious products are deemed inferior by supply-side advocates. And so, while supply-side theorists began from the perspective that religious diversity increases religious vitality, they ended with the expectation that only conservative sects will grow in a market governed by individual rationality and freely chosen religious commitments.

But, just as the secularization perspective overestimated the impact of science and modernity on religious vitality, supply-side theorists' assumptions led to erroneous explanations of historical processes and flawed expectations about the future. Indeed, a key mistake of both perspectives is making the assumption that individuals freely choose religious commitments in accordance with their preferences for religious explanations. The history of American religion is instead the history of people coming to a new land and finding or maintaining solidarity with coethnics in religious organizations. Finke and Stark (1992) are correct that the initial waves of European immigrants to the United States were disconnected from religion, in large part because of their key demographic—young men trying to establish a life in what was then a dangerous frontier backwater. But the main reason why English, Scottish, and Welsh settlers did not identify with or participate in the established "mainline" Episcopalian, Congregationalist, and Presbyterian churches had nothing to do with their preferences for particular theologies or worship styles. Instead, new settlers were unwelcome in these established churches, and their only pathway to community respectability would come from the Anglo-focused Methodist and Baptist movements of the 19th century. Further, attraction to these movements was not about their superior religious products but about their open invitation for social benefits and social participation—so long as you were from England, Scotland, or Wales, you could be someone in the community by joining a church. And, until the mid-20th century, religious organizations were one of the very few places for social interaction in the rural areas of the United States, and they remain profoundly important for maintaining family ties, supporting marriage markets, providing opportunities for education and business, and mobilizing politically.

The flourishing of Protestant denominations in the United States is seen by many liberal Protestant and Catholic scholars as the result of the negative influence of fundamentalism and widespread ignorance which hinders ecumenicalism (Niebuhr 1929; Troeltsch 1931). Supply-side theorists argue that diversity is a natural product of diverse preferences combined with limited religious regulation. But the history of American denominationalism is much more complex. The United States lacked substantial religious institutions with the resources and authority to control ministers and congregations. This gave both ministers and congregations considerable latitude to forge associations with other ministers and congregations. Congregations banded together to form denominations, which often merged with other denominations, and frequently spurred movements for a variety of reasons—theological, political, ethnic, and regional factors influenced the birth, merging, and death of denominations. Denominationalism was more a function of organizational dynamics and the elite control of religious groups than it was a product of individuals' freely chosen religious identifications.

Demography drives membership in and identification with voluntary organizations through establishing solidarity based on homophily. People like to associate with people from common ethnic backgrounds, who hold the same occupations, have similar levels of educational attainment, and have comparable family structures (McPherson, Smith-Lovin, and Cook 2001; Munch, McPherson, and Smith-Lovin 1997; Popielarz and McPherson 1995). Religious organizations are no different from other voluntary commitments, and we have seen that many people belong to and identify with religious groups while not sharing the beliefs espoused by the denomination. Indeed, in contradiction to the assumption that people choose religious commitments on the basis of individual preferences, research shows that religious participation is highest in the United States in areas characterized by religious homogeneity and strong social ties—participation is driven by social benefits and normative pressures to show solidarity with the community (Ellison and Sherkat 1995b, 1999; Hunt and Hunt 1999; Sherkat and Cunningham 1998). This is particularly true for ethnic minorities, who tend to have high rates of religious participation and low rates of religious switching. We see this in the stability of identification with ethnic denominations such as Lutherans and Catholics and for ethnic religious traditions such as Judaism, Islam, and Hinduism. We have also seen how religious identities are influenced by social status—people are more likely to leave religious groups when their income and educational attainment are higher or lower than the average identifier from that group. We have seen this dynamic come full circle as religious identification also impacts socioeconomic status.

The "decline" of mostly Anglo-American mainline religious denominations such as Methodists, Presbyterians, and Disciples of Christ was not caused by individuals choosing more exclusivist religious groups but instead was driven by differences in immigration streams, the assimilation of European ethnicity, differential birth rates, and decreasing pressure to identify with religious groups. Changes in immigration laws after World War II meant that an increasing proportion of U.S. immigrants hailed from eastern Europe and eventually from elsewhere in the world. These new sources of American immigrants helped solidify the proportion of Americans who identify with Catholicism, but these new immigration streams also reduced the numbers of Americans identifying with the traditional "white Anglo-Saxon Protestant" denominations. Indeed, the assimilation of western and even eastern European immigrants broke down many of the barriers between Protestant denominations, leading to widespread mergers and a loss of ethnic distinctiveness (Form 2000; Hamilton and Form 2003; Herberg 1983). Identification with religious groups was no longer a marker of ethnic identity, particularly for western Europeans, as many ethnic identities became less salient because of assimilation.

This book has demonstrated two key areas where decreasing social pressure to identify with religious groups has transformed the distribution of religious identification: the increasing proportion of Americans who identify as "Protestant" with no particular denomination and the increasing fraction who reject any religious identification. As we saw earlier in the book, the decreasing proportion of people identifying with Protestant denominations is attributable to increasing numbers of people embracing only a generic Protestant identification or rejecting identification altogether. Across all ethnic groups, identifying as a Protestant with no particular denomination is a growing option over time and across generations. And identifying as a Protestant with no particular denomination is especially popular for western Europeans and Native Americans. Indeed, regardless of ethnicity, it is increasingly common for people to have been raised with no particular denominational identity and to maintain this generic Protestant identity. In many ways, and particularly for western Europeans, these generic Protestants look very much like moderate Protestants or Catholics in their beliefs about religion, social values, family commitments, and political values and behaviors. However, these other Protestants have somewhat lower rates of religious participation—more akin to liberal Protestants or Episcopalians. It is these nominal Protestant identifiers who look more like the "believers who don't belong."

Yet many people who embrace a generic Protestant identity do "belong" to some congregation, and many of them attend quite regularly. Some may attend nondenominational congregations, and many others may not know the denominational association of the church they attend —this is increasingly likely with denominations such as the Southern Baptist Convention that are attempting to jettison their "southernness" by naming churches after places (such as Rick Warren's Saddleback Church) or generically. As noted earlier, in my college town, First Baptist Church was renamed "The View." In a sense, this trend bolsters the claim made by Robert Wuthnow and others (Hunter 1991; Wuthnow 1988, 1993) that denominationalism is in decline. However, as we have seen throughout this research, denominational identities continue to persist and to influence many aspects of American social life.

Two trends are forging a new perspective on religious diversity in the United States: the growth of non-Christian religious identities and the rejection of religious identity. In the older generations, the vast majority of non-Christians in the United States were Jews; however, in the youngest generations, the GSS finds over three times as many non-Christians from other religious traditions as Jews. Non-Christians make up over 5% of the youngest generation, and Hindu, Buddhist, and Muslim religious identities are nearly as prevalent as Jewish identities. Indeed, we have seen that American Hindus are also rivaling American Jews in their educational and income attainment, as other research using data from the New Immigrant Survey has also shown (Amin and Sherkat 2014). Immigration is slowly reshaping the American religious marketplace, and it is likely that the connection between ethnic identification and religious identification will remain strong for these new immigrants. We have seen that, unlike in earlier generations, the younger generations of Hindus, Buddhists, Muslims, and other religions are increasingly likely to retain their religious identification rather than switching to a Christian faith. Religious diversity in the United States will increasingly be about diverse religious traditions and not simply Christian denominationalism.

The most substantial trend in religious identification is the rejection of religious identity. While many commentators have assumed that those who reject a religious identification are simply Christians without a particular denominational connection, this book has shown that the rejection of religious identity is an indication of growing secularism in the United States. Indeed, in the youngest generation, nearly one in four GSS respondents have no religious identification, and almost 60% of people who reject identification are atheist, are agnostic, or believe in a "higher power but not a god." The rejection of religious identification is also tied to increasing levels of educational attainment (Sherkat 1998, Sherkat and Wilson 1995) and to the rejection of politicized Christianity (Hout and Fischer 2002). Paying attention to religious diversity requires increasing acknowledgment that the United States is no longer simply a Christian nation and that a large plurality of Americans reject religion. Indeed, organized atheism and secularism are on the rise, with groups such as the Secular Student Alliance (SSA) and the Freedom From Religion Foundation enjoying substantial mobilization success. Between 2007 and 2012, the SSA grew from having affiliated student organizations at 80 schools to having them at 413 (Niose 2012). People who reject religion are beginning to push back against the hegemonic authority of exclusivist Christianity (J. Smith 2011; Zuckerman 2009). And, as we have seen throughout this book, people who reject religious identification are quite distinctive in many social arenas.

This research has shown that the American religious marketplace is undergoing a market correction. The religious hyperactivity of Americans was rooted in ethnic competition and social expectations to identify with a Christian religious group, but ethnic assimilation combined with increased immigration from non-Christian nations no longer makes identification compulsory—particularly not for people of European and Asian descent. Indeed, we have seen that the majority of Asian Americans either identify with a non-Christian religious tradition or have no religious identification. We can expect that future generations of Americans will be much less likely to identify with Christian religious groups and that this exceptional characteristic of the American religious landscape will fade.

## The Social Impact of Religious Identification

Despite the clear trend of declining Protestant denominational identification, religious identities matter, and they continue to influence social life across generations and ethnic groups. People who maintain identifications with religious denominations are quite distinctive in their religious commitments, their family structure and functioning, their social status, and their political orientations. Among Protestants, these differences are consistent across ethnicities—confirming the longstanding social sources of denominationalism that divide religious bodies into exclusivist sects and more universalistic denominations. Further, we have seen that there is a middle ground of Christian identification in the United States and that moderate Protestants, Lutherans, and Catholics make up the middle—though with some variation for non-European Catholics. Jews and people who identify with other non-Christian religious traditions also have distinctive patterns of social engagement, and Mormon identification sometimes structures social life in a way similar to exclusivist sectarian identities—yet Mormon identity and its consequences differs from sectarian Protestantism.

Religious identifications influence how often people engage in public religious activities such as church or mosque attendance, as well as private religious behaviors such as prayer. Many treatments of these associations set the standard for attendance at the poles of the distribution—people who identify with exclusivist sects and Mormons attend very frequently, while those who identify with more universalistic religious groups are less regular in their attendance. As we have seen, this tendency to use exclusivist groups as a positive standard misses the point. The hyperactivity of exclusivist groups overshadows the regular patterns of attendance found among those who identify with more universalistic religious groups. Research has shown that social desirability biases play a role in Americans' self-reported church attendance—people report attending more often than they do (Hadaway, Marler, and Chaves 1993), and people who hold identifications with exclusivist sectarian groups may feel more compelled to exaggerate their religious participation than those who identify with groups with less rigid expectations. Also, we have seen that non-Christians—Jews, Hindus, Muslims, Buddhists, and others—have low rates of public religious activity. As supply-side theorists would argue, for many non-Christians, low participation may well be a function of limited availability—most American communities lack a mosque or a Hindu, Buddhist, or Sikh temple. As the new immigrants establish more of a foothold, we can expect burgeoning development of religious services and greater diversity for these "other" religious traditions.

Religious identifications continue to have a strong influence on what people believe about the supernatural—about whether there is a god and if this god inspired instructions found in sacred texts. Mormons and sectarians tend to believe in their god with no doubts, while people from more universalistic denominations and Catholics are more circumspect. Again, we should not privilege the sectarian pole of the distribution, since the proper belief to hold for good Catholics, Lutherans, Episcopalians, and others is that doubt is a part of faith. Similarly, people who identify with universalistic Christian groups are not "supposed" to believe that the Bible is the inerrant word of god, and a good Episcopalian may well view the Bible as largely a book of fables. Hence, the importance of denominational identification is revealed both in the tendency of sectarians to embrace exclusivist beliefs and the prevalence of doubt and secularism among more universalistic religious identifiers.

Another key finding of this book has been that the influence of religious identification on religious participation and beliefs is relatively uniform across ethnic groups. Exclusivist Protestant groups command participation and socialize members into narratives that reinforce certainty about the existence of god, an afterlife, eternal punishment for sinners, and the inerrancy of sacred texts. Moderate Protestants, Catholics, and Lutherans form a middle ground, while liberal Protestants and Episcopalians are satisfied with monthly participation and view the Christian narratives as primarily allegorical.

Indeed, interethnic similarities in the effects of religious identifications are evident across other realms of social life as well. Across all ethnic groups, exclusivist sectarian Protestants tend to marry earlier, have more children, and value obedience in their children, enforced by corporal punishment, when compared to more universalistic Christian traditions, non-Christians, and people who reject religious identification. And, across all ethnic groups, people identifying with exclusivist sects are opposed to nonmarital sexuality of any kind; yet they are just as likely as people who identify with other religious groups to engage in premarital sex, extramarital sex, and homosexuality, and sectarians also have higher rates of divorce than do people with most other religious identifications. Religious identities are closely linked to orientations toward family and to decisions about marriage and fertility. Indeed, the close connection between religion and family helps to ensure the continued impact of religious identifications on other arenas of social life. People from universalistic traditions grow up seeking their own path to knowledge, with parents who value independent thought and who trust their children to make the correct decisions. People who identify with universalistic religious traditions tend to be raised accepting human sexuality as normal, even in the absence of marriage, and viewing marriage and fertility as requiring considerable maturity and planning. Exclusivist religious groups view sexuality as problematic and prescribe early marriage to prevent premarital sex. Contraception and sex education is also viewed in a negative light, and high fertility and female subordination are prescribed functions of the family for those who identify with exclusivist groups. Family life is more omnipresent for those who embrace exclusivist identifications, and the pressure of early marriage, high fertility, and sacralized expectations of family roles puts strain on marriages, often leading to divorce. The most marked contrast to the experiences of exclusivist sectarian Protestants is with those who hold Jewish identifications. We have seen that Jews have the highest rates of premarital sex, very tolerant views of nonmarital sexuality, older ages of marriage, and fewer children—and they have the lowest rates of divorce.

The impact of religious identifications on family factors has consequences far beyond family life. While many sociological investigations link social-status differences across religious groups to the confluence of inherited wealth and inherited religion (Davidson 1994; Davidson and Pyle 2011; Davidson, Pyle, and Reyes 1995), more recent investigations are increasingly amplifying how the religion-and-family connection influences social-status differences across religious identifications (Fitzgerald and Glass 2012; Keister 2011; Lehrer 2008). Over the course of the 20th century, the United States went from being a predominantly agrarian nation, where the inheritance of land or benefiting from confiscations from the indigenous populations determined fortunes, to being a modern industrial and postindustrial society, where stratification outcomes are in much larger part determined by educational and occupational attainment processes (Blau and Duncan 1967; Kerckhoff 1976). Religious identifications help direct stratification outcomes and reproduce patterns of social status by influencing educational attainment, occupational choices, and even patterns of saving and investing. In this book, we have seen how religious identities are associated with the completion of college, labor-force participation for women, and income—and these patterns are fairly consistent across ethnic groups.

What is clear is that across all ethnic groups, sectarian Protestant and Baptist identification is associated with low educational achievement, limited occupational attainment, and lower incomes. Hostility toward education is considerable in sectarian Protestant circles, and this consistently has translated into lower rates of postsecondary educational attainment, particularly for women (Darnell and Sherkat 1997; Lehrer 1999a, 2008; Sherkat and Darnell 1999). Exclusivist sectarian identities are also associated with low levels of verbal ability and scientific literacy—even after controlling for educational attainment—and this could undermine occupational attainment and performance (Sherkat 2010b, 2011). Because sectarian communities tend to be insular and to discourage social ties with nonbelievers, the social networks of people with sectarian identities have a limited capacity to assist with educational and occupational attainment. The strong ties to fellow coreligionists and distrust of people who do not identify with one's own religious group may prevent the development of weak social ties, which often translate into socioeconomic benefits (DiPrete et al. 2011; Granovetter 1973, 1985). Sectarian income disadvantages are particularly evident when household incomes are calculated per family member, since larger family sizes divide the scarce resources of sectarian and Baptist families. Worse yet is the economic position of women in sectarian religion and in the Latter-Day Saints. Women are discouraged from gaining educational attainment and from pursuing permanent careers. The results are clear: women who identify as Baptist, sectarian, or Mormon are less likely to be employed and earn less money if they are. And, as we have seen, early ages of marriage, high fertility, and high rates of divorce create a disastrous economic situation for women from these religious groups. Divorced women who identify with these religious groups are shouldered with the burden of children and with minimal human-capital resources to attain careers or earn money. Religious identifications have consequences, and patriarchal religious strictures help to anchor sectarians, Baptists, and Mormons at the bottom of the socioeconomic ladder—and women and female-headed families bear the brunt of the negative effects of religious identification on socioeconomic outcomes.

One exception to the relative invariance of the association between religious identity and socioeconomic outcomes is that Latin American Catholics lag far behind their European counterparts. Yet Catholics in general have enjoyed social mobility across the generations—and now they are roughly equal to moderate Protestants and Lutherans in their levels of educational attainment and income, and studies show considerable progress in European Catholics' wealth accumulation (Keister 2007, 2011). Notably, over the course of the 20th century, European Catholics altered their family behaviors, and over the generations, Catholics began to have rates of fertility and ages of marriage that were comparable to moderate and liberal Protestants. Further, Catholic women have high rates of labor-force participation, and they tend to work in professional and career-type jobs, rather than in the service sector (Sherkat 2012). Catholic schools may also have played a role in fostering upward mobility, and there is some evidence that later generations of Latin American Catholics are following the upward trajectory of Catholics of other ethnicities (Keister 2007; Keister and Borelli 2014). Given the large numbers of immigrants from Latin America who identify with Catholicism—and the higher rates of defection from the Catholic Church among Europeans from younger generations—Latin Americans are poised to demographically define the Catholic Church in the 21st century. Given this fact, the social status of Latin American Catholics will determine whether Catholicism is a religious identity of the middle class or an identity associated with limited social status.

Jewish and Unitarian identities are associated with positive socio-economic outcomes, and these two identifications are squarely at the top of the stratification hierarchy—eclipsing even Episcopalians. Interestingly, though, we have seen that the social-status advantage of rejecting religious identification has declined somewhat across generations. In older generations, rejecting religious identification was most often a choice, while in younger generations, many people were raised with no religious identification. Still, rather than being marginal or advantaged, those who reject a religious identity look very much like the average American in their social status. Another interesting finding in this research is the relative status of minority religious groups and particularly the Hindu advantage. While much has been made of the changes in immigration laws that opened up immigration to people from Asia, the fact is that immigration is strictly controlled, and only the most "desirable" immigrants are granted entrance (Jasso and Rosenzweig 1990; Jasso, Rosenzweig, and Smith 2000). Most of these "new immigrants" are coming to America on work visas for professional jobs, and they have considerable human capital. Indeed, we have seen that GSS respondents who identify as Hindu have higher rates of college-degree attainment and higher personal and household incomes than Jews do. Buddhists are almost neck and neck with Episcopalians, the highest-status Christian group, in their educational and income attainment. And, while Muslims sit somewhere in the middle of the status hierarchy of religious identifications, there is considerable variation—suggesting that Muslims from different nations or migration circumstances have variable fortunes (Amin and Sherkat 2014). In the future, we can expect high-status non-Christian groups to have a profound influence on the American religious landscape, just as Judaism has.

Religious identification continues to be consequential for religious beliefs and behaviors, for sexuality and family life, and for influencing social status. We have also seen how these religious influences are interrelated. Distinctive religious beliefs are a product of religious identifications, and they mandate particular patterns of religious participation. Religious beliefs and religious communities reinforce prescriptions and proscriptions regarding sexuality, marriage, fertility, and gender equality and inequality. Marital timing and fertility and female labor-force participation influence educational attainment, occupational attainment, and income. The interconnections between these social forces are common across generations and ethnic groups, and we can expect this to continue in the future.

## The Religious and Ethnic Foundations of Polarized Politics

The connection between religious identification and political orientations and alignments is a definitive feature of American religion and politics, and ethnic and religious cleavages contour the American political landscape. Many of the connections between religious identification and political beliefs and values are relatively invariant across ethnic groups; however, other political orientations and alignments are deeply affected by race and ethnicity. Indeed, one of the key findings in this book is that many political values and commitments that predominate in ethnic groups are mostly a function of the distribution of religious identifications by ethnicity.

The politicization of the family is largely tied to the political mobilization of religious beliefs, and exclusivist sectarian identifications are strongly predictive of opposing abortion rights, denying marriage rights for gays and lesbians, making divorce more difficult, banning pornography, mandating school prayer, eliminating sex education in schools, and limiting access to contraception. Interestingly, while the Catholic Church hierarchy is quite animated in the political realm regarding issues of family and sexuality, American Catholics across ethnic groups are no different from moderate and even liberal Protestants on most of these issues (abortion being the only exception). At the other pole of political values on the family are people who reject religious identification, Unitarians, Episcopalians, Jews, and liberal Protestants. Notably, these conservative and liberal ends of the political-religious spectrum are of roughly equal size—with about 30% of Americans identifying with exclusivist sectarian groups and about the same proportion identifying with universalistic liberal groups or rejecting religious identity. However, in younger generations, we have seen that rejection of religious identity is growing, and we can expect that in the future the more liberal pole of family values will dominate.

On many issues, the political values of ethnic groups are defined largely by the distribution of religious identities. Eastern Europeans are relatively liberal on sexuality and family issues in large part because they are heavily Catholic and Jewish and are much less likely to identify with sectarian groups. In contrast, African Americans' high rates of identification with sectarian Protestant groups lead them to be more conservative on some sexuality and family issues, particularly marriage rights for same-sex couples (Sherkat, de Vries, and Creek 2010). Asians are more liberal on a variety of political concerns in part because they tend to reject religious identification or identify with non-Christian religious traditions. Latin Americans' embrace of Catholic identity places them in the middle of the road on most political issues—though Latin American Catholics differ quite substantially from European Catholics on political identification and voting behavior.

European Protestants are quite distinctive in many of their political orientations and commitments, particularly regarding crime and punishment, immigration, and political identification and voting. European Protestants are much more likely than non-Europeans to support the death penalty, to oppose gun laws, and to oppose the legalization of marijuana. Racial antipathy and anti-immigrant sentiment is especially common among European sectarian Protestants. As we have seen, European Protestants are in decline as a proportion of the population, and this trend will continue because of higher fertility in other ethnic groups and continued immigration from Asia, Africa, and Latin America. This may well set the stage for widespread changes in policy on immigration, gun control, and capital punishment.

The religious and ethnic polarization of politics is most apparent in party alignment and voting, and we have seen that voting for conservative presidential candidates and Republican identification is most prevalent among European Christians (particularly western Europeans). While Mormons of most ethnicities are staunchly Republican in identification and voting, African Americans of all religious identifications are unlikely to identify as Republican or to vote for conservative presidential candidates. Latin American Catholics are also quite different from their European peers, and attempts by Republicans to reach out to Latin Americans do not seem to be working—though European Catholics have become more aligned with the Republican Party over the past forty years (Brooks and Manza 2004). While the Republicans were traditionally a party of the Anglo-European establishment who tended to identify with liberal and moderate Protestant denominations, across generations, European Americans from sectarian groups and even Catholics of European ancestry have become more attracted to the Republican Party and its candidates. While European Catholics appear to be increasingly conservative in their political identifications and voting behavior, Latin American Catholics continue to embrace Democratic political identities and to vote for more liberal presidential candidates. This has created a growing divide between European Catholics and Latin American Catholics that will certainly fragment the political character of the Catholic Church in the decades to come. This divide within American Catholicism may become particularly salient given Pope Francis's amplification of the social justice teachings of the Catholic Church.

The political mobilization of religious identities continues to be relevant, and we have seen the rise of a new coalition of secular Americans and religious liberals to counter the hegemony of sectarian Protestantism. We have also seen the political division of the Catholic Church along ethnic lines, and in the future, the political polarization within the Catholic Church will play an important role in determining how religious identifications influence political commitments.

## The Future of Religious Identification in America

The U.S. Census Bureau predicts that the United States will be "majority minority" by 2060 (U.S. Census Bureau 2012). In 2012, U.S. Census Bureau estimates showed that 63% of Americans were non-Hispanic whites, and this figure is expected to fall to 43% by 2060. During the same period, the Census Bureau predicts that Hispanics will increase from 17% of the population to 31%, and 8% of Americans will be Asian, while another 6% will be of two or more racial identifications by 2060. These projections bode well for the future of the Catholic Church and for various non-Christian traditions. However, this change also could be a source of conflict within Catholicism as Latin Americans and other non-Europeans will come to dominate numerically. We can also expect that the proportion of Muslims, Hindus, Buddhists, and Sikhs will continue to grow, as will nonidentification. Questions remain about how this burgeoning diversity will impact religious beliefs and practices, family life, socioeconomic positioning, and political alignments.

Growing diversity does not necessarily reduce commitment to distinctive faiths, as supply-side theorists have correctly argued. And people with exclusivist religious identities have ensured the intergenerational transmission of their religious commitments through self-segregation. This pattern is readily evident for ethnic minorities, and Muslim, Hindu, Buddhist, and Jewish areas abound in our major cities. Indeed, my old neighborhood in Tulsa, Oklahoma, has become something of a Muslim neighborhood, and my former elementary school is now a mosque, complete with an Islamic school. Sectarian Christians have also gravitated toward distinctive enclaves in the outer suburbs of urban areas, and the dominance of European and African American sectarian Christianity in rural areas has scarcely been challenged. Organizationally, however, both Protestant and Catholic religious groups face considerable challenges as their members grow old and younger generations move. Organizational innovation will be needed to bring people into the pews and to reproduce subsequent generations of identifiers. The organizational crisis is most acute for Catholicism, which faces a tremendous shortfall of priests and a decline in Catholic-school attendance (Ewert 2013; Schoenherr, Young, and Cheng 1993).

Another issue for the future of American religious identification is how denominationalism will play out for the various "other religions." Will Hindus become another high-status non-Christian group, as the Jews did in the 20th century? Can they sustain their advantages across generations? Will they fragment into denominations based on regional religious traditions—or even boundaries of social status and caste? The same can be asked of Buddhists, Muslims, and Sikhs. For Muslims, this issue is already apparent in many communities where concentrations are high. At a recent talk on the politics of same-sex marriage in Fresno, California, my host pointed out a dapper gentleman in the audience and explained that he was the imam of a local mosque and the president of the interfaith coalition which helped sponsor the talk. Later as we walked across campus past a mosque, I asked if that was the congregation of the imam at my talk, and my host replied, "No, his mosque is out in the suburbs where the doctors and rich people live. That mosque seems mostly for cab drivers and restaurant workers, and I've never met their imam."

Family factors will also loom large in the future of religious identification, and it remains to be seen whether religious identities will lose salience for the choice of marriage partners and how ethnic diversity will play a role in the shifting commitments to family and faith. In the past, it was most common for American immigrants from non-Christian backgrounds to convert to Christianity if they married someone of European descent. Now, with greater ethnic diversity and declining salience of specific religious identities, it seems likely that religious and ethnic intermarriage may lead to a rejection of religious identification and the accelerated growth of secularism.

Religious identification is often influenced by educational attainment, and many religious groups have set up private school systems to counter the potentially negative impact of secularism and/or Protestant hegemony on the religious beliefs and identifications of the young. Indeed, the decline of compulsory public education has led many parents to avoid institutional education entirely and to "homeschool" their children. Homeschooling is particularly common among sectarian Protestants, though we do not have strong research identifying the extent of this practice—much less its consequences for children's socioeconomic outcomes (Kunzman 2009). Indeed, the segmented world of religious schools raises questions about the social and political values being taught to children under the guise of religious instruction. While Catholic schools in the 20th century successfully integrated European ethnic immigrants into American society, the new breed of religious schools seems more focused on reproducing religious distinctiveness than on preparing young people to be successful citizens in a diverse nation. Maintaining distinctive religious identities in the face of increasing religious and ethnic diversity may be a costly endeavor for the coming generations.

# REFERENCES

Aarts, Olav, Ariana Need, Manfred Te Grotenhuis, and Nan Dirk De Graaf. 2008. "Does Belonging Accompany Believing? Correlations and Trends in Western Europe and North America between 1981 and 2000." *Review of Religious Research* 50:16–34.

Aho, James Alfred. 1995. *The Politics of Righteousness: Idaho Christian Patriotism.* Seattle: University of Washington Press.

Akerlof, George A. 1997. "Social Distance and Social Decisions." *Econometrica* 65: 1005–1027.

Akerlof, George A., and Rachel E. Kranton. 2000. "Economics and Identity." *Quarterly Journal of Economics* 65:715–752.

———. 2010. *Identity Economics: How Our Identities Shape Our Work, Wages, and Well-Being.* Princeton: Princeton University Press.

Alanezi, Fawaz, and Darren E. Sherkat. 2008. "The Religious Participation of U.S. Immigrants: Exploring Contextual and Individual Influences." *Social Science Research* 37:844–855.

Alston, Jon P. 1971. "Religious Mobility and Socioeconomic Status." *Sociology of Religion* 32:140–148.

Amin, Nadia, and Darren E. Sherkat. 2014. "Religion, Gender, and Educational Attainment among U.S. Immigrants: Evidence from the New Immigrant Survey." In *Religion and Inequality in America*, edited by Lisa Keister and Darren E. Sherkat, 52–74. Cambridge: Cambridge University Press.

Ammerman, Nancy T. 1997. "Golden Rule Christianity: Lived Religion in the American Mainstream." In *Lived Religion in America: Toward a History of Practice*, edited by David Hall, 196–216. Princeton: Princeton University Press.

Andrews, Kenneth T. 2002. "Movement-Countermovement Dynamics and the Emergence of New Institutions: The Case of 'White Flight' Schools in Mississippi." *Social Forces* 80:911–936.

Babchuk, Nicholas, and Hugh P. Whitt. 1990. "R-Order and Religious Switching." *Journal for the Scientific Study of Religion* 29:246–254.

Bagwell, Laurie Simon, and B. Douglas Bernheim. 1996. "Veblen Effects in a Theory of Conspicuous Consumption." *American Economic Review* 86:349–373.

Barkun, Michael. 1997. *Religion and the Racist Right: The Origins of the Chistian Identity Movement.* Chapel Hill: University of North Carolina Press.

Bartkowski, John P., and W. Bradford Wilcox. 2000. "Conservative Protestant Child Discipline: The Case of Parental Yelling." *Social Forces* 79:265–290.

Baunach, Dawn Michelle. 2011. "Decomposing Trends in Attitudes toward Gay Marriage, 1988–2006." *Social Science Quarterly* 92:346–363.

Bellah, Robert N. 1970. *Beyond Belief: Essays on Religion in a Post-traditional World.* New York: Harper and Row.

———. 1976. "New Religious Consciousness and the Crisis in Modernity." In *The New Religious Consciousness*, edited by Charles Y. Glock and Robert Bellah, 333–352. Berkeley: University of California Press.

———. 2008. *Habits of the Heart: Individualism and Commitment in American Life.* Berkeley: University of California Press.

Berger, Peter L. 1967. *The Sacred Canopy: Elements of a Sociological Theory of Religion.* Garden City, NY: Doubleday.

Berkman, Michael B., Julianna Sandell Pacheco, and Eric Plutzer. 2008. "Evolution and Creationism in America's Classrooms: A National Portrait." *PLoS Biology* 6: 920–924.

Bernheim, B. Douglas. 1994. "A Theory of Conformity." *Journal of Political Economy* 102:841–877.

Beyerlein, Kraig. 2004. "Specifying the Impact of Conservative Protestantism on Educational Attainment." *Journal for the Scientific Study of Religion* 43:505–518.

Bibby, Reginald W. 1978. "Why Conservative Churches Really Are Growing: Kelley Revisited." *Journal for the Scientific Study of Religion* 17:129–137.

Bibby, Reginald W., and Merlin B. Brinkerhoff. 1973. "The Circulation of the Saints: A Study of People Who Join Conservative Churches." *Journal for the Scientific Study of Religion* 12:273–283.

———. 1983. "Circulation of the Saints Revisited: A Longitudinal Look at Conservative Church Growth." *Journal for the Scientific Study of Religion* 22:253–262.

Blau, Peter. M., and Otis Dudley Duncan. 1967. *The American Occupational Structure.* New York: Wiley.

Booth, Alan, and John N. Edwards. 1985. "Age at Marriage and Marital Instability." *Journal of Marriage and the Family* 47:67–75.

Bowles, Samuel, and Herbert Gintis. 1976. *Schooling in Capitalist America: Educational Reform and the Contradictions of Economic Life.* New York: Basic Books.

Breen, Richard, and Bernadette C. Hayes. 1996. "Religious Mobility in the UK." *Journal of the Royal Statistical Society, Series A: Statistics in Society* 159:493–504.

Brooks, Clem, and Jeff Manza. 2004. "A Great Divide? Religion and Political Change in U.S. National Elections, 1972–2000." *Sociological Quarterly* 45:421–450.

Bruce, Steve. 2011. *Secularization: In Defence of an Unfashionable Theory.* Oxford: Oxford University Press.

Busto, Rudy V. 1996. "The Gospel According to the Model Minority? Hazarding an Interpretation of Asian American Evangelical College Students." *Amerasia Journal* 22:133–147.

Butler, Jon, Grant Wacker, and Randall Balmer. 2007. *Religion in American Life: A Short History*. Updated ed. Oxford: Oxford University Press.

Card, Josefina J., and Lauress L. Wise. 1978. "Teenage Mothers and Teenage Fathers: The Impact of Early Childbearing on the Parents' Personal and Professional Lives." *Family Planning Perspectives* 10:199–205.

Carsey, Thomas M., and Geoffrey C. Layman. 2006. "Changing Sides or Changing Minds? Party Identification and Policy Preferences in the American Electorate." *American Journal of Political Science* 50:464–477.

Chaves, Mark. 1994. "Secularization as Declining Religious Authority." *Social Forces* 72: 749–774.

Cherlin, Andrew J. 1992. *Marriage, Divorce, Remarriage*. Cambridge: Harvard University Press.

Chong, Kelly H. 1998. "What It Means to Be Christian: The Role of Religion in the Construction of Ethnic Identity and Boundary among Second-Generation Korean Americans." *Sociology of Religion* 59:259–286.

Civettini, Nicole H. W., and Jennifer Glass. 2008. "The Impact of Religious Conservatism on Men's Work and Family Involvement." *Gender & Society* 22:172–193.

Connor, Phillip. 2008. "Increase or Decrease? The Impact of the International Migratory Event on Immigrant Religious Participation." *Journal for the Scientific Study of Religion* 47:243–257.

———. 2011. "Religion as Resource: Religion and Immigrant Economic Incorporation." *Social Science Research* 40:1350–1361.

D'Antonio, William V., and Dean R. Hoge. 2006. "The American Experience of Religious Disestablishment and Pluralism." *Social Compass* 53:345–356.

Darnell, Alfred, and Darren E. Sherkat. 1997. "The Impact of Protestant Fundamentalism on Educational Attainment." *American Sociological Review* 62:306–316.

Davidson, James D. 1994. "Religion among America's Elite: Persistence and Change in the Protestant Establishment." *Sociology of Religion* 55:419–440.

Davidson, James D., and Ralph E. Pyle. 2011. *Ranking Faiths: Religious Stratification in America*. Lanham, MD: Rowman and Littlefield.

Davidson, James D., Ralph E. Pyle, and David V. Reyes. 1995. "Persistence and Change in the Protestant Establishment, 1930–1992." *Social Forces* 74:157–175.

Davie, Grace. 1990. "Believing without Belonging: Is This the Future of Religion in Britain?" *Social Compass* 37:455–469.

———. 1994. *Religion in Britain since 1945: Believing without Belonging*. Oxford, UK: Blackwell.

Deckman, Melissa M. 2002. "Holy ABCs! The Impact of Religion on Attitudes about Education Policies." *Social Science Quarterly* 83:472–487.

———. 2004. *School Board Battles: The Christian Right in Local Politics*. Washington, DC: Georgetown University Press.

Demerath, N. Jay. 1965. *Social Class in American Protestantism*. Chicago: Rand McNally.

Dillon, Michele. 1999. *Catholic Identity: Balancing Reason, Faith, and Power.* Cambridge: Cambridge University Press.

DiPrete, Thomas A., Andrew Gelman, Tyler McCormick, Julien Teitler, and Tian Zheng. 2011. "Segregation in Social Networks Based on Acquaintanceship and Trust." *American Journal of Sociology* 116:1234–1283.

Dynan, Karen, and Enrichetta Ravina. 2007. "Increasing Income Inequality, External Habits, and Self-Reported Happiness." *American Economic Review* 97:226–231.

Easterlin, Richard A. 2001. "Income and Happiness: Towards a Unified Theory." *Economic Journal* 111:465–484.

Ebaugh, Helen Rose. 2003. "Religion and the New Immigrants." In *Handbook of the Sociology of Religion*, edited by Michele Dillon, 225–239. Cambridge: Cambridge University Press.

Ebaugh, Helen Rose, and Janet Saltzman Chafetz. 2000. *Religion and the New Immigrants: Continuities and Adaptations in Immigrant Congregations.* Lanham, MD: AltaMira.

Edgell, Penny. 2005. *Religion and Family in a Changing Society.* Princeton: Princeton University Press.

Edgell, Penny, Joseph Gerteis, and Douglas Hartmann. 2006. "Atheists as 'Other': Moral Boundaries and Cultural Membership in American Society." *American Sociological Review* 71:211–234.

Ellison, Christopher G., and Darren E. Sherkat. 1990. "Patterns of Religious Mobility among Black Americans." *Sociological Quarterly* 31:551–568.

———. 1993a. "Conservative Protestantism and Support for Corporal Punishment." *American Sociological Review* 58:131–144.

———. 1993b. "Obedience and Autonomy: Religion and Parental Values Reconsidered." *Journal for the Scientific Study of Religion* 32:313–329.

———. 1995a. "Is Sociology the Core Discipline for the Scientific Study of Religion?" *Social Forces* 73:1255–1266.

———. 1995b. "The 'Semi-Involuntary Institution' Revisited: Regional Variations in Church Participation among Black Americans." *Social Forces* 73:1415–1437.

———. 1999. "Identifying the Semi-Involuntary Institution: A Clarification." *Social Forces* 78:793–802.

Elster, Jon. 1979. *Ulysses and the Sirens: Studies in Rationality and Irrationality.* Cambridge: Cambridge University Press.

Emerson, Michael O., and Christian Smith. 2000. *Divided by Faith: Evangelical Religion and the Problem of Race in America.* Oxford: Oxford University Press.

Ewert, S. 2013. "The Decline in Private School Enrollment." U.S. Census Bureau. SEHSD Working Paper FY12-117.

Finke, Roger, and Rodney Stark. 1988. "Religious Economies and Sacred Canopies: Religious Mobilization in American Cities, 1906." *American Sociological Review* 53: 41–49.

———. 1992. *The Churching of America: Winners and Losers in Our Religious Economy.* New Brunswick: Rutgers University Press.

Fitzgerald, Scott T., and Jennifer L. Glass. 2008. "Can Early Family Formation Explain the Lower Educational Attainment of US Conservative Protestants?" *Sociological Spectrum* 28:556–577.

———. 2012. "Conservative Protestants, Early Transitions to Adulthood, and the Intergenerational Transmission of Class." *Research in the Sociology of Work* 23:49–72.

Form, William. 2000. "Italian Protestants: Religion, Ethnicity, and Assimilation." *Journal for the Scientific Study of Religion* 39:307–320.

Francis, Leslie J., and Mandy Robbins. 2007. "Belonging without Believing: A Study in the Social Significance of Anglican Identity and Implicit Religion among 13–15 Year-Old Males." *Implicit Religion* 7:37–54.

Frazier, Edward Franklin. 1964. *The Negro Church in America*. New York: Schocken Books.

Frijters, Paul, John P. Haisken-DeNew, and Michael A. Shields. 2004. "Money Does Matter! Evidence from Increasing Real Income and Life Satisfaction in East Germany Following Reunification." *American Economic Review* 94:730–740.

Gamson, Joshua. 1995. "Must Identity Movements Self-Destruct? A Queer Dilemma." *Social Problems* 42:390–407.

———. 1996. "The Organizational Shaping of Collective Identity: The Case of Lesbian and Gay Film Festivals in New York." *Sociological Forum* 11:231–261.

———. 1997. "Messages of Exclusion: Gender, Movements, and Symbolic Boundaries." *Gender & Society* 11:178–199.

Garroutte, Eva M., Janette Beals, Ellen M. Keane, Carol Kaufman, Paul Spicer, Jeff Henderson, Patricia N. Henderson, Christina M. Mitchell, Spero M. Manson, and the A.I. SUPERPFP Team. 2009. "Religiosity and Spiritual Engagement in Two American Indian Populations." *Journal for the Scientific Study of Religion* 48:480–500.

Giles, Micheal W., and Kaenan Hertz. 1994. "Racial Threat and Partisan Identification." *American Political Science Review* 88:317–326.

Glass, Jennifer, and Jerry Jacobs. 2005. "Childhood Religious Conservatism and Adult Attainment among Black and White Women." *Social Forces* 83:555–579.

Glass, Jennifer, and Leda E. Nath. 2006. "Religious Conservatism and Women's Market Behavior Following Marriage and Childbirth." *Journal of Marriage and Family* 68:611–629.

Glenn, Norval D. 1964. "Negro Religion and Negro Status in the United States." In *Religion, Culture, and Society*, edited by Louis Schneider, 623–639. New York: Wiley.

Glock, Charles Y., Robert N. Bellah, and Randall H. Alfred. 1976. *The New Religious Consciousness*. Berkeley: University of California Press.

Goodman, Leo A., and Clifford C. Clogg. 1992. "New Methods for the Analysis of Occupational Mobility Tables and Other Kinds of Cross-Classifications." *Contemporary Sociology* 21:609–622.

Goodman, Leo A., and Michael Hout. 1998. "Statistical Methods and Graphical Displays for Analyzing How the Association between Two Qualitative Variables Differs among Countries, among Groups, or over Time: A Modified Regression-Type Approach." *Sociological Methodology* 28:175–230.

Granovetter, Mark. 1973. "The Strength of Weak Ties." *American Journal of Sociology* 79:1360–1380.

———. 1985. "Economic Action and Social Structure: The Problem of Embeddedness." *American Journal of Sociology* 91:481–510.

Greeley, Andrew, and Michael Hout. 1999. "Americans' Increasing Belief in Life after Death: Religious Competition and Acculturation." *American Sociological Review* 64:813–835.

———. 2001. "Getting to the Truths That Matter." *American Sociological Review* 66: 152–158.

———. 2006. *The Truth about Conservative Christians: What They Think and What They Believe.* Chicago: University of Chicago Press.

Gusfield, Joseph R. 1986. *Symbolic Crusade: Status Politics and the American Temperance Movement.* Urbana: University of Illinois Press.

Hadaway, C. Kirk, Penny Long Marler, and Mark Chaves. 1993. "What the Polls Don't Show: A Closer Look at US Church Attendance." *American Sociological Review* 58: 741–752.

Hadden, Jeffrey K. 1987. "Toward Desacralizing Secularization Theory." *Social Forces* 65:587–611.

Hamilton, Richard F., and William H. Form. 2003. "Categorical Usages and Complex Realities: Race, Ethnicity, and Religion in the United States." *Social Forces* 81: 693–714.

Harrison, Michael I., and Bernard Lazerwitz. 1982. "Do Denominations Matter?" *American Journal of Sociology* 88:356–377.

Harrod, Howard L. 1995. *Becoming and Remaining a People: Native American Religions on the Northern Plains.* Tucson: University of Arizona Press.

Hayes, Bernadette C., and Ian McAllister. 1995. "Religious Independents in Northern Ireland: Origins, Attitudes, and Significance." *Review of Religious Research* 36:65–83.

Herberg, Will. 1983. *Protestant–Catholic–Jew: An Essay in American Religious Sociology.* Chicago: University of Chicago Press.

Hoge, Dean R., Gregory H. Petrillo, and Ella I. Smith. 1982. "Transmission of Religious and Social Values from Parents to Teenage Children." *Journal of Marriage and the Family* 44:569–580.

Hoge, Dean R., and David A. Roozen. 1979. *Understanding Church Growth and Decline, 1950–1978.* Cleveland: Pilgrim.

Hout, Michael, and Claude S. Fischer. 2002. "Why More Americans Have No Religious Preference: Politics and Generations." *American Sociological Review* 67:165–190.

Hout, Michael, Andrew Greeley, and Melissa J Wilde. 2001. "The Demographic Imperative in Religious Change in the United States 1." *American Journal of Sociology* 107: 468–500.

Hunsberger, Bruce. 1995. "Religion and Prejudice: The Role of Religious Fundamentalism, Quest, and Right-Wing Authoritarianism." *Journal of Social Issues* 51:113–129.

Hunsberger, Bruce, and Lynne M. Jackson. 2005. "Religion, Meaning, and Prejudice." *Journal of Social Issues* 61:807–826.

Hunt, Larry L., and Janet G. Hunt. 1975. "A Religious Factor in Secular Achievement among Blacks: The Case of Catholicism." *Social Forces* 53:595–605.

Hunt, Larry L., and Matthew O. Hunt. 1999. "Regional Patterns of African American Church Attendance: Revisiting the Semi-Involuntary Thesis." *Social Forces* 78: 779–791.

———. 2001. "Race, Region, and Religious Involvement: A Comparative Study of Whites and African Americans." *Social Forces* 80:605–631.

Hunter, James Davison. 1991. *Culture Wars: The Struggle to Define America*. New York: Basic Books.

Hyer, Marjorie. 1980. "Evangelist Reverses Position on God's Hearing Jews." *Washington Post*, October 11. http://www.washingtonpost.com/wp-dyn/content/article/2007/05/15/AR2007051501197.html.

Iannaccone, Laurence R. 1988. "A Formal Model of Church and Sect." *American Journal of Sociology* 94:s241–s268.

———. 1990. "Religious Practice: A Human Capital Approach." *Journal for the Scientific Study of Religion* 29:297–314.

———. 1991. "The Consequences of Religious Market Structure: Adam Smith and the Economics of Religion." *Rationality and Society* 32:156–177.

———. 1992. "Sacrifice and Stigma: Reducing Free-Riding in Cults, Communes, and Other Collectives." *Journal of Political Economy* 100: 271–291.

———. 1994. "Why Strict Churches Are Strong." *American Journal of Sociology* 99: 1180–1211.

Jasso, Guillermina, Douglas S. Massey, Mark R. Rosenzweig, and James P. Smith. 2004. "The US New Immigrant Survey: Overview and Preliminary Results Based on the New-Immigrant Cohorts of 1996 and 2003." In *Immigration Research and Statistics Service Workshop on Longitudinal Surveys and Cross-Cultural Survey Design: Workshop Proceedings*, 29–46. London: Crown.

Jasso, Gullermina, and Mark R. Rosenzweig. 1990. *The New Chosen People: Immigrants in the United States*. New York: Russell Sage Foundation.

Jasso, Guillermina, Mark R. Rosenzweig, and James P. Smith. 2000. "The Changing Skill of New Immigrants to the United States: Recent Trends and Their Determinants." In *Issues in the Economics of Immigration*, edited by George Borjas, 185–226. Chicago: University of Chicago Press.

Jelen, Ted G. 1991. *The Political Mobilization of Religious Beliefs*. New York: Praeger.

Jennings, M. Kent, and Richard G. Niemi. 1981. *Generations and Politics: A Panel Study of Young Adults and Their Parents*. Princeton: Princeton University Press.

Johnson, Benton. 1963. "On Church and Sect." *American Sociological Review* 28: 539–549.

Johnson, Jennifer L. 2011. "Mobilizing Minutewomen: Gender, Cyberpower, and the New Nativist Movement." *Research in Social Movements, Conflicts and Change* 32: 137–161.

Johnson, Robert Alan. 1980. *Religious Assortative Marriage in the United States*. New York: Academic Press.

Keister, Lisa A. 2003. "Religion and Wealth: The Role of Religious Affiliation and Participation in Early Adult Asset Accumulation." *Social Forces* 82:173–205.

———. 2007. "Upward Wealth Mobility: Exploring the Roman Catholic Advantage." *Social Forces* 85:1195–1226.

———. 2008. "Conservative Protestants and Wealth: How Religion Perpetuates Asset Accumulation Processes." *American Journal of Sociology* 113:1237–1271.

———. 2011. *Faith and Money: How Religion Contributes to Wealth and Poverty*. Cambridge: Cambridge University Press.

Keister, Lisa A., and E. Paige Borelli. 2014. "Religion and Wealth Mobility: The Case of American Latinos." In *Religion and Inequality in America*, edited by Lisa A. Keister and Darren E. Sherkat, 119–145. Cambridge: Cambridge University Press.

Kerckhoff, Alan. C. 1976. "The Status Attainment Process: Socialization or Allocation?" *Social Forces* 552:368–381.

Klatch, Rebecca. 1999. *A Generation Divided: The New Left, the New Right, and the 1960s*. Berkeley: University of California Press.

Kluegel, James. 1980. "Denominational Mobility: Current Patterns and Recent Trends." *Journal for the Scientific Study of Religion* 19:26–39.

Kosmin, Barry A., and Ariela Keysar. 2006. *Religion in a Free Market: Religious and Non-religious Americans: Who, What, Why, Where*. Ithaca, NY: Paramount Market.

Kunzman, Robert. 2009. *Write These Laws on Your Children: Inside the World of Conservative Christian Homeschooling*. Boston: Beacon.

Kuran, Timur. 1993. "The Unthinkable and the Unthought." *Rationality and Society* 5: 473–505.

———. 1995. *Private Truths, Public Lies*. Cambridge: Harvard University Press.

Lauer, Robert H. 1975. "Occupational and Religious Mobility in a Small City." *Sociological Quarterly* 16:380–392.

Lawson, Ronald, and Ryan T. Cragun. 2012. "Comparing the Geographic Distributions and Growth of Mormons, Adventists, and Witnesses." *Journal for the Scientific Study of Religion* 51:220–240.

Layman, Geoffrey C. 2001. *The Great Divide: Religious and Cultural Conflict in American Party Politics*. New York: Columbia University Press.

Layman, Geoffrey C., Thomas M. Carsey, and Juliana Menasce Horowitz. 2006. "Party Polarization in American Politics: Characteristics, Causes, and Consequences." *Annual Review of Political Science* 9:83–110.

Lechner, Frank J. 1991. "The Case against Secularization: A Rebuttal." *Social Forces* 69: 1103–1119.

Lehrer, Evelyn L. 1995. "The Effects of Religion on the Labor Supply of Married Women." *Social Science Research* 24:281–301.

———. 1996. "Religion as a Determinant of Fertility." *Journal of Population Economics* 9: 173–196.

———. 1999a. "Married Women's Labor Supply Behavior in the 1990s: Differences by Life-Cycle Stage." *Social Science Quarterly* 80:574–590.

———. 1999b. "Religion as a Determinant of Educational Attainment: An Economic Perspective." *Social Science Research* 28:358–379.

———. 2004. "Religion as a Determinant of Economic and Demographic Behavior in the United States." *Population and Development Review* 30:707–726.

———. 2008. *Religion as a Determinant of Economic and Demographic Behavior*. New York: Routledge.

Lehrer, Evelyn L., and Carmel U. Chiswick. 1993. "Religion as a Determinant of Marital Stability." *Demography* 30:385–404.

Levitt, Peggy. 2003. " 'You Know, Abraham Was Really the First Immigrant': Religion and Transnational Migration." *International Migration Review* 37:847–873.

Lincoln, C. Eric, and Lawrence H. Mamiya. 1990. *The Black Church in the African-American Experience*. Durham: Duke University Press.

Lindsay, D. Michael. 2007. *Faith in the Halls of Power: How Evangelicals Joined the American Elite*. New York: Oxford University Press.

Lofland, John, and Rodney Stark. 1965. "Becoming a World-Saver: A Theory of Conversion to a Deviant Perspective." *American Sociological Review* 30:862–875.

Loftus, Jeni. 2001. "America's Liberalization in Attitudes toward Homosexuality, 1973 to 1998." *American Sociological Review* 66:762–782.

Luker, Kristin. 1985. *Abortion and the Politics of Motherhood*. Berkeley: University of California Press.

Manza, Jeff, and Clem Brooks. 1997. "The Religious Factor in US Presidential Elections, 1960–1992." *American Journal of Sociology* 103:38–81.

Marchisio, Roberto, and Maurizio Pisati. 1999. "Belonging without Believing: Catholics in Contemporary Italy." *Journal of Modern Italian Studies* 4:236–255.

Marsden, George M. 1980. *Fundamentalism and American Culture*. New York: Oxford University Press.

Marshall, Susan E. 1985. "Ladies against Women: Mobilization Dilemmas of Antifeminist Movements." *Social Problems* 32:348–362.

———. 1986. "In Defense of Separate Spheres: Class and Status Politics in the Antisuffrage Movement." *Social Forces* 65:327–351.

———. 1991. "Who Speaks for American Women? The Future of Antifeminism." *Annals of the American Academy of Political and Social Science* 515:50–62.

Marty, Martin E. 1999. *Modern American Religion*. Chicago: University of Chicago Press.

Marty, Martin E., and R. Scott Appleby. 2004. *Accounting for Fundamentalisms: The Dynamic Character of Movements*. Chicago: University of Chicago Press.

Massengill, Rebekah Peeples. 2008. "Educational Attainment and Cohort Change among Conservative Protestants, 1972–2004." *Journal for the Scientific Study of Religion* 47:545–562.

McCarthy, John, and Mayer Zald. 1977. "Resource Mobilization and Social Movements." *American Journal of Sociology* 82:1212–1241.

McPherson, J. Miller, and Thomas Rotolo. 1996. "Testing a Dynamic Model of Social

Composition: Diversity and Change in Voluntary Groups." *American Sociological Review* 61:179–202.

McPherson, J. Miller, Lynn Smith-Lovin, and James M. Cook. 2001. "Birds of a Feather: Homophily in Social Networks." *Annual Review of Sociology* 27:415–444.

Meares, Tracey L. 1997. "Charting Race and Class Differences in Attitudes towards Drug Legalization and Law Enforcement: Lessons for Federal Criminal Law." *Buffalo Criminal Law Review* 1:137–174.

Melton, J. Gordon. 2003. *Encyclopedia of American Religions*. Farmington Hills, MI: Gale/Cengage Learning.

Montgomery, James D. 1996. "The Dynamics of the Religious Economy: Exit, Voice, and Denominational Secularization." *Rationality and Society* 8:81–110.

Morris, Aldon D. 1986. *Origins of the Civil Rights Movement*. Detroit: Free Press.

Munch, Alison, J. Miller McPherson, and Lynn Smith-Lovin. 1997. "Gender, Children, and Social Contact: The Effects of Childrearing for Men and Women." *American Sociological Review* 62:509–520.

Murray, Charles. 2012. *Coming Apart: The State of White America, 1960–2010*. New York: Crown Forum.

Myers, Scott M. 1996. "An Interactive Model of Religiosity Inheritance: The Importance of Family Context." *American Sociological Review* 61:858–866.

———. 2000. "The Impact of Religious Involvement on Migration." *Social Forces* 79: 755–783.

Nagel, Joane. 1996. *American Indian Ethnic Renewal: Red Power and the Resurgence of Identity and Culture*. Oxford: Oxford University Press.

Nash, Dennison. 1968. "A Little Child Shall Lead Them: A Statistical Test of an Hypothesis That Children Were the Source of the American 'Religious Revival.'" *Journal for the Scientific Study of Religion* 7:238–240.

Nash, Dennison, and Peter Berger. 1962. "The Child the Family and the 'Religious Revival' in Suburbia." *Journal for the Scientific Study of Religion* 2:85–93.

Neitz, Mary Jo. 1987. *Charisma and Community: A Study of Religious Commitment within the Charismatic Renewal*. Piscataway, NJ: Transaction.

Newport, Frank. 1979. "The Religious Switcher in the United States." *American Sociological Review* 44:528–552.

Nie, Norman H., Sidney Verba, and John R. Petrocik. 1979. *The Changing American Voter*. Cambridge: Harvard University Press.

Niebuhr, H. Reinhold. 1929. *The Social Sources of Denominationalism*. New York: Holt.

Niose, David. 2012. *Nonbeliever Nation: The Rise of Secular Americans*. New York: Macmillan.

Palmer, Susan J. 1994. *Moon Sisters, Krishna Mothers, Rajneesh Lovers: Women's Roles in New Religions*. Syracuse: Syracuse University Press.

Park, Jerry Z., and Elaine Howard Ecklund. 2007. "Negotiating Continuity: Family and Religious Socialization for Second-Generation Asian Americans." *Sociological Quarterly* 48:93–118.

Pearce, Lisa D. 2002. "The Influence of Early Life Course Religious Exposure on Young

Adults' Dispositions toward Childbearing." *Journal for the Scientific Study of Religion* 41:325–340.

———. 2010. "Religion and the Timing of First Births in the United States." In *Religion, Families, and Health: Population-Based Research in the United States*, edited by Robert A. Hummer and Christopher G. Ellison, 19–39. New Brunswick: Rutgers University Press.

Pearce, Lisa D., and Arland Thornton. 2007. "Religious Identity and Family Ideologies in the Transition to Adulthood." *Journal of Marriage and Family* 69:1227–1243.

Phillips, Rick, and Ryan Cragun. 2013. "Contemporary Mormon Religiosity and the Legacy of 'Gathering.'" *Nova Religio* 16:77–94.

Popielarz, Pamela, and J. Miller McPherson. 1995. "On the Edge or In Between: Niche Position, Niche Overlap, and the Duration of Voluntary Association Memberships." *American Journal of Sociology* 101:698–720.

Powers, Daniel A., and Yu Xie. 2008. *Statistical Methods for Categorical Data Analysis*. Bingley, UK: Emerald.

Putnam, Robert D., and David E. Campbell. 2012. *American Grace: How Religion Divides and Unites Us*. New York: Simon and Schuster.

Read, Jen'nan Ghazal, and Sharon Oselin. 2008. "Gender and the Education-Employment Paradox in Ethnic and Religious Contexts: The Case of Arab Americans." *American Sociological Review* 73:296–313.

Regnerus, Mark D. 2009. *Forbidden Fruit: Sex and Religion in the Lives of American Teenagers*. New York: Oxford University Press.

Regnerus, Mark D., and Jeremy Uecker. 2011. *Premarital Sex in America: How Young Americans Meet, Mate, and Think about Marrying*. New York: Oxford University Press.

Riley, Naomi Schaefer. 2008. "What Saddleback's Pastor Really Thinks about Politics." *Wall Street Journal*, August 23. http://online.wsj.com/article/SB121944811327665223 .html.

Rochford, E. Burke. 1985. *Hare Krishna in America*. New Brunswick: Rutgers University Press.

———. 2007. *Hare Krishna Transformed*. New York: NYU Press.

Roof, Wade Clark. 1989. "Multiple Religious Switching: A Research Note." *Journal for the Scientific Study of Religion* 28:530–535.

Roof, Wade Clark, and Bruce Greer. 1993. *A Generation of Seekers: The Spiritual Journeys of the Baby Boom Generation*. San Francisco: Harper.

Roof, Wade Clark, and William McKinney. 1987. *American Mainline Religion: Its Changing Shape and Future*. New Brunswick: Rutgers University Press.

Sandomirsky, Sharon, and John Wilson. 1990. "Processes of Disaffiliation: Religious Mobility among Men and Women." *Social Forces* 68:1211–1229.

Schoenherr, Richard A., Lawrence Alfred Young, and Tsan-Yuang Cheng. 1993. *Full Pews and Empty Altars: Demographics of the Priest Shortage in United States Catholic Dioceses*. Madison: University of Wisconsin Press.

Sen, Amartya. 1973. "Behavior and the Concept of Preference." *Economica* 40:241–259.

Sen, Amartya. 1993. "Internal Consistency of Choice." *Econometrica* 61:495–521.

Sewell, William H., Jr. 1992. "A Theory of Structure: Duality, Agency, and Transformation." *American Journal of Sociology* 98:1–29.

Sherkat, Darren E. 1991. "Leaving the Faith: Testing Theories of Religious Switching Using Survival Models." *Social Science Research* 20:171–187.

——. 1997. "Embedding Religious Choices: Integrating Preferences and Social Constraints into Rational Choice Theories of Religious Behavior." In *Rational Choice Theory and Religion: Summary and Assessment*, edited by Lawrence Young, 65–86. London: Routledge.

——. 1998. "Counterculture or Continuity? Examining Competing Influences on Baby Boomers' Religious Orientations and Participation." *Social Forces* 76: 1087–1114.

——. 2000. " 'That They Be Keepers of the Home': The Effect of Conservative Religion on Early and Late Transitions into Housewifery." *Review of Religious Research* 41: 344–458.

——. 2001a. "Investigating the Sect-Church-Sect Cycle: Cohort Specific Attendance Differences across African American Denominations." *Journal for the Scientific Study of Religion* 40: 221–233.

——. 2001b. "Tracking the Restructuring of American Religion: Religious Affiliation and Patterns of Mobility 1973–1998." *Social Forces* 79:1459–1492.

——. 2002. "African American Religious Affiliation in the Late 20th Century: Trends, Cohort Variations, and Patterns of Switching, 1973–1998." *Journal for the Scientific Study of Religion* 41:485–494.

——. 2003. "Religious Socialization: Sources of Influence and Influences of Agency." In *Handbook of the Sociology of Religion*, edited by Michele Dillon, 151–163. Cambridge: Cambridge University Press.

——. 2004. "Religious Intermarriage in the United States: Trends, Patterns, and Predictors." *Social Science Research* 33:606–625.

——. 2006. "Politics and Social Movements." In *Handbook of Religion and Social Institutions*, edited by Helen Rose Ebaugh, 3–19. New York: Springer.

——. 2008. "Beyond Belief: Atheism, Agnosticism, and Theistic Certainty in the United States." *Sociological Spectrum* 28:438–459.

——. 2010a. "Immigrants, Migration, and Religious Economies." In *Handbook of Economics of Religion*, edited by Rachel M. McCleary, 151–168. Oxford: Oxford University Press.

——. 2010b. "Religion and Verbal Ability." *Social Science Research* 39:2–13.

——. 2010c. "The Religious Demography of the United States: Dynamics of Affiliation, Participation, and Belief." In *Religion, Families, and Health: Population Based Research in the United States*, edited by Christopher G. Ellison and Robert A. Hummer, 403–430. New Brunswick: Rutgers University Press.

——. 2011. "Religion and Scientific Literacy in the United States." *Social Science Quarterly* 92:1134–1150.

———. 2012. "Religion and the American Occupation Structure." *Research in the Sociology of Work* 23:75–102.

Sherkat, Darren E., and T. Jean Blocker. 1997. "Explaining the Political and Personal Consequences of Protest." *Social Forces* 75:1049–1076.

Sherkat, Darren E., and Shannon A. Cunningham. 1998. "Extending the Semi-Involuntary Institution: Social Constraints and Regional Differences in Private Religious Consumption among African Americans." *Journal for the Scientific Study of Religion* 37:383–396.

Sherkat, Darren E., and Alfred Darnell. 1999. "The Effect of Parents' Fundamentalism on Children's Educational Attainment: Examining Differences by Gender and Children's Fundamentalism." *Journal for the Scientific Study of Religion* 38:23–35.

Sherkat, Darren E., Kylan M. de Vries, and Stacia Creek. 2010. "Race, Religion, and Opposition to Same-Sex Marriage." *Social Science Quarterly* 91:79–97.

Sherkat, Darren E., and Christopher G. Ellison. 1991. "The Politics of Black Religious Change: Disaffiliation from Black Mainline Denominations." *Social Forces* 70: 431–454.

———. 1999. "Recent Developments and Current Controversies in the Sociology of Religion." *Annual Review of Sociology* 25:363–394.

Sherkat, Darren E., Melissa Powell-Williams, Gregory Maddox, and Kylan de Vries. 2011. "Religion, Politics, and Support for Same-Sex Marriage in the United States, 1988–2008." *Social Science Research* 40:167–180.

Sherkat, Darren E., and John Wilson. 1995. "Preferences, Constraints, and Choices in Religious Markets: An Examination of Religious Switching and Apostasy." *Social Forces* 73:993–1026.

Smith, Christian. 2000. *Christian America? What Evangelicals Really Want*. Berkeley: University of California Press.

———. 2003. "Religious Participation and Network Closure among American Adolescents." *Journal for the Scientific Study of Religion* 42:95–104.

Smith, Christian, and Michael O. Emerson. 1998. *American Evangelicalism: Embattled and Thriving*. Chicago: University of Chicago Press.

Smith, Jesse. M. 2011. "Becoming an Atheist in America: Constructing Identity and Meaning from the Rejection of Theism." *Sociology of Religion* 72:215–237.

Smith, Tom W. 1990. "Classifying Protestant Denominations." *Review of Religious Research* 31:225–245.

Smock, Pamela J., Wendy D. Manning, and Sanjiv Gupta. 1999. "The Effect of Marriage and Divorce on Women's Economic Well-Being." *American Sociological Review* 64: 794–812.

Stark, Rodney. 1999. "Secularization, RIP." *Sociology of Religion* 60:249–273.

———. 2008. *What Americans Really Believe*. Waco, TX: Baylor University Press.

Stark, Rodney, and William Sims Bainbridge. 1980. "Networks of Faith: Interpersonal Bonds and Recruitment to Cults and Sects." *American Journal of Sociology* 85: 1376–1395.

Stark, Rodney, and William Sims Bainbridge. 1985. *Future of Religion: Secularization, Revival, and Cult Formation*. Berkeley: University of California Press.

———. 1987. *A Theory of Religion*. Toronto: Lang.

Stark, Rodney, and Roger Finke. 2000. *Acts of Faith: Explaining the Human Side of Religion*. Berkeley: University of California Press.

Stark, Rodney, and Charles Y. Glock. 1965. *American Piety: The Nature of Religious Commitment*. Berkeley: University of California Press.

Stark, Rodney, and Reid Larkin Neilson. 2005. *The Rise of Mormonism*. New York: Columbia University Press.

Starks, Brian, and Robert V. Robinson. 2005. "Who Values the Obedient Child Now? The Religious Factor in Adult Values for Children, 1986–2002." *Social Forces* 84: 343–359.

Steensland, Brian, Jerry Z. Park, Mark D. Regnerus, Lynn D. Robinson, W. Bradford Wilcox, and Robert D. Woodberry. 2000. "The Measure of American Religion: Toward Improving the State of the Art." *Social Forces* 79:291–318.

Stoll, David. 1990. *Is Latin America Turning Protestant? The Politics of Evangelical Growth*. Berkeley: University of California Press.

Stolzenberg, Ross M. 2001. "True Facts, True Stories, and True Differences." *American Sociological Review* 66:146–152.

Stolzenberg, Ross M., Mary Blair-Loy, and Linda J. Waite. 1995. "Religious Participation in Early Adulthood: Age and Family Life Cycle Effects on Church Membership." *American Sociological Review* 60:84–103.

Stouffer, Samuel Andrew. 1992. *Communism, Conformity, and Civil Liberties: A Cross-Section of the Nation Speaks Its Mind*. New Brunswick, NJ: Transaction.

Strate, John M., Charles J. Parrish, Charles D. Elder, and Coit Ford. 1989. "Life Span Civic Development and Voting Participation." *American Political Science Review* 83: 443–464.

Stryker, Robin. 1981. "Religio-ethnic Effects on Attainments in the Early Career." *American Sociological Review* 46:212–231.

Sullins, D. Paul. 1993. "Switching Close to Home: Volatility or Coherence in Protestant Affiliation Patterns?" *Social Forces* 72:399–419.

Taylor, Charles, and James Heft. 1999. *A Catholic Modernity? Charles Taylor's Marianist Award Lecture, with Responses by William M. Shea, Rosemary Luling Haughton, George Marsden, and Jean Bethke Elshtain*. Oxford: Oxford University Press.

Thoits, Peggy A. 2003. "Personal Agency in the Accumulation of Multiple Role-Identities." In *Advances in Identity Theory and Research*, edited by Peter J. Burke, 179–194. New York: Springer.

Thornton, Russel. 1987. *American Indian Holocaust and Survival: A Population History since 1492*. Norman: University of Oklahoma Press.

Tilly, Charles. 1978. *From Mobilization to Revolution*. Reading, MA: Addison-Wesley.

Tipton, Steven M. 1982. *Getting Saved from the Sixties: Moral Meaning in Conversion and Cultural Change*. Berkeley: University of California Press.

Tolsma, Jochem, Nan Dirk De Graaf, and Lincoln Quillian. 2009. "Does Intergenerational Social Mobility Affect Antagonistic Attitudes towards Ethnic Minorities?" *British Journal of Sociology* 60:257–277.

Troeltsch, Ernst. 1931. *The Social Teachings of the Christian Churches*. New York: Macmillan.

Tzeng, Jessie M., and Robert D. Mare. 1995. "Labor Market and Socioeconomic Effects on Marital Stability." *Social Science Research* 24:329–351.

Udis-Kessler, Amanda. 2008. *Queer Inclusion in the United Methodist Church*. New York: Routledge.

Unitarian Universalist Association of Congregations. 2013. "Unitarian Universalist LGBTQ History & Facts." May 16. http://UUa.org/lgbt/history/185789.shtml.

U.S. Census Bureau. 2012. "U.S. Census Bureau Projections Show a Slower Growing, Older, More Diverse Nationa a Half Century from Now." December 12. http://www.census.gov/newsroom/releases/archives/population/cb12-243.html.

Veblen, Thorstein. 2005. *The Theory of the Leisure Class: An Economic Study of Institutions*. Delhi: Aakar Books.

Voas, David, and Alasdair Crockett. 2005. "Religion in Britain: Neither Believing nor Belonging." *Sociology* 39:11–28.

Weber, Max. 1978. *Economy and Society*. Berkeley: University of California Press.

White, Harrison C. 2008. "Notes on the Constituents of Social Structure. Social Relations 10—Spring 1965." *Sociologica* 1. http://www.sociologica.mulino.it/doi/10.2383/26576.

Whittier, Nancy E. 1995. *Feminist Generations: The Persistence of the Radical Women's Movement*. Philadelphia: Temple University Press.

Wilcox, Clyde. 1996. *Onward Christian Soldiers? The Religious Right in American Politics*. Boulder, CO: Westview.

Wilcox, Clyde, and William Clyde Wilcox. 1992. *God's Warriors: The Christian Right in Twentieth-Century America*. Baltimore: Johns Hopkins University Press.

Wilcox, W. Bradford. 2004. *Soft Patriarchs: How Christianity Shapes Fathers and Husbands*. Chicago: University of Chicago Press.

Wilcox, W. Bradford, Andrew J. Cherlin, Jeremy E. Uecker, and Matthew Messel. 2012. "No Money, No Honey, No Church: The Deinstitutionalization of Religious Life among the White Working Class." *Research in the Sociology of Work* 23:227–250.

Wilder, Esther I., and William H. Walters. 1998. "Ethnic and Religious Components of the Jewish Income Advantage, 1969 and 1989." *Sociological Inquiry* 68:426–436.

Wilson, John, and Darren E. Sherkat. 1994. "Returning to the Fold." *Journal for the Scientific Study of Religion* 33:148–161.

Wright, Stuart A. 2009. "Strategic Framing of Racial-Nationalism in North America and Europe: An Analysis of a Burgeoning Transnational Network." *Terrorism and Political Violence* 21:189–210.

Wuthnow, Robert. 1976. *The Consciousness Reformation*. Berkeley: University of California Press.

———. 1988. *The Restructuring of American Religion: Society and Faith since World War II*. Princeton: Princeton University Press.

Wuthnow, Robert. 1993. *Christianity in the Twenty-First Century: Reflections on the Challenges Ahead.* New York: Oxford University Press.

Yang, Fenggang, and Helen Rose Ebaugh. 2001. "Transformations in New Immigrant Religions and Their Global Implications." *American Sociological Review* 66: 269–288.

Zald, Mayer N. 1982. "Theological Crucibles: Social Movements in and of Religion." *Review of Religious Research* 23:317–336.

Zuckerman, P. 2009. "Atheism, Secularity, and Well-Being: How the Findings of Social Science Counter Negative Stereotypes and Assumptions." *Sociology Compass* 36: 949–971.

# INDEX

Darren E. Sherkat is Professor of Sociology at Southern Illinois University. His research examines the intersections between religion, family, stratification, and politics. He has published over sixty peer-reviewed articles and book chapters and recently coedited *Religion and Inequality in America* with Lisa Keister of Duke University.